SOUTH AMERICA

University of California, Los Angeles

SOUTH AMERICA

OBSERVATIONS AND IMPRESSIONS

BY

JAMES BRYCE

AUTHOR OF "THE HOLY ROMAN EMPIRE"
"THE AMERICAN COMMONWEALTH," ETC.

PUBLISHED FOR THE

BAY VIEW READING CLUB

CENTRAL OFFICE, BOSTON BOULEVARD

DETROIT, MICHIGAN

BY

THE MACMILLAN COMPANY

Set up and electrotyped. Published September, 1912. Reprinted
October, November, December, 1912; January, 1913.
New edition with corrections, July, 1913.

Norwood Press
J. S. Cushing Co. — Berwick & Smith Co.
Norwood, Mass., U.S.A.

TO MY FRIENDS OF THE
ENGLISH ALPINE CLUB

PREFACE

This book records observations made and impressions formed during a journey through western and southern South America from Panama to Argentina and Brazil *via* the Straits of Magellan. The nature of its contents is briefly outlined in the Introduction which follows, so all that I have to do here is to acknowledge gratefully the many kindnesses I received in every part of South America which I visited, and in particular from the following persons : Colonel Goethals, Chief Engineer of the Panama Canal, and other officers of the United States engineers stationed there, and Colonel Gorgas, head of the medical staff ; the officials of the Peruvian Corporation in Lima and of the Peruvian Southern Railways in Mollendo, Arequipa, and La Paz ; the officials of the Antofagasta and Bolivia Railroad Company ; those of the Transandine Railway Company in Chile and those of the Buenos Aires and Pacific and Argentine Great Western Railways Companies in Mendoza and Buenos Aires, and also those of the Leopoldina Railway in Brazil. Nor must I fail to express my obligations to the heads in New York of the firm of Messrs. W. R. Grace Co., who advised me regarding my journey, and to my friend Professor Bingham of Yale University, who, familiar with South

America from his own travels and studies, has given me valuable help in many ways.

I have also to return my respectful thanks to the Governments of Chile and Brazil, who were good enough to extend to me facilities for travel on their railways, and to the Governments of Peru, Bolivia, Argentina, and Uruguay for other courtesies. To many statesmen and scholars in these six republics, too numerous to mention by name, as also to not a few of my own fellow-countrymen from Britain and Canada who are there settled, I am indebted for hospitality, for private acts of kindness, and for valuable information.

JAMES BRYCE.

June 27, 1912.

NOTE TO REVISED EDITION

This edition has been carefully revised and many corrections have been made in it.

February 26th, 1913.

TABLE OF CONTENTS

PAGE

PREFACE vii

INTRODUCTION xvii

CHAPTER I

THE ISTHMUS OF PANAMA

The Part of the Isthmus and the Strait in History . . . 1

The Isthmus of Suez and the Isthmus of Panama: The Route
    from Colon to Culebra and Panama 2

View from the Hill of Ancon 9

The Natives of the Isthmus: The San Blas Indians . . . 13

The English Raiders: Drake and Morgan 15

The Canal: Gatun Locks and Lake 19

The Great Cutting at Culebra 24

Administration and Sanitation of the Canal Zone . . . 26

Failure of the French Undertaking due Primarily to Disease . 28

Commercial Prospects of the Canal 33

General Impressions made by the Isthmus and the Canal . . 35

CHAPTER II

THE COAST OF PERU

Cold Climate of the West Coast 37

The Antarctic Current 38

Aridity and Barrenness of the Peruvian Coast 39

Payta: The Guano Islands 40

Lima: General Aspect and Buildings 46

Life and Society in Lima 51

Mollendo and the Peruvian Southern Railway 54

First View of the Andes 56

The Desert of Western Peru 57

The City of Arequipa 60

ix

PAGE

The Volcano of El Misti 61
Oriental Aspect of Arequipa 64
Character of the People of Arequipa 66
A Story from Colonial Days 69

CHAPTER III

CUZCO AND THE LAND OF THE INCAS

Physical Character of Peru 75
Crossing of the Andes from Arequipa to the Central Plateau of
    Lake Titicaca 80
Scenery of the Valley from the Plateau to Cuzco . . . 81
One of the Sources of the Amazon 86
Market Day at Sicuani: The Quichua Indians 88
Cuzco: Its Situation and Aspect 95
The Spanish Buildings at Cuzco 96
The Ancient Buildings: Inca Walls 102
The Prehistoric Fortress of Sacsahuaman 107
Impression made by the Remains of Ancient Peruvian Work . 114
Historical Associations of Cuzco 114
[Note on the Fortress Walls of Sacsahuaman] 118

CHAPTER IV

LAKE TITICACA AND THE CENTRAL ANDES

The Central Plateau and the Lake 119
Inhabitants of the Plateau: The Aymará Indians . . . 121
Scenery of Lake Titicaca 124
The Shrine of Copacavana 128
Voyage to the Sacred Islands 130
Koati: The Island of the Moon 131
The Island of the Sun 132
The Bath and Garden of the Inca 133
The Sacred Rock of the Wild Cat 135
View of the Snowy Range of Sorata or Illampu . . . 141
The Lake of Vinamarca 143
Tiahuanaco and its Ruins 144
Impression made by the Ruins 147
Character of the Ancient Peruvian Civilization 152
The Primitive Religion of Peru 156
Government and the Policy of the Incas 160

CHAPTER V

LA PAZ AND THE BOLIVIAN DESERT

PAGE

Origin of the Bolivian Republic 166
General Physical Character of Bolivia 167
Approach to La Paz: The *Barranca* 168
Climate of La Paz: The Mountain Sickness or *Soroche* . . 171
The City and its Environs 174
Character and Habits of the Bolivian Indians 179
The Plateau from La Paz to Oruro 186
Uyuni: The Great Bolivian Desert 191
Passage through the Andes 198
The Borax Lake and the Volcanoes 199
View of the Western Cordillera 203
The Desert of Atacama 204

CHAPTER VI

CHILE

The Three Regions of Chile 206
Northern Chile: The Nitrate Fields 207
Megillones and Antofagasta 210
Valparaiso 212
Santiago 216
Pedro de Valdivia and the Rock of Santa Lucia . . . 218
Chilean Society and Politics 220
Southern Chile: Its Climate and Scenery 223
The Coast Cities: Concepcion and Talcahuano . . . 225
Lota Valdivia and Corral 227
The Araucanian Indians: Their History, Customs, and Religion 232
Osorno and its German Colony 239
Rio Bueno 242
Attractiveness of Southern Chile 241
Lake Rinihue and the Chilean Forests 244

CHAPTER VII

ACROSS THE ANDES

The Andean Range 248
The Uspallata Pass from Chile into Argentina . . . 250
Construction of the Transandine Railway 251

PAGE

Scenery on the Chilean Side 253
The Tunnel under the Summit of the Cordillera . . . 256
Scenery on the Argentine Side 256
Aconcagua and Tupungato 257
The City of Mendoza 260
Argentines and Chileans 264
Return across the Mountains and Ascent to the Cumbre . . 267
The Christ of the Andes 269
Observations on the Scenery of the Andes in General . . 271
Comparison with the Himalayas 276
[Note on the Passage of the Andes, in 1817, by the Army of
    General San Martin] 280

CHAPTER VIII

THE STRAITS OF MAGELLAN

Discovery of the Straits, and Circumnavigation of the Globe, by
    Magellan 284
Voyage of Sir Francis Drake 286
The Coast of Southern Chile : The Sea-birds 286
Approach to, and Entrance of, the Straits 290
The Scenery of the Western Half of the Straits 291
Punta Arenas and Tierra del Fuego 300
The Eastern Half of the Straits 304
General Observations on the Character of the Straits . . 305
Their Historical Importance 307
The Falkland Isles, their Character and Products . . . 308
Their History 311
Their Scenery 313

CHAPTER IX

ARGENTINA

The Approach to Buenos Aires 315
Aspect of the City 316
Society in Buenos Aires 318
Physical Character of Argentina 324
Inhabitants of Argentina : The Gaucho 327
Agriculture and Ranching 329
The Process of Settlement : Labour 330

PAGE

The Scenery of the Pampas 334
Economic Prospects of Argentina 336
The European Immigrants 338
Character and Tendencies of Society in Argentina . . . 341
Argentina the Most Modern of South American Countries . 346

CHAPTER X

URUGUAY

How Uruguay became an Independent Republic . . . 349
Resources of the Country 350
The City of Montevideo 351
Population of Uruguay: Immigrants and Natives . . . 355
A Revolution in Uruguay 356
The Whites and the Reds 357
Causes of the Revolutionary Habit 358
Prosperity of Uruguay 362

CHAPTER XI

BRAZIL

How Brazil fell to the Portuguese 366
Physical Features of the Different Parts of the Country . . 368
Voyage from Montevideo to Santos 370
Santos and the Railway to São Paulo 372
The City of São Paulo and its People 374
Approach to Rio de Janeiro 377
Aspect of Rio: The Bay and the Mountains 378
Scenery of the Environs of Rio 382
Petropolis the " Hill Station " of Rio 384
Excursion through the Mountains 386
A Brazilian Forest 390
Naval Mutiny at Rio 395
Economic Resources of Brazil 402
The People: German and Italian Immigrants . . . 405
The Negroes and Indians 407
Recent History of Brazil 410
Character and Tendencies of the Brazilians . . . 416
The Future of Brazil 420

CHAPTER XII

THE RELATIONS OF RACES IN SOUTH AMERICA

PAGE

Importance of the Aboriginal Element in Spanish-American Countries 424

How the Native Tribes came to Survive 425

Probable Present Numbers of the Indian Population . . . 428

The Indians in Peru and Bolivia 430

Present State of these Indians, Social and Religious . . . 430

Ulloa's Report on their Condition in the Eighteenth Century . 433

Universal Illiteracy of the Indians: Their Civil and Political Status 435

Relations of Indians and Whites: No " Colour Line " in Latin America 440

How the Presence of the Aborigines has affected the Whites . 445

The Negroes in Brazil 449

Three General Conclusions regarding the Native Indians of South America 450

It is not certain that they have injured the White Race by Intermixture 451

Demoralization of the Peruvian Indians by the Spanish Conquest, and Subsequent Oppression 451

Racial Repugnance not a Universal Phenomenon in the Relations of Peoples of Different Colour 452

INTRODUCTION

WHOEVER read as a boy the books of old travellers in the Andes, such as Humboldt's *Aspects of Nature*, or pored over such accounts of the primitive American peoples as are given in Prescott's *Conquest of Peru* must have longed to visit some day the countries that fired his imagination. These had been my experiences, and to them there was subsequently added a curiosity to learn the causes which produced so many revolutions and civil wars in Spanish America, and, still later, a sense that these countries, some of them issuing from a long period of turbulence, were becoming potent economic factors in the modern world. So when after many years the opportunity of having four clear months for a journey to South America presented itself, I spent those months in seeing as much as I could within the time, and was able to make some observations and form certain impressions regarding the seven republics I visited. These observations and impressions are contained in the following pages. They are, of course, merely first impressions, but the impressions which travel makes on a fresh mind have their value if they are tested by subsequent study and by being submitted to persons who know the country thoroughly. I have tried so to test these impressions of mine, and hope they may be of service to those who desire to learn something about South America, but have not time to peruse the many books of travel that have been written about each of its countries.

The chief points of interest which these countries have for Europeans and North Americans may be summed up as follows : —

1. The aspects of nature.

2. The inhabitants, the white part of whom are of Spanish origin, except the. Brazilians, who come from Portugal.

3. The economic resources of the several countries.

4. The prospects for the development of industry and commerce.

5. The relics of prehistoric civilization.

6. The native Indian population.

7. The conditions of political life in the several republics.

It may be convenient that I should explain how far and in what order each of these topics is dealt with.

The first eleven chapters of the book contain a description of what I saw of scenery and of social and economic phenomena in the seven republics of Panama, Peru, Bolivia, Chile, Argentina, Uruguay, and Brazil, and in these chapters the first three of the above-mentioned subjects are dealt with when and as each country is described. It is Nature that chiefly engages the traveller's mind in Peru and Bolivia, as it is economic development which interests him in Argentina and Uruguay. In Chile and Brazil he must be always thinking of both. The fourth topic has been treated so fully by many writers who have brought special knowledge to it and have written professedly for the information of business men, that I have not thought it necessary to fill this book with statistical tables or, indeed, to do more than indicate the possibilities for commercial development or agricultural immigration which the natural resources of each country seem to promise.

It is only in Peru and Bolivia that any prehistoric monuments exist. Some of the most important and interesting of these I saw, and in describing them I have endeavoured to convey an idea of the character of the ancient Peruvian civilization (if that name can properly be applied to it) and of the people who produced it. This is done in Chapters III, IV, and V.

Only in Peru, Bolivia, and Chile did I have opportunities of seeing the native Indians. In the two former states they constitute a far larger part of the total population than in any other state (except Paraguay): they are nominally Christians, and they lead a settled agricultural life. In Chile there is only one considerable Indian tribe remaining, the famous Araucanians. Of these warriors, of the Quichuas in Peru and of the Aymarás in Bolivia, some account will be found in Chapters III to VI.

In the above-mentioned eleven descriptive chapters I have endeavoured to individualize, so to speak, the chief countries of South America, so as to bring out the chief characteristics, natural and human, of each of them.

But marked as are the differences between the various republics, they have all something in common, something that belongs to South America as opposed to Europe or North America or Australia. There are also certain general questions affecting the whole Continent which present themselves to the traveller's mind and need to be discussed upon broad and general lines. To these questions the last five chapters of the book have been devoted. One chapter endeavours to indicate the causes which have divided the vast Spanish-American dominion (including Mexico and Central America) as it stood in A.D. 1810 into the sixteen independent republics of to-day, some of which have become, others of which are becoming, true nations with marked national characteristics. Another chapter deals with the relations to the white population of the aborigines in the Spanish countries and of the negroes in Brazil, the only state in which negroes are numerous. It is a subject of study all the more interesting because these relations are altogether different from those borne by the European element to the coloured races in the British colonies, in India, and in the United States of North America, and also because the intermixture of races which is now going on in South America suggests physiological and ethnological problems of high interest.

A third chapter (Chapter XIV) briefly compares the conditions of settlement and of government which determined the course of economic and political development in North and in South America respectively and enquires how far the latter Continent is to be considered any more closely related to the former than it is to Europe. Is there, in fact, such a thing as that which the word Pan-Americanism is intended to describe, or does the expression denote an aspiration rather than a fact?

Of the political history of these republics very little
is said in this book, and of their current politics nothing
at all. That is a topic on which it would not be
fitting for me to enter. But in travelling through the
seven countries, in observing their physical features and
the character of their people, and the state of knowledge and education among them, as well as in reading
accounts of the kind of administration which the Spanish
Crown gave them during nearly three centuries, I
was struck by the influence which all these facts must
have had upon the free governments which the Revolutionary leaders tried to set up when they broke away
from the mother country. The history of Spanish
America since 1810 cannot be understood or fairly
judged, without taking these things into account.
They have been the fundamental and determinative
conditions of political life in these countries; and to
them Chapter XV has been devoted.

In the last Chapter (XVI) I have touched upon
several subjects relating to the South American lands
and peoples in general for which no appropriate earlier
place could be found, and have indulged in a few conjectures as to the future both of the several states and
of the Continent as a whole. These are not meant as
predictions, but rather as suggestions of possibilities
which may serve to set others thinking.

Lest some of the views presented, especially those regarding the native races and political conditions should
be deemed unduly optimistic, let me try to meet any
such criticism by a few words on optimism in general.

Pessimism is easier than optimism, as it is easier to destroy than to construct. There was an old dictum in the Middle Ages, "*Omnia tendunt naturaliter in non esse,*"[1] and Mephistopheles in Goethe's *Faust* tells us that

Alles was entsteht
Ist werth dass es zu Grunde geht.[2]

If pessimism is easy, the more need to stand on guard against it.

The duty of a traveller, or a historian, or a philosopher is, of course, to reach and convey the exact truth, and any tendency either to lighten or to darken the picture is equally to be condemned. But where there is room for doubt, and wherever that which may be called the "temperamental equation" of the observer comes in, an optimistic attitude would seem to be the safer, that is to say, likely to be nearer to the truth. We are all prone to see faults rather than merits, and in making this remark I do not forget the so-called "log-rolling critics," because with them the question is of what the critic says, not of what he sees, which may be something quite different. If this maxim holds true, it is especially needed when a traveller is judging a foreign country, for the bias always present in us which favours our own national ways and traits makes us judge the faults of other nations more severely than we do those with which we are familiar. As this unconscious factor present in our minds darkens

[1] All things tend naturally towards non-existence. So in the original statutes of Oriel College, Oxford (founded in A.D. 1327).

[2] All that comes into being deserves to perish.

the picture that a traveller draws, it is safer for him, if in doubt, to throw in a little light so as to secure a just result. Moreover, we are all apt, when we deal with another country, to be unduly impressed by the defects we actually see and to forget to ask what is, after all, the really important question, whether things are getting better or worse. Is it an ebbing or a flowing tide that we see? Even in reflecting on the past of our own country, which we know better than we do that of other countries, we are apt, in noting the emergence of new dangers, to forget how many old dangers have disappeared. Much more is this kind of error likely to affect us in the case of a country whose faults are more repellent than our own national faults, and whose recuperative forces we may overlook or undervalue.

Such considerations as these have made me believe that the natural propensity of a West European or North American traveller to judge Spanish Americans by his own standards needs to be corrected not only by making allowance for differences of intellect and character, but also by a comprehension of the history of these peoples and of the difficulties, many of them due to causes outside their own control, which have encompassed and entangled them ever since their ancestors first set foot in the Western world. Whoever compares these difficulties as they stand to-day with those of a century ago will find grounds not only for more lenient judgments than most Europeans have passed, but also for brighter hopes.

Neither in this matter, however, nor anywhere in

the chapters which deal with the social and political conditions of South America have I ventured to dogmatize. My aim has rather been to start questions and to indicate various sides from which South American problems may be approached. The interest of these new countries lies largely in the fact that while some problems, already familiar to the Old World, have here taken on new aspects, others appear here almost for the first time in history. Some of them involve phenomena of race growth and race intermixture for the investigation of which the data we possess are still insufficient. Others turn upon the still unascertained capacity of European races for working and thriving in tropical countries. It may take many years before science can tell us half of what we desire to know regarding the economic possibilities of the central regions of the Continent, for the development of which no labour is now available. The future of the temperate South is more certain, for all the material conditions that make for prosperity in North America and Australia are present there also. These countries will be the home of rich and populous nations, and possibly of great nations. The most interesting of all the questions which a journey in South America suggests are those which concern the growth of these young nations. What type of manhood will they develop ? What place in the world will they ultimately hold ? They need fear no attacks from the powers of the Northern Hemisphere, and they have abundant resources within. Their future is in their own hands.

SOUTH AMERICA

CHAPTER I

THE ISTHMUS OF PANAMA

SOUTH AMERICA is bounded at its northern end by an isthmus and at its southern by a strait. They are the two gateways by which the western side of the Continent, cut off from the western and central portions by a long and lofty mountain range, can be approached from the Atlantic. It was by crossing the Isthmus that Vasco Nuñez de Balboa discovered the South Sea. It was by penetrating the Strait that Magellan, seven years later, discovered that this South Sea was a vast ocean stretching all the way to the coasts of Asia. In old Spanish days all the commerce of the west coast passed over the Isthmus,[1] but when the days of steam navigation arrived, that commerce passed through Magellan's Strait. Now the Isthmus itself is to be turned into a strait and will be a channel for sea-borne trade, the main gateway to the West.

An isthmus and a strait are, to the historical geographer and to the geographical historian, the most interesting things with which geographical science has to deal. Commerce and travel and naval warfare concentrate themselves at the spot where a narrow channel connects wide seas, and the strip of land which severs two seas from one another interposes a barrier to water-borne trade and turns it off into other directions. It

[1] The trade to the Philippines crossed the Continent at Tehuantepec.

B   1

becomes a point the control of which can stop the march of armies, and it furnishes a central stronghold whence ships can go forth to threaten the neighbouring coasts. Thus every strait and every isthmus has a high commercial importance, and almost always a political importance also, since lines of commerce have usually been, and are now more than ever, potent factors in human affairs, while the command of a water passage for fleets, or that of a land passage for armies, may be of capital importance in war.

The Eastern Hemisphere has an isthmus which has been significant for world commerce and for world history almost from the beginning of civilization. It is the Isthmus of Suez. So the Western Hemisphere has its isthmus of supreme importance, — that of Panama. It is a link between continents and a barrier between seas, which, though its history is far shorter than is that of Suez, yet has been at some moments in the last four centuries, and may be still more hereafter, of high significance for the movements of the world.

There are some notable points of similarity between these two isthmuses. Their breadth is not very different, — Suez sixty miles, Panama about fifty-four. The shortest line across each runs nearly due north and south. The continents which each unites are gigantic. Each lies in what is, or was till quite lately, a practically uninhabited country.

Here, however, the likeness ends; and we come to points of contrast that are more remarkable. The Isthmus of Suez is flat as a table from one end to the other ; that of Panama is covered with high and generally steep hills. Suez is an arid waste, where there is not a brook and scarcely even a well, and by consequence not a tree, nor any growing thing save a few thin and thorny shrubs. Panama has a tremendous rainfall in places, varying from one hundred and forty inches a year on the north side to sixty on the south, and is covered with wood so dense that roads have to be not only hewn through the forest but defended by incessant cutting against the efforts of a prolific nature, always seeking to reassert her rights. Having a keen, dry, desert air, the whole Suez region is a healthy one, where man need fear disease only in those few spots which he has in recent years brought under irrigation. Panama had for centuries a climate so deadly that even passing travellers feared to halt more than a few hours on either side of the Isthmus. Yellow fever, intermittent and remittent fevers, and all sorts of other tropical maladies made it their favourite home.

A still more remarkable contrast, however, between these two necks of land lies in the part they have respectively played in human affairs. The Isthmus of Panama must, in far-off prehistoric days, have been the highway along which those wandering tribes whose forefathers had passed in their canoes from northeastern Asia along the Aleutian Isles into Alaska found their way, after many centuries, into the vast spaces of South America. But its place in the annals of mankind during the four centuries that have elapsed since

Balboa gazed from a mountain top rising out of the forest upon the far-off waters of the South Sea has been small, indeed, compared to that which the Isthmus of Suez has held from the beginning of history. It echoed to the tread of the armies of Thothmes and Rameses marching forth on their invasions of western Asia. Along the edge of it Israel fled forth before the hosts of Pharaoh. First the Assyrian and afterwards the Persian hosts poured across it to conquer Egypt; and over its sands Bonaparte led his regiments to Palestine in that bold adventure which was stopped at St. Jean d'Acre. It has been one of the great highways for armies for forty centuries, as the canal cut through it is now one of the great highways of commerce.

The turn of the Isthmus of Panama has now come, and curiously enough it is the Isthmus of Suez that brought that turn, for it was the digging of a ship canal from the Mediterranean to the Red Sea, and the vast expansion of Eastern trade which followed, that led to the revival of the old designs, mooted as far back as the days of the Emperor Charles the Fifth, of piercing the American Isthmus. Thus the comparison of the two isthmuses becomes now more interesting than ever, for our generation will watch to see whether the commerce and politics of the western world will be affected by this new route which is now being opened, as those of the Old World have been affected by the achievement of Ferdinand de Lesseps.

So many books have been written, and so many more will be written, about the engineering of the

Panama Canal and about its commercial possibilities, that of these very little need be said in such a sketch as this. But as everybody is already curious, and will, two years hence, be still more curious regarding the region it traverses, I shall try to convey some sort of notion of the physical aspects of the Isthmus and of the impressions its past and its present make on the traveller's mind. In taking the reader with me across the neck of land, I shall in the first instance say nothing of the works of the canal which I saw in course of execution, but will ask him to remember that it runs, as does the Trans-Isthmian railway, from north to south, the coast line both on the Atlantic and on the Pacific side trending in this region east and west.[1]

Approaching in the steamer from Europe or New York across the Caribbean Sea one sees low hills rising gently from the shore, fringed with palms and dotted with small white houses half hidden among the trees. In front, on an islet now joined to the mainland, is the town of Colon, a new town, with a statue of Christopher Columbus "protecting" a female Indian figure of America, but no buildings of interest and little history, for it is only sixty years old, built as the terminal point of the railway. The old fortified ports where the Spanish galleons used to lie at anchor in former days, Nombre de Dios and Puerto Bello, stand farther to the east. Behind the town, higher hills, covered with those thick, light green woods that characterize the

[1] The reader will find at the end of the volume a small map which may help him to understand the topography of the region.

tropics, cut off the view to the south.   No depression
in the land is visible.   There is nothing to suggest that
another ocean lies beyond, only fifty miles away, and
that here the great backbone which traverses two
continents for many thousands of miles sinks to a
point a few hundreds of feet above sea level.

The traveller on landing steps into the railroad car,
and after running for three miles along the shore of the
shallow bay of Limon into which the Canal is to issue,
strikes in four miles more the valley of the Chágrés
River.   Here is the point (to be described later) at
which the huge Gatun Dam is being built across that
valley to flood it and turn it into a navigable lake.
Thence the line keeps in the same general south-southeast direction on the east side of the Chagres River,
parallel to its course.   The Chagres, a muddy and
rather languid stream, has in the dry season about as
much water as the Scottish Tweed and in the wet season rather more than the Potomac and much more
than the Shannon.   There are few stations on the way,
and at first no dwellings, for the country was uninhabited till the work of canal construction began.   Mo-
rasses are crossed, and everywhere there is on each side a
dense, dark forest.   So deep and spongy are the swamps
that in places it has been found impossible to fill them
up or to lay more than one set of rails upon the surface.
So dense is the forest, the spaces between the tree trunks
filled by shrubs and the boughs bound together by
climbing plants into a wall of living green, that one
cannot see more than a few yards into the thicket,

and can force a way through it only by the help of the *machete*, — that long, cutlass-like knife which people carry in Spanish America. Hardly a trail running into the woods is seen, and a mile or two back the wild cats and monkeys, and their terrible enemies, the ana-condas or boa constrictors, have the place all to them-selves.

After some twenty-three miles of this sort of country, beautiful when the outer boughs of the trees are gay with brilliant blossoms, and pendulous orchids sway in the breeze between their stems, but in September rather monotonous in color, the railway crosses and leaves the Chagres River, whose valley turns north-east far in among higher hills. The line continues to run southward, rising gently between slopes from which the wood has been lately cut away so that one can see the surrounding landscape. All around there is a sort of tossing sea of miniature moun-tains — I call them mountains because of their steep slopes and pointed crests, though few of them exceed a thousand feet in height. These are set so close together that hardly a dozen yards of level ground can be found between the bases of their declivities, and are disposed so irregularly that they seem as if the product of scattered outbreaks and uplifts of igneous rock. Their sides are clothed and their tops plumed with so thick a growth of wood that the eye cannot discover crags or cliffs, if any there be, and the tops of all are practi-cally unapproachable, because no trails have yet been cut, except to one conspicuous summit. This one

rises boldly to a height of about 1200 feet, and has
received the name of Balboa Hill, because from it
alone in this region — so one is told — can both oceans
in a season of fair weather be descried.   The gallant
Vasco Nuñez deserves the honour of being thus com-
memorated; but it is to be feared that before long the
legend will have struck root among those who dwell
here, and will be repeated to those who pass along the
canal, that it was from this height, and not from a peak
in Darien, seventy or eighty miles farther to the east,
that the bold adventurer first looked out over the
shining expanse of the South Sea.

We are now more than halfway to the Pacific and
may pause to survey the landscape.   Though there is
moisture everywhere, one sees no water, for neither
ocean can be seen, the Chagres is hidden among the folds
of the hills, and the brooks at the valley bottoms are
insignificant.   But otherwise it is cheerful and pleasant
in its bright green and its varied lines, — a country in
which a man might be content to live, faintly reminding one of the Trossachs in Scotland by the number of
steep little peaks crowded together and by the profusion
of wood.   The luxuriance of nature is, however, far
greater than in any temperate clime, and the trees
have that feathery lightness which belongs to the
tropics, their tops springing like green bubbles into the
soft blue air.

Here, at a place called Culebra, is the highest part of
the crossing from ocean to ocean, 110 feet above sea-
level; and as it was here that the deepest cutting had

to be made for the canal it is here that the head-quarters of the engineering staff has been fixed. Of the cutting more anon. The railway follows a devious course among the hills, rattling here and there through cuttings in hard igneous rock, and in a few miles, descending gently, it passes out into a wide valley, the farther end of which, to the south, is open, with a bold hill guarding it on the east side and several more distant rocky eminences visible far away against the horizon. The hill is Ancon, overlooking Panama city on the one side, and, on the other, the bay which the canal enters. The eminences are islands lying out in the Pacific. Being now quite down on the level of the ocean, we do not see its waters till the railway, passing along the edge of a brackish tidal swamp, reaches the city of Panama, forty-six miles from Colon.

As the Pacific side of the Isthmus is much the most picturesque part of the whole, and impresses itself most on the imagination, the visitor who desires to enjoy the scenery and grasp the configuration of land and sea, ought to climb, if he is an active walker, to the top of the hill of Ancon, on the lower slopes of which, rising just above Panama city, are the United States government offices and the villas of its officials. Steep everywhere, and in parts slippery also, is the foot-path that leads over pastures and through thickets to the top of the hill, some six hundred feet high. But it is worth while to make the ascent, for from the summit one obtains an ample prospect worthy of the historic greatness of the spot.

From this breezy height let the traveller turn his eyes first to the north, and look back over that maze of low forest-covered mountains through which he has passed from Colon and which form the watershed between the two seas. No more from this side of the Isthmus than from the other does one discern any depression in the watershed, any break in the range sufficient to indicate that at this point there is an easy passage from the Atlantic to the Pacific. The hollows through which both railroad and canal pass are hidden deep in the folds of the hills, which stand so thick together that it is hard to believe any waterway could ever be carved out between them and impossible to tell the spot where the cutting is being made.

Very different is the view when the gaze is turned east-ward along the far-winding bays and promontories of the Gulf of Panama. There the coast is for a long space flat, and a plain runs back toward distant hills. Beyond this plain other ranges rise to the southeast, bordering the Pacific till they sink below the horizon opposite the Pearl Islands. Somewhere among those ranges is the height to which Balboa climbed and whence he made the great discovery; somewhere along those shores the place where, clad in armour, he strode into the waves, and with sword drawn, took possession of the sea on behalf of the king of Spain. It is rather across that plain that any one looking from this side might fancy the lowest passage from sea to sea would be found. Yet not there, but much farther to the southeast, far behind the hills, in the Gulf of Darien, there is a point still lower, where between the Atrato River which falls into the Caribbean and the River San Juan running to the Pacific a few miles of cut would enable a ship to pass from sea to sea. Now let the traveller turn round and face to the west. His eyes will follow a long mountain chain which rises high and bold from the opposite shore of the Gulf of Panama and runs out southwest until it too is lost to sight beneath the far horizon. In front, a group of rocky isles lies basking in the sunny sea. Just beneath the Ancon hill, at its eastern foot, the little city of Panama stands on its promontory, a mass of grey, red-roofed houses with a half-demolished Spanish fort of the eighteenth century guarding the shallow roadstead, while on the opposite side of the hill, at the base of its steep slopes, is the mouth of the Canal.

The landscape spread out under this hill of Ancon is the finest in all the Isthmian region. The northern side at Colon, although pretty with its abundant verdure, is commonplace; but here there is a view which appeals at once to the eye and to the imagination, ranging over vast stretches of land and sea, rich with varied colour, bringing together the past and the future. Over these smooth ocean plains, which the Spaniards, accustomed to their own stormy Atlantic, called the Peaceful Sea, Vasco Nuñez de Balboa looked eagerly out as he planned that expedition to Peru which the jealous cruelty of Pedrarias, the Spanish viceroy, cut short. Over them the less worthy but more fortunate Pizarro sailed to those far southern lands, where he won, in two years, an empire vaster than that which in the Old World obeyed his sovereign, Charles the Fifth. Backward and forward across these waters came the fleets that bore to the south swarms of fierce adventurers to plunder the native peoples, and that brought back the treasures which supported the European wars of Spain and helped to work her ruin. Three miles off there can be just discerned amid the trees the ancient cathedral tower of the now ruined city of old Panama, where those fleets used to anchor till the English buccaneer Morgan sacked and destroyed the place in 1679. And just beneath, on the opposite side of the hill from these traces of the vanished colonial empire of Spain, the long mole that is to shield the mouth of the Canal is rising, and the steamships lying along the wharves, and cars standing beside them on the railway tracks, presage a commerce vaster than ever was seen in the great days of Spain, for they speak of the passage of men from all the nations along the new waterway through these forests and out over this sea to the ends of the earth. Here, as at the Straits of Gibraltar and on the Bosphorus, nature and history have joined to give delight for the eyes, and to the mind musings on the past and dim forecasting visions of the future.

Save for these few points where human dwellings are seen, — the little Spanish city below and the offices and warehouses that mark the beginnings of the new commercial port and some houses on the islets in the bay, where the inhabitants of Panama seek in summer a cooler air, — it is a lonely landscape, with scarcely a sign of life on land, and as yet few ships flecking the water. The region has always been thinly peopled and its tribes never reached the semi-civilization of the Maya peoples of Yucatan, Honduras, and Guatemala to the north of them, nor of the Chibchas of Bogota to the south. There are, anyhow, no traces of prehistoric progress here, though some have been found in Costa Rica. The aborigines were not numerous in this region, and, after the Spaniards came, were quickly reduced by the attacks which gold-seeking adventurers made upon them. Thus one hears of but few now, except at one place, called San Blas, on the shore of the Caribbean Sea, some forty miles east of Colon. There an Indian tribe has kept itself quite apart from the white intruders, having maintained a practical independence both of Spanish viceroys and republican presidents of Colombia. These Indians are short, strong men, good sailors and fine fighters, men of the same stock that repulsed the first settlers whom Columbus planted near by on his second voyage, and so jealous of their freedom and their own ways that they will not suffer a white stranger to spend the night in one of their villages. They are reported to be still heathens, having their own medicine men, the efficiency of whom is secured by a rule which terminates the professional career together with the life of a practitioner who has lost to death seven patients in succession. These Indians come to Colon in their canoes to trade, and show themselves passably friendly to the Americans there, though less effusively so than their ancestors were to the English in those far-away days when they guided English buccaneers across the Isthmus to pounce upon their Spanish enemies at Panama. When in 1698 the Scottish colonists arrived on their ill-starred expedition to found a colony at Darien, the San Blas men welcomed them with open arms and shewed their good feeling by frequently coming on board and drinking a great deal of liquor. These kindly dispositions lasted down till our own time, for a tale goes that in one of their struggles against the Colombians they declared themselves subjects of Queen Victoria. The Republic of Panama, having plenty of troubles of its own, wisely leaves them alone.

As there are few Indians now in the narrowest part of the Isthmus, so also there are few white people. The Spaniards never tried to settle the country, though they built towns here and there on the coast for trade. There was neither gold nor silver to attract adventurers. The land was covered with jungle, and there was a lack of native labourers to be enslaved and set to clear and till it. The jealous policy of the home government excluded the subjects of all other powers, so most of this region remained a wilderness, unimproved, and parts of it unexplored. A paved road was constructed across the Isthmus from old Panama, the town built by Pedrarias when he crossed to the Pacific side in 1520, to Nombre de Dios, which became the chief port on the Atlantic side; and along this road pack mule trains carried the silver that had come up from Peru to be shipped for Cadiz or Vigo in those great galleons for which the English seamen used to lie in wait. On the Atlantic coast there was held once a year a great fair which lasted six weeks, and to which trading folk came by sea from far and wide. Nearly all the manufactured goods which were consumed in Peru and all down the west coast were sold and bought here. Little else broke the monotonous annals of these remote provinces except the exploits of the English sea-rovers who carried on the war of Protestantism against Spain for the benefit of their own pockets. Sir Francis Drake, the least sordid and most gallant among them, began his exploits by establishing himself in a creek on the At-lantic side of the Isthmus, and thence took Nombre de Dios with a ridiculously small force, and laid ambushes for the silver-carrying mule trains that crossed from Pa-nama, raiding at intervals such Spanish ports as his small force enabled him to capture. In one early expedition, he climbed a tree on a hilltop, and seeing the Pacific from it, fell on his knees and prayed God to give him life till he could sail upon that sea in an English ship — a prayer which was amply fulfilled when he issued from the Straits of Magellan and ravaged the coasts of Peru in 1578. In the last of all his cruises it was in his ship off Puerto Bello that he died in 1596. Eighty years later, Morgan, the famous English buc-caneer, gathered a large force of adventurers and sea-faring ruffians, crossed the Isthmus by sailing in small boats up the Chagres and thence after a short land journey falling upon Panama, which he took and pillaged, bringing back his booty to the Caribbean Sea. The city was burned, whether by him or by the Spaniards remains in doubt, and thereafter it lay deserted.

Thirty years after Morgan's raid the commercial possibilities of the Isthmus fascinated a Scotsman who had more than the usual fervour and less than the usual caution of his nation. William Paterson, the founder of the Bank of England, led a colony, chiefly composed of Scottish people, and well supplied with Scottish ministers, to a place near Acla in the Gulf of Darien, on the Atlantic side of the Isthmus, one hundred miles southeast of Colon, meaning to make it a great centre of trade over both oceans. They went out, however, imperfectly equipped and ignorant of climatic conditions. Many perished from disease; King William III gave them no support; the Spaniards at last attacked and compelled the surrender of the few who remained. Thereafter nobody disturbed the subjects of the Catholic king. New Panama, planted in a better site where the roadstead is a little deeper, although too shallow for the ocean liners of our own day, continued to enjoy a certain prosperity as the gateway to all western South America, for there was and could be no land transit through the trackless forests and rugged mountains that lie along the coast between the Isthmus and the Equator. But the decline and decay of the colonial empire of Spain under the most ill-conceived and ill-administered scheme of government that selfishness and stupidity ever combined to devise, steadily reduced the importance of the city. Nothing was done to develop the country, which remained, outside Panama and a few other ports, an unprofitable solitude. Neither did the extinction of the rule of Spain, which came quietly here because the local governor did not resist it, make any difference. Occupied with domestic broils, the new republic, first called New Granada and now Colombia, had not the capital nor the intelligence nor the energy to improve the country or develop the commercial possibilities of the Isthmus. This was a task reserved for children of the race which had produced Drake and Morgan.

Thus we come down to the events which have given Panama its present importance. In 1846 Mexico was forced to cede to the United States, as the price of peace, the territories which now constitute the States of California, Nevada, Arizona, and New Mexico. Soon afterwards gold was discovered in California, and a great inrush of settlers followed. There was urgent need for some shorter and safer route to San Francisco than the voyage round Cape Horn or the waggon trail over plains and mountains from the Missouri. Three enterprising Americans obtained in 1848 a concession of the right to build a railway across the Isthmus. The line was opened in 1855, and had, till taken over by the United States government, paid higher dividends continuously (an average down to 1895 of about 15 per cent per annum) than any other line in the world. Being exposed to no competition, it could charge what fares it pleased. A better service of passenger steamers began to run from Panama southward as

c

well as northward; and thenceforward, despite its
deadly climate, the Isthmus became a world highway.
Though the subsequent opening of railroads across
the North American continent reduced the passenger
traffic from the eastern United States to California via
Panama, the goods or freight traffic continued; and as
trade to western South America increased, so the old idea
of constructing an interoceanic canal took more definite
shape and led to the propounding of scheme after
scheme.   Finally, in 1878, the success which Ferdinand
de Lesseps had achieved at Suez encouraged him to
form a company in France to make a sea-level waterway through the Isthmus.   This company, formed
without sufficient preliminary investigation of the conditions and the cost, collapsed in 1889, having exhausted its funds.   A second one, formed in 1894 to
resume and complete the enterprise, failed in its turn,
after spending many millions, and in 1904 transferred
all its rights and interests, together with its plans and
its machinery, to the United States government, who,
after about two years usefully spent in examining
the problem they had to face, began in 1907 that
effective work of digging and lock-building which they
expect to complete in 1913.   They had for some time
been trying to obtain a grant from the republic of Colombia of the strip of land required for the excavation of
the Canal, but could not secure terms which they thought
reasonable.   Then, in 1903, a revolt took place at Panama against the authority of Colombia, and the new
republic of Panama, which forthwith emerged, gave to

the United States a perpetual lease of a strip of ten miles wide, being the space through which the purposed canal was to run. This strip — now called the Canal Zone — is forty-five miles long, with an area of about 448 square miles. The United States Government is practically supreme in it, — though it has been held not to be a part of the United States for the purposes of the Constitution, — and rules it by a Commission under the War Department, being also owner of more than two-thirds of its surface. In return for the lease it has paid a large sum to the little republic and guaranteed its independence. With the strip it has also acquired four small islands, deemed valuable strategically, which lie a little way off the shore opposite the Pacific end of the Canal. They are now to be fortified to protect the approach. The colonial city, with its picturesque fort looking out over the sea, its pretty little plazas planted with trees, its winding old-fashioned streets and big dark churches, stands within the Canal Zone, but is administered by its own government, being the capital of this smallest of all the South American republics. The poorer classes occupy themselves with fishing and sitting in the shade, the upper classes with politics. There is hardly any cultivated land near, but it is hoped that on the high undulating ground some miles to the west the cultivation of vegetables and fruits and whatever else passing vessels may need will presently be established.

Of the Canal itself a few words must now be said, just enough to convey some preliminary general notion of it to those who two years hence, when the time for its formal opening arrives, will be deluged with details.

It will be fifty miles in length, from deep water to deep water, though only forty from tide-end to tide-end. The minimum bottom width will be three hundred feet, the minimum depth forty-one feet, the breadth and depth being, however, for the larger part of its length, greater than these figures. Its highest point above sea-level will be eighty-five feet at the surface of the water and forty feet at the bottom, the depth at this point being forty-five feet; *i.e.* it will be cut down through the dividing ridge of the Continent to a point forty feet above the two oceans.

The simplest way to realize its character is to consider it as consisting of four sections which I will call (*a*) the Atlantic Level, (*b*) the Lake, (*c*) the Cutting, and (*d*) the Pacific·section (in two levels separated by a lock). The Atlantic Level is a straight channel, unbroken by locks, of eight miles, from deep water at the mouth of the shallow Bay of Limon, a little west of Colon, to Gatun, where it reaches the valley of the Chagres River. Now the Chagres River had always been reckoned as one of the chief difficulties in the way of making a canal. It occupied the bottom of that natural depression along which all surveyors had long ago perceived that any canal must run. But the difficulty of widening and deepening the river channel till it should become a useable canal, was a formidable one, because in the wet season the river swells to an unmanageable size under the tropical rains, sometimes rising over forty feet in twenty-four hours. This difficulty was at last met and the stream ingeniously utilized by erecting right across the course of the Chagres a stupendous dam at Gatun, which by impounding the water of the river turns its valley into a lake. This lake will have along the central channel a depth of from eighty-five to forty-five feet of water, sufficient for the largest ship. At the Gatun dam there are three locks, built of concrete, with a total rise of eighty-five feet, by which vessels will be lifted up into the lake. The lake will fill not only the valley of the Chagres itself, but the bottom of its tributary valleys to the east and west, so that it will cover 164 square miles in all, and will be dotted by many islands. The central and deepest line of this artificial piece of water, nearly twenty-four miles long, is the second of our four canal sections, and will be the prettiest, for the banks are richly wooded. At the point called Bas Obispo, where the Chagres valley, which has been running south-southeast towards the Pacific turns away to the northeast among the hills, the line of the canal leaves the Gatun river-lake, and we enter the third section, which I have called the Cutting. Here hills are encountered, so it became necessary, in order to avoid the making of more locks, to cut deep into the central line of the continent, with its ridge of rock which connects the Cordilleras of the southern continent with the Sierras of the northern. After five miles of comparatively shallow cutting southward from the Lake, a tall and steep eminence, Gold Hill, the continental watershed, its top 665 feet high, bars the way.   Through it there has been carved out a mighty gash, the " Culebra Cut," of which more anon.   A little further south, eight miles from the Lake, the ground begins to fall rapidly towards the other sea, and we reach the fourth or Pacific section at a point called Pedro Miguel.   Here is a lock by which the Canal is lowered thirty feet to another but much smaller artificial lake, formed by a long dam built across the valley at a spot called Miraflores, where we find two more locks, by which vessels will be lowered fifty-five feet to the level of the Pacific.   Thence the Canal runs straight out into the ocean, here so shallow that a deep-water channel has been dredged out for some miles, and a great dyke or mole erected along its eastern side to keep the southerly current from silting up the harbour.   From Pedro Miguel to Miraflores it is nearly two miles, and from the locks at the latter to the Pacific eight miles, so the length of this fourth Pacific section, which, unlike the Atlantic section, is on two different levels divided by the Miraflores dam and locks, is ten miles.   In it there has been comparatively little land excavation, because the ground is flat, though a great deal of dredging, both to carry a sea channel out through the shallow bay into the open Pacific, and also to provide space for vessels to lie and load or discharge without blocking the traffic.

Thus the voyager of the future, in the ten or twelve hours of his passage from ocean to ocean, will have much variety.   The level light of the fiery tropic dawn will fall on the houses of Colon as he approaches it in the morning, when vessels usually arrive. When his ship has mounted the majestic staircase of the three Gatun locks from the Atlantic level, he will glide slowly and softly along the waters of a broad lake which gradually narrows toward its head, a lake enclosed by rich forests of that velvety softness one sees in the tropics, with vistas of forest-girt islets stretching far off to right and left among the hills, a welcome change from the restless Caribbean Sea which he has left. Then the mountains will close in upon him, steep slopes of grass or brushwood rising two hundred feet above him as he passes through the great Cut. From the level of the Miguel lock he will look southward down the broad vale that opens on the ocean flooded with the light of the declining sun, and see the rocky islets rising, between which in the twilight his course will lie out into the vast Pacific. At Suez the passage from sea to sea is through a dreary and monotonous waste of shifting sand and barren clay. Here one is for a few hours in the centre of a verdant continent, floating on smooth waters, shut off from sight of the ocean behind and the ocean before, a short sweet present of tranquillity between a stormy past and a stormy future.

In these forty miles of canal (or fifty if we reckon from deep water to deep water) the two most remarkable pieces of engineering work are the gigantic dam (with its locks) at Gatun and the gigantic cutting at Culebra, each the hugest of its kind that the world has to shew. The dam is nearly a mile and a half long; its base nearly half a mile thick, and it is 400 feet wide at the water line of the lake which it will support. Each of the three locks is double, so that one of the pair can be used by vessels passing from north to south, the other by those passing from south to north. Each has a useable length of 1000 feet, a useable width of 110 feet. They are big enough in length, width, and depth for the largest vessels that were afloat in 1911. He who stands inside one of them seems, when he looks up, to be at the bottom of a rocky glen, "a canyon of cement." Nothing less than an earthquake will affect them, and of earthquakes there is no record in this region, though they are frequent in Costa Rica, two hundred miles away. The locks will be worked, and vessels will be towed through them, by electric power, which is to be generated by the fall of the Chagres River over the spillway which carries its water from the lake to the Atlantic.

The great Culebra Cut is interesting not only to the engineer, but also to the geologist, as being what he calls a Section. It is the deepest open cutting anywhere in the world, and shows curious phenomena in the injection of igneous rocks, apparently very recent, among the loose sedimentary beds, chiefly clays and soft sandstones of the latest tertiary epoch. A troublesome result, partly of this intermixture, and partly of the friability and instability not only of the sedimentary strata but also of some of the volcanic rocks, has been noted in the constant slips and slides of rock and earth down the sides of the cutting into the bed of the canal that is to be. This source of expense and delay was always foreseen by those who knew the character of the soil and the power of torrential tropical rains, and was long dwelt upon as a fatal objection to a sea-level canal. It has caused even more delay and more expenditure than was expected. But it has now been overcome, though to avert the risk of future damage to the work when completed the engineers have been obliged to give a much lower slope to the sides of the cutting than was originally contemplated, so that the width of the cutting at the top is also greater than had been planned, and the quantity of material excavated has been correspondingly larger.[1] In order to lessen further washing down, the slopes will be sown with creeping grasses and other plants calculated to hold the surface soil.

The interior of the Culebra Cut presented, during the period of excavation, a striking sight. Within the nine miles of the whole cutting, two hundred miles of railroad track had been laid down side by side, some on the lowest level on terraces along which the excavating shovels were at work. Within the deepest part of the cutting, whose length is less than a mile, many hundreds of railroad construction cars and many thousands of men were at work, some busy in setting dynamite charges for blasting, some clearing away the

[1] The highest point of excavation at Gold Hill is 534 feet above sea level and the highest elevation of the original surface of the ground along the centre line of the Canal was 312 feet above sea level. The vertical depth of the cut on the centre line is thus 272 feet, the bottom of the cut being 40 feet above sea level.

rubbish scattered round by an explosion, some working the huge moving shovels which were digging into the softer parts of the hill or were removing the material loosened by explosions, the rest working the trains of cars that were perpetually being made up and run out of the cutting at each end to dump the excavated material wherever it was needed somewhere along the line of the Canal. Every here and there one saw little puffs of steam, some from the locomotives, some where the compressed air by which power was applied to the shovels was escaping from the pipes, and condensing the vapour-saturated atmosphere.

There is something in the magnitude and the methods of this enterprise which a poet might take as his theme. Never before on our planet have so much labour, so much scientific knowledge, and so much executive skill been concentrated on a work designed to bring the nations nearer to one another and serve the interests of all mankind.

Yet a still more interesting sight is that which meets the visitor when, emerging from the cutting, he crosses to where, behind the western hill, are the quarters of the workers,[1] with the cottages of the chief engineer and his principal assistants on the top. The chief engineer, Colonel Goethals, is the head not only of the whole scheme of construction but of the whole ad-

[1] The unskilled labourers employed are mostly West Indian negroes from Jamaica and Barbadoes, with some Spaniards, but no Chinese. The skilled men are from the United States. Many Chinese were here in the French days and died in great numbers.

ministration, and his energy, judgment, and power of swift decision are recognized to have been a prime factor in the progress of the work and the excellence of the administrative details. The houses, erected by the United States government, are each of them surrounded on every floor by a fine wire netting which, while freely admitting the air, excludes winged insects. All the hospitals have been netted so carefully that no insect can enter to carry out infection from a patient. Every path and every yard is scrupulously clean and neat. Not a puddle of water is left where mosquitoes can breed, for every slope and bottom has been carefully drained. Even on the grass slopes that surround the villas at Ancon there are little tile drains laid to carry off the rain. With the well-kept lawns and the gay flower-beds, the place has the air of a model village. And one sees the same in the other quarters of the employés all along the canal line, at Gatun, at Miraflores, at Ancon, where is the great hospital and where have been set up the offices of the civil government which does everything for its employés, both white and coloured. Nowhere perhaps in the world are workpeople so well cared for, and such ample and almost luxurious provision made for comfort and amusement as well as for health by the benevolent autocracy which presides over everything. Its' success in escaping all charges of partiality or corruption, as well as in producing efficiency in the work and contentment among the workers, has indeed been such as to make some persons draw from it an argument in favour of State control of all great enterprises. To the unbiassed observer it is rather an instance of the efficiency obtainable by vesting full administrative control in men whose uprightness and capacity have already been proved beyond question, who have not risen by political methods, and who have nothing to gain by any misuse of their powers. So far as any political moral can be drawn from the case, that moral recommends not democratic collectivism but military autocracy.

In these wire nettings and drainage arrangements and hospital precautions, to which I have referred, more than in anything else is to be found the reason why, after the French effort to build the canal had twice failed, the present enterprise is succeeding. The French engineers had shown great skill and were doing their work well. No one admits their merits more fully than do, with the generous candour that belongs to true soldiers and true men of science, the American engineers who have come after them. But they had no means of fighting the yellow fever and the malaria that were frustrating all their skill and exhausting all their resources. The discovery, made while the United States troops were occupying Cuba after the war of ·1898, that yellow fever is due to the bite of the *Stegomyia* carrying infection from a patient to a healthy person, and that intermittent fevers are due to the bite of the *Anopheles*, similarly bearing poison from the sick to the sound, made it possible to enter on a campaign for the prevention of these diseases among the workers on the Isthmus. This was done before excavation began, and done so efficiently that the Isthmus is now as healthy as any part of the United States. No case of yellow fever has occurred since 1905. The mortality is no higher than in the United States army generally. In 1910 the death rate among 50,802 employés of both colours in the Canal Zone was 10.98 per thousand, in 1911, among 48,876, it was 11.02, — an extraordinarily low rate when compared with the average of European and North American cities. Among the American white employés and their families the rate was only 6.01.[1] The white employés and their families are healthy and fresh-looking, with none of that sickly brownish-yellow hue which usually marks the inhabitants of malarial districts. And I can confirm what many other visitors have told me, that one may be for days and nights on the Isthmus and neither see nor hear nor feel a mosquito. To have made one of the pest-houses of the world, a place with a reputation like that of the Pontine Marshes, or Poti on the Black Sea, or Sierra Leone itself, as healthy as Boston or London is an achievement of which the American medical staff, and their country for them, may well be proud ; and the name of Colonel Gorgas, the head of that medical staff to whose unwearied zeal and care this achievement is largely due, deserves to stand on

---

[1] Among the white population of the Zone, excluding the cities of Panama and Colon, the rate was higher, viz. 16.47 for 1910 and 15.32 for 1911, the part of the population not under official control being less careful to observe health rules.

the roll of fame beside that of Colonel Goethals, the chief engineer and Chairman of the Commission, who has directed, and is bringing to its successful issue, this whole great enterprise.

The sanitation of the Canal Zone, following that of Havana, has done more than make possible the piercing of the Isthmus. It has opened up possibilities for the settlement by Europeans of, and for the maintenance of permanent European population in, many tropical districts hitherto deemed habitable by their natives only. To the effect of such an example one can hardly set bounds.

In no previous age could an enterprise so vast as this have been carried through; that is to say, it would have required a time so long and an expenditure so prodigious that no rational government would have attempted it. Pharaoh Necho may have, as Herodotus relates, dug a canal across the Isthmus of Suez by the labour of hundreds of thousands of his subjects accustomed to implict obedience, but his ditch was probably a small and shallow one, and it was through a dead level of sand and clay that it was dug. Here there was a mountain to pierce and a torrent to bridle, and the locks had to provide for vessels a thousand feet long. Nothing but the new forces which scientific discovery has placed in the hands of the modern engineer — steam, electricity, explosives of high power, machinery capable of raising and setting in their place one above another huge masses of cement — would have made the work possible. Yet even that was not enough. The French company possessed such appliances, and though their estimates of cost turned out to be based on totally inadequate data, the competence and energy of their engineers have never been questioned. And the French company failed hopelessly; and failed not merely because the work turned out heavier, and the loose strata giving way under the downpours of rain made the slides and landslips far worse, than was expected.[1] These things doubtless told against them, and much of the money raised never found its way to the Isthmus. But it was a more terrible force that foiled them. It was Pestilence, Pestilence coming on the gauzy wings of the mosquito. So little did they recognize their foe that when they built the large and commodious hospital at Ancon they provided, outside the windows, flower-boxes where stagnant water gathered and mosquitoes were hatched. Engineers died, foremen died, labourers were mown down by hundreds. Yet even if all the French capital had been properly spent and better sanitary measures had reduced the pestilential conditions, it may be doubted whether the French company could have made a success of the undertaking. More capital would have

[1] Fascinated by the example of Suez, and not realizing how greatly the problem of construction was affected by the difference between the very wet climate of Panama and the absolutely dry climate of Suez, the French engineers originally planned a sea-level canal. To have carried out that plan would have added enormously to the cost, for the Culebra cutting must have been not only eighty feet deeper, but immensely wider. Few who examine the spot seem now to doubt that the decision to have a lock canal has been a wise one.

been needed, capital which must have been raised on onerous terms, and when it had all been spent and the work completed the profits of the canal could not, after providing for working expenses, have paid interest on half of the money borrowed. Whoever looks at this prodigious work feels that it could be carried through only by a nation commanding resources so overflowing that it does not need to care how much it spends, a nation which can borrow as much money as it pleases without sensibly affecting the quotations of its existing national debt.

It is expected that the construction of the Canal will be found, when it is finished, to have cost nearly £80,000,000 ($400,000,000).[1] To this there will have to be added the cost of the fortifications it is intended to erect at Colon and on the islands that lie in the Gulf of Panama, opposite the south end of the Canal, as well as of barracks for the large garrison which is to defend it. The visitor who sees the slopes where these forts and batteries are to be placed asks who are the enemies whom it is desired to repel. Where is the great naval power that has any motive either of national enmity or of self-interest sufficient to induce it to face the risks of a war with a country so populous, so wealthy, and so vigorous as the United States? He is told that there is at present no such naval power, and that no quarter can be indicated whence danger will arise; but that it is possible that

---

[1] The last estimate presented puts the amount at $375,000,000. The fortifications are expected to cost about $12,000,000 more.

at some future time, from some unknown direction, some yet unconjectured enemy may arise against whose possible attacks provision ought now to be made.

When the Canal has been opened and the interest now felt in getting it completed by the appointed day has ended, hardly less keen will be the interest in that other question on which men have speculated so long. What difference will this new waterway from ocean to ocean make to world commerce and therewith also, though probably in a less degree, to world politics? And what difference, to descend to smaller matters, will it make to the West Indies, and to the ports of the Gulf of Mexico, and (not so much commercially as politically) to the neighbouring states of Central and South America? The political side of the matter is one too delicate to be discussed here, but upon the commercial one a word or two may be said.

The new route will doubtless become an important route for the traffic in heavy freight from the Atlantic ports of the United States, and from European ports also, to the ports of western North America.

It will similarly become the main freight line for goods of all kinds from both European and eastern North American ports to the west coast of South America as far south as Callao, and also from Gulf of Mexico ports as far as Coquimbo or Valparaiso. Whether the freight traffic from Europe to Valparaiso and the other ports of Chile will be greatly affected, is deemed more doubtful. Much will, of course, depend on the tolls fixed for transit through the Canal, which, by the treaty of 1901 be-

D

tween Great Britain and the United States, are to be, like those at Suez, equal between all nations.

The most interesting, because the largest, and also the most doubtful and complicated, question is as to the result upon European commerce to the Far East, —Japan, China, New Zealand, and Australia. It is the most complicated, because many factors enter into it, some of them political as well as commercial. Here the Canal will compete with the Suez Canal route, and (as respects Australia in particular) with the Cape of Good Hope route, and it will also compete with the steamship lines which now ply from Australia and New Zealand to England round Cape Horn. From England to all the Australasian and east Asiatic ports, except those of New Zealand, the Suez route will be shorter than that by Panama.[1] From New York, however, the route by Panama to Sydney, Auckland (New Zealand), and Shanghai will be shorter than that via Suez, while to Hong Kong and Manila it will be of practically the same length. It is generally supposed that the Panama tolls will be lower than those now imposed at Suez. Commerce, like other things, changes more quickly in our age than it did in any previous age; yet years may elapse before the full results of the opening of the Canal disclose themselves. Some of the commercial as well as the political consequences which have been due to the making of the Suez Canal were altogether unforeseen. If a dozen of the

---

[1] London to Sydney via Suez 11,531 miles, via Panama 12,525 ; London to Auckland via Suez 12,638 miles, via Panama, 11,404.

most important experts were, in 1914, to write out
and place in the library of the British Museum and
the library of Congress their respective forecasts bearing on this subject, sealed up and not to be opened till
A.D. 2000, they might make curious reading in that
latter year.

The chief impressions which the scenery of the Isthmus
makes on the traveller have already been indicated, —
the contrast of the wildness and solitude of the region
with its wonderful geographical position, which long
ago seemed destined to make it a centre of commerce
and population, the contrast of the advantages offered
by that position with the slothful neglect of those advantages by its Spanish rulers, the contrast one sees
to-day between the busy crowd of workers along this
narrow line cut out from the vast forest and the un-
touched unpeopled nature on each side, the contrast
between the black cloud of death that hung over it
for four centuries and the sunshine of health and energy
which medical science has now poured around it.

But the strongest impression of all is that here one
sees the latest, so far as can be foreseen, of any large
changes which man is likely to try to work upon the
surface of the earth. Tunnels longer than any yet
made may be bored through mountains or carried under
arms of the sea. The courses of rivers may be diverted.
Reservoirs vaster than any we know may be constructed
to irrigate arid tracts or supply electric power to cities,
and bridges may be built to span straits like the Bosphorus, or railroads, like that recently opened in south-

ern Florida, be carried through the sea along a line of reefs. But nowhere else do there remain two continents to be divided, two oceans to be connected, by a water channel cut through a mountain range.

There is a tale that when the plan for digging a canal at Panama was first mooted, Philip the Second of Spain was deterred from it by the argument, pressed by his clerical advisers, that if the Almighty had wished the seas to be joined, He would have joined them, just as, according to Herodotus, the people of Knidus were deterred by the Delphic oracle from cutting through the isthmus along which their Persian enemies could advance by land to attack them. If Zeus had wished the place to be an island, said the oracle, he would have made it one. But when an age arrived in which commercial and scientific views of nature prevailed against ecclesiastics, it became certain that here a canal would be some time or other made. Made it now has been. It is the greatest liberty Man has ever taken with Nature.

CHAPTER II

THE first part of the voyage from Panama down the coast towards Peru is enjoyable when made in a steamer, for the sea is smooth, the southerly breeze is usually light, and after passing through the picturesque isles that lie off Panama one sees at no great distance those Pearl Islands which at one time rivalled the isles of Bahrein in the Persian Gulf as the chief pearl fishery of the world. One wonders at the difficulties experienced by the first Spanish adventurers, Vasco Nuñez de Balboa, and after him Pizarro, in their efforts to get south, but the reason is that a strong current sets into the Gulf, and against it and the prevailing south winds it was hard for the clumsy craft of those days to make progress. But on the second morning when we had got four or five hundred miles to the south, what was our surprise to find the temperature getting lower and the sky cloudier as we approached the equator. It was chilly that evening and we asked for blankets. Dreams of a delightful basking in the soft air of a sunlit sea were dispelled! We were entering cold weather, and it was to continue with us for thousands of miles, all the way to the Straits of Magellan.

Everybody knows nowadays how largely the cli-

mate and the flora and the civilization of western
Europe are due to the Gulf Stream. But one may
suspect that few people have heard of an ocean current
on the other side of America equal in length and volume and scarcely less important in its influence on
climate. The great Antarctic current, or Humboldt
current, as it is sometimes called from the illustrious
German who first scientifically observed and explained it, carries up from southern Chile to some distance north of the Equator a vast body of cold water
which chills the atmosphere of the ocean and the coast
and frequently covers them both with a roof of cloud.
Before he crosses the Line, the traveller encounters
this murky and ungenial weather, which excited the
wonder of the early Spanish writers, who expected to find
a zone just as torrid as they had found on the Atlantic.
Seldom thereafter (during fully half the year) does he
see clear blue sky, save for perhaps an hour or two
each day, all the way southward as far as Valparaiso.
The mists and clouds which this mass of cold water
brings give the sun, the chief deity of the ancient Peruvians of the inner country, no chance on the coast,
while the fogs are so frequent as to be a source of
anxiety to the navigator, and the clouds so thick that
the great peaks of the Andes, though at some points
only fifty or sixty miles distant, can rarely be seen from
the ocean.

But its cool and cloudy climate is only one of the
singular features of the coast. From the Isthmus till
one gets a little way south of the Equator at the Gulf

of Guayaquil, the usual wet summer season of the
tropics prevails and the abundant rains give to the
highlands along the coast of Colombia and Ecuador
splendid forests, which will one day be a source of
wealth to those countries. But at this point, or to be
more precise, about the boundary of Ecuador and Peru,
near the town of Tumbez where Pizarro landed, the
climatic conditions suddenly change, and there begins
a rainless tract which extends down the coast as far as
Coquimbo in 30° S. latitude. The vaporous moisture
which the southeasterly trade winds bring up from
the other side of the continent is most of it spent in
showers falling on the eastern side of the Andes, and
what remains is absorbed by the air of the dry plateaux
between the parallel chains of that range, so that hardly
any passes over to the western side of the mountains.
The Antarctic current, cooling the air of the warmer
regions it enters, creates plenty of mists but no rain,
the land being warmer than the sea. Thus so much
of the coast of western South America as lies between
the ocean and the Cordillera of the Andes from
Tumbez nearly to Valparaiso, for a distance of some
two thousand miles, is dry and sterile. This strip of
land varies in width from forty to sixty miles. It is
crossed here and there by small rivers fed by the snows
of the Andes behind, and along their banks are
oases of verdure. Otherwise the whole coast of
the strip is a bare, brown, and dismally barren
desert.

We had hoped before reaching the arid region to

touch at the city of Guayaquil, which is the chief port and only place of commercial importance in the mountain republic of Ecuador. It had, however, been put under quarantine by Peru, owing to the appearance in it of yellow fever and the Oriental plague, so we had to pass on without landing, as quarantine would have meant a loss of eight or ten days out of our limited time. Ecuador is not the most progressive of the South American countries, and Guayaquil enjoys the reputation of being the pest-house of the continent, rivalling for the prevalence and malignity of its malarial fevers such dens of disease as Fontesvilla on the Pungwe River in South Africa and the Guinea coast itself, and adding to these the more swift and deadly yellow fever, which has now been practically extirpated from every other part of South America except the banks of the Amazon. The city stands in a naturally unhealthy situation among swamps at the mouth of a river, but since Havana and Colon and Vera Cruz and Rio de Janeiro and even Santos, once the deadliest of the Brazilian ports, have all been purified and rendered safe, it seems to be high time that efforts should be made to improve conditions at a place whose development is so essential to the development of Ecuador itself.

Seeing far off the dim grey mountains around the Gulf of Guayaquil, but not the snowy cone of Chimborazo which towers behind them, we touched next morning at our first Peruvian port, the little town of Payta, and here got our first impression of those South American deserts with which we were to become so familiar. It is a row of huts constructed of the whitish sun-baked mud called adobe which is the usual building material in the flat country, with two or three shipping offices and stores and a railway station, for a railway runs hence up the country to the old town of Piura. A stream from the Andes gives fertility to the long Piura valley which produces much cotton of an extremely fine quality. There are also oil wells not far off, so Payta does some business, offering as good an anchorage as there is on this part of the coast. We landed and climbed to the top of the cliffs of soft strata that rise steeply from the water, getting a wide view over the bay and to the flat-topped hills that rise fifteen miles or more inland. The sun had come out, the air was clear and fresh, and though the land was as unmitigated a bit of desert as I had ever seen, with only a few stunted, prickly, and woody stemmed plants supporting a feeble life in the hollows of the ground, still it was exhilarating to tread at last the soil of a new continent and receive a new impression.

The first view of Peru answers very little to that impression of a wealthy land called up by the name of this country, more familiar and more famous in the olden days than that of any other part of the colonial empire of Spain. Nevertheless, it is a curious fact that the wealth of Spanish Peru belonged more to her barren than to her fertile and populous regions. In the days of the Incas it was otherwise. They ruled over an agricultural people, and though they had gold in plenty, gold to them was not wealth, but material for ornaments. Apart, however, from agriculture, of which I shall speak later, the riches of Peru have consisted of three natural products, which belong to the drier tracts. These are the guano of the rainless islands off the coast, the nitrate deposits in the province of Tarapaca and the mines of silver and copper. Of these three, the guano has now been nearly exhausted, and while it lasted it enriched, not the country, but a succession of military adventurers. The nitrate provinces have been conquered by Chile and seem unlikely ever to be restored. The most productive of the silver mines were taken away when Bolivia, in which they are situated, was erected into a separate republic, and such mines as remain in the High Andes, doubtless of great and not yet fully explored value, are in the hands of foreign companies and syndicates. Little good have these bounties of nature done to the people of Peru, whether Spanish or Indian.

From Panama to Payta the direct steamers take five days, and from Payta to Callao it is two days more, so the whole voyage is about as long as that from New York to Liverpool in the quick liners. This is one of the least troubled parts of the ocean; that is to say, gales are rare, and hurricanes, like those of the Caribbean, unknown. There is, however, usually a pretty heavy swell, and when there has been a storm some two or three hundred miles out to the west, the great rollers come in and make landing along the coast no easy matter. As the ship keeps too far out for the details of the coast to be visible, the voyage is rather monotonous, especially in the cloudy weather we encountered. Here in the Antarctic current one has lost the pleasure of watching the gauzy gleam of the flying fish, but sea-birds appear circling round the ship and pelicans abound in the harbour. Whales, following the cold water northward, are seen spouting and are beset and attacked by their enemy the thresher, while whenever the ship anchors in a roadstead to discharge or take in cargo, seals and sea lions gambolling among the waves give a little amusement. The crew were Chileans,—they are the only South Americans with a taste for the sea—the passengers mostly natives of the various re-publics along the coast, for these steamers furnish the only means of communication north and south, but there are usually some English commercial men and some Americans looking after their mining interests or pros-pecting for railways across the Andes. There is much more variety than one usually finds in an Atlantic liner, but much less than in a Mediterranean or Black Sea steamer, where on the same deck you may see the cos-tumes and hear the tongues of seven or eight nations. The Spanish-Americans are not very communicative to strangers, but whoever speaks their language can learn a good deal from them about minerals and revolutions, — the two chief products of the northwest coast.

To sail along a coast without a chance of examining its natural beauties or the cities that stud it, is in most cases mortifying, but here in the six hundred miles be-tween Payta and Callao one has this consolation, that there is nothing to see, and you cannot see it. The shores are brown, bare and unpeopled, while the heavy cloud roof that hangs over the sea, hides the tops of the hills also, and cuts off all view of the snowy Cordillera far behind. The towns are few and small, because the land is sterile save where one of the Andean streams gives fertility to a valley. One would naturally suppose that the country had always been even as it is now. But the ruins of ancient cities here and there prove that it must once have been far more populous. A census taken soon after the Conquest shewed that there were in the Valley of Piura 193,000 Indians. In 1785 the inhabitants, then mostly negroes, numbered only 44,500. Of these ruins the largest are those of a city often called Chimu, from the title of the king who ruled there, near the town of Truxillo, to which Pizarro, when he founded it, gave the name of his own Estremaduran birthplace. The remains cover a wide space and shew that the people who dwelt here and in the other coast valleys must have made considerable advances toward civilization, for the pottery and other utensils are better in artistic style than any other remains found in South America. The kingdom of the Chimu was overthrown by the Incas a century before the Spanish Conquest, and nothing is known of the race except that its language, called Mochica, was quite different from that of the mountain tribes who obeyed the Incas. Whether the people perished under Spanish oppression, or whether they moved away, when in the confusion that followed the Conquest, the irrigation works that made cultivation possible were allowed to fall into decay—this is one of the many riddles of Peruvian history.

Gazing from the deck hour after hour on this dreary coast, and remembering that the Atlantic side of the Continent in the same latitude is one of the best watered and richest parts of the tropics, one is struck by the unfortunate physical conditions that make useless a region whose climate, kept so cool by the Antarctic current would otherwise have fitted it for the development of progressive communities. Such communities did exist among the subjects of the Chimu, but being confined to a few valleys, they were not strong enough to resist the impact of the more numerous mountain tribes. Thus it was only on the plateau behind that a great nation could grow up. With a moderate rainfall these six hundred miles of coast might have been one of the most fertile parts of South America, and the history of Perú would have been altogether different. The absence of rain has provided a compensation in the form of a product which, though it cannot be used on the spot, became serviceable to other countries, and might have given Peru the means of developing mines or building railroads. The droppings of the swarms of sea-birds that frequent the rocky islands along the coast instead of being, as in other countries, washed away by showers, have accumulated till they formed those huge masses of guano which eighty years ago began to be carried away and sold to European countries as the most efficient fertilizers. The Inca sovereigns knew their value and are said to have protected the birds.

Unfortunately, this easily obtained source of national wealth excited the cupidity of revolutionary leaders, each of whom fought for power because power meant the command of the revenue derivable from these deposits. Not much is now left, and the republic has been none the better for them. Some of the largest were on the Chincha Islands. The islets are all bare, some shewing bold lines and sharp peaks which remind one of those that fringe the coast of Norway about the Arctic circle.

The entrance to Callao, the port of the city of Lima, which lies seven miles inland and is five hundred feet higher, has a certain grandeur. A range of hills abuts on the sea, forming a bold cape, and opposite to it, leaving an entrance a mile or two wide, rises a lofty island, steep, bare and brown like the islands of the Red Sea, which reduces the long surges of the Pacific and gives a comparatively quiet anchorage in the spacious bay within. The town of Callao, consisting of steamship offices and warehouses and shops dealing in the things ships need, offers nothing of interest, except the remains of the fort of St. Philip, the last building where the flag of Spain floated on the mainland of the New World. So the traveller hurries by the steam railroad or the electric line up to Lima.

We came full of the expectations stirred long ago by the fame of the city Pizarro built, and in which he ruled and perished, hoping to find in it another and a still more picturesque and more truly Spanish Mexico. It was long the first city of South America, into which the silver mines poured fabulous wealth. Its Viceroy was the greatest man in the Continent, a potentate whose distant master could seldom interfere with him, for there were no telegraphs or steam vessels in those days. Nobody but the archbishop could oppose him; nor need he fear anybody but the head of the Inquisition and the head of the Jesuits. The pomp that surrounded him, the pageants with which his entrance was celebrated, were like those of a Mogul Emperor.

Lima was called by Pizarro the City of the Kings, *i.e.* the Three Wise Men of the East, but the name it now bears, a variant from that of the river Rimac, soon prevailed. It stands in a wide flat valley, guarded by steep mountains to the north, on both banks of the broad stony bed of the Rimac, a large part of whose waters has been diverted for irrigation. Except where this river water has made cultivation possible, the plain is bare, being part of the coastal desert. The high range of hills already mentioned guards the city on the north, and runs out to the sea on the northwest. Lofty spurs of the Andes are visible to the east, but for much of the year the clouds hang so low that the hills are hardly part of the landscape and the great peaks are seldom seen.

As in most Spanish-American cities, the streets are narrow and straight, cutting one another at right angles. One is at first surprised to find the houses extremely low, many of one story and hardly any (save a few new residences on the outskirts) exceeding two stories, and to be told that they are built of bricks, or more commonly

of cane and reeds, plastered with mud. It is commonly said that in Lima a burglar needs nothing
more than a bowl of water and a sponge to soften the
plaster, and a knife to cut the canes. But the reason
is apparent when one remembers that no place on the
West coast has suffered more from earthquakes. Thus,
except the convents and some of the older churches,
everything looks modern, unsubstantial, and also un-
picturesque, having little variety and little ornament
in the architecture except the long wooden balcony which
usually projects above the gateway. The bridge that
spans the Rimac is hardly worthy of a great capital.
The shops are small and mediocre, and only in one or
two thoroughfares is there any throng of passers to
and fro. One notes little of the life and stir, and still
less of the stateliness, that befits an ancient and famous
capital.

Yet to this mediocrity there is one exception. It is
the great central square. In a Spanish, as in an Italian,
city, one usually enquires first for the Square, for whatever nobleness a place has is sure to be there. The Plaza
de Armas at Lima has much dignity in its ample space,
and beauty in its fine proportions, in its central fountain, in the palms and flowering trees and statues which
adorn it, besides a wealth of historic associations in the
buildings that stand around it. Most conspicuous is
the Cathedral, with its rich façade, its two quaint
towers; its spacious interior, not broken, as are most of
the great churches of Old Spain, by a central choir, its
handsome carved choir stalls, its side chapel shrines, in

one of which a glass case holds bones which tradition declares to be those of the terrible Pizarro. That pious conqueror founded the church in 1540, but earthquakes have made such havoc with the walls that what one sees now is of much later date. At the opposite corner of the Plaza are the government offices, comparatively recent buildings, low, and of no architectural interest. In the *open arcade which borders them a white marble slab in the pavement marks the spot where Pizarro, cut down by the swords of his enemies, the men of Chile, made the sign of the cross with his own blood as he expired. The passage is still shown whence the assassins emerged from a house hard by the Cathedral, where they had been drinking together to nerve themselves, and crossed the Plaza to attack him in his palace. Also on the Plaza, facing the Cathedral, is the municipal building, from the gallery of which, nearly four centuries after the Inca power had fallen under the assault of Pizarro, General San Martin, the heroic Argentine who led the revolutionary forces to the liberation of Peru, proclaimed to the crowd beneath the end of Spanish rule in South America. Of the old Palace of the Viceroys, which also fronted on the Plaza, there remains only the chapel, now desecrated and used as a storehouse for archives, whose handsome ceiling and walls, decorated with coloured tiles of the sixteenth century, carry one back to the Moorish art of Spain. Other churches there are in plenty, — seventy-two used to be enumerated, — and some of them are large and grandiose in style, but all

E

are of the same type, and none either beautiful or imposing.

Few relics of antiquity are left in them or indeed anywhere in Lima. The library of the University, the oldest seat of learning in America, which was formerly controlled and staffed by the Society of Jesus, suffered sadly at the hands of the Chilean invaders when they took the city in the war of 1882. The old hall of the Inquisition, in which the Peruvian Senate now sits, has a beautiful ceiling of dark red cedar richly carved, a work worthy of the best days of Spain. What scenes may it not have looked down upon during the three centuries when the Holy Office was a power at the name of which the stoutest heart in Lima trembled! And out of the many fine old mansions of colonial days one has been preserved intact, with a beautiful gallery running along its four sides of a spacious *patio* (internal court), and in front a long-windowed, richly decorated balcony, a gem of the domestic architecture of the seventeenth century, perhaps the most perfect, that earthquakes, fire, and war have permitted to survive in Spanish America. There is so little else to remember with pleasure from the days of the Viceroys and the Inquisitors that these relics of expiring artistic skill may be valued all the more.

I am forced to confess that the high expectations with which we came to Lima were scarcely realized. The environs are far less beautiful than those of Mexico, and the city itself not only much smaller, but less stately, and wearing less of the air of a capital. Our appreciation may perhaps have been dulled by the weather. We were told that the hills were pretty, but low clouds hid all but their bases from us; nor was there any sunshine to brighten the Plaza. For more than half the year, Lima has a peculiar climate. It is never cold enough to have a fire, but usually cold enough to make you wish for one. It never rains, but it is never dry; that is to say, it is not wet enough to make one hold up an umbrella, yet wet enough to soak one's clothes. September was as dark as a London November, and as damp as an Edinburgh February, for the fog was of that penetrating and wetting kind which in the east of Scotland they call a "haar." The climate being what it is, we were the more surprised to hear what the etiquette of courtship requires from a Limeno lover. Every *novio* (admirer) is expected to shew his devotion by standing for hours together in the evening under the window of the house in which the object of his admiration lives. He may or not cheer himself during these frequently repeated performances by a guitar, but in so moist an atmosphere the guitar strings would discourse feeble music.

Despite her earthquakes, and despite her damp and murky air, which depresses the traveller who had looked for brilliant sunshine, the City of the Kings retains that light-hearted gaiety and gift for social enjoyment for which she was famous in the old days. Not even political disasters, nor revolutions more frequent than earthquakes, have dulled the edge of pleasure. There had been an attempted revolution shortly before my

visit.   The President, an excellent man, courageous
and intelligent, had been suddenly seized by a band
of insurgents, dragged through the streets, threatened with death unless he should abdicate, fired at,
wounded and left for dead, until his own troops,
having recovered from their surprise and found how
few their assailants were, began to clear the streets
of the revolutionaries, and discovered their chief under
a heap of slain.   The insurgent general fled over the
frontier into Bolivia, where he was pointed out to me
some weeks later, planning, as was believed, another
descent upon Lima.   Such events disturb the even
tenor of Peruvian life little more than a street railway
strike disturbs Philadelphia or Glasgow.

Lima retains more of an old Spanish air than do the
much larger capitals of the southern republics, Argentina, Chile, and Uruguay.   Its viceregal court was long
the centre of the best society of the Continent.   Its
archbishop was the greatest ecclesiastical potentate in
the Southern Hemisphere.   It had a closer connection
with Spain through its leading families, as well as
through official channels, than any other place.   Loyalty to the Spanish monarchy was strongest here.   It
was the last great city that held out for the Catholic
King, long after all the other countries, both to the
north and south, had followed the examples of revolt
set by Mexico and Argentina.   And it is also, with the
exception of remote and isolated Bogotá, where some
few Spanish families are said to have kept their European blood least touched by native immixture, the

place in which the purest Castilian is spoken and the Castilian pride of birth is most cherished.

That a city so ancient and famous should not have more of the past to shew, that the aspect of streets and buildings should not be more stately, that there should be so little of that flavour of romance which charms one in Spanish cities like Seville or Avila — these things might be expected in a centre of industry or commerce, losing its antique charm, like Nürnberg or Venice, under the coarsening touch of material prosperity. But there is here no growth of industry or commerce. The Limeños are not what a North American would call either "progressive" or "aggressive." The railways and mines of Peru are mostly in the hands of men from the United States, shipping business in the hands of Englishmen and Germans, retail trade in those of Frenchmen, Spaniards, and others from continental Europe. But the people of Lima may answer that there are more ways than one of being happy. They enjoy life in their own way, with more civil freedom, and very much more religious freedom, than under the Viceroys, and occasional revolutions — now less sanguinary than they used to be — are better than a permanent rule of inquisitors and officials sent from Spain. Some day or other Lima will be drawn into the whirlpool of modern progress. But Europe and North America are still far off, and in the meantime the inhabitants, with their pleasant, courteous manners and their enjoyment of the everyday pleasures of life, are willing enough to leave mines and commerce to the foreigner.

From Callao it is two days more on to Mollendo, over a cold, grey, tumbling sea, along a brown and cloud-shadowed coast. We had, however, changed into a much larger steamer, for at Callao begins the through ocean service all the way to Liverpool of the Pacific Steam Navigation Company. Their vessels, not so large nor so luxuriously fitted up as the Atlantic liners that ply between Europe and New York, are excellent sea boats, and commanded by careful British captains.

Next to Callao in its importance as a Peruvian port, is the little town of Mollendo, for it is the starting point of the principal railway in the country of southern Peru, which climbs the Andes, traverses the central plateau, and sends out branches to Cuzco on the north, and on the southeast to the frontier of Bolivia, on the shore of Lake Titicaca. It is the main avenue to the interior of the country. Unfortunately there is at Mollendo no harbour, only an open roadstead, where vessels lie rolling and pitching in the ocean swell, which is sometimes heavy enough to make landing in boats difficult or even dangerous. A sort of break-water has been made enclosing a tiny port, but even in its shelter, the sweep of the great billow round the rocky semicircle forces the disembarking passenger to jump hastily ashore and scurry up before the next bil-low overtakes him. No more dreary spot than this could be imagined. Payta in its desert was doleful enough, but Payta had sun; and this place, under a thick roof of cloud, was far more gloomy. Hills brown and barren rise steeply from the beach, leaving room only for one row of houses, brown as the cliff itself. There is not a blade of grass visible, nor a drop of fresh water within many miles, save what a pipe brings from a distant river. Yet, gloomy as the place looked under the grey cloud roof which was hanging over land and sea, the inhabitants find it more tolerable than such an arid and treeless land would be were the blaze of the sun reflected from the rocky hill face behind.

The railroad runs south for some miles between the cliffs along a stretch of flat sand, on which the surf booms in slow thunder, leaves the shore and turns up into the clouds, mounting in long zigzags the steep acclivities of the mountain, and following here and there what were hardly to be called glens, but rather waterless hollows, down which once in nine or ten years a rain storm may send a torrent. The mists grow thicker and damper as one rises, and with the cooler and damper air there begins to be a little vegetation, some flowers, most of them at this season withered, and low, thorny shrubs, such as are usually found on arid soils. Away off to the south, occasional glimpses are caught of a river valley far below, where the bright green and yellow of crops on the irrigated banks make a pleasant relief to the monotony of the brown or black slopes, up which we keep our way. Curiosity grew more intense to know what lies behind those dreary mountains. At last, after two hours of steady climbing to a height of over four thousand feet, the train reaches what seems to be the top of the range, but proves to be really the edge of a tableland, as it emerges on to level ground, it suddenly passes out of the mists into dazzling sunshine, and stops at a spot called Cachendo. We step out, and have before us a view, the like of which we had never seen before. In front, looking eastward, was a wide plain of sand and pebbles with loose piles and shattered ridges of black rock rising here and there from its surface, all shimmering in the sunlight. Beyond the plain, thirty miles away, is a long line of red and grey mountains, their sides all bare, their crags pierced by deep, dark gorges, so that they seem full of shadows. Behind these mountains again, and some fifty or sixty miles away, three gigantic mountains stand up and close the prospect. That farthest to the south is a long line of precipices, crowned here and there by spires and towers of rock, seventeen thousand feet in height. This is Pichu Pichu. Its faces are too steep for snow, save in the gorges that scar them here and there, but lower down, where the slopes are less abrupt, every gully is white with desert sand blown up by the winds. Next to the north is a huge purplish black cone, streaked near its top with snow beds, and lower down by lines of red or grey ash and black lava. This is El Misti, a volcano not quite extinct, for though there has been no eruption for centuries, faint curls of steam still rise from the crater. It stands quite alone, evidently of far more recent origin than the third great mass, its neighbour on the north, Chachani, which, though also of volcanic rock, has long since lost its crater, and rises in three great black pinnacles, divided by valleys filled with snow. Both it and Misti exceed nineteen thousand feet. They are not, however, the loftiest ground visible. Far, far away to the north, there tower up two white giants, Ampato, and (farther west) the still grander Coropuna, whose height, not yet absolutely determined, may exceed twenty-two thousand feet and make it the rival of Illampu in Bolivia and Aconcagua in Chile. It stands alone in a vast wilderness, a flat-topped cone at the end of a long ridge, based on mighty buttresses all deep with snow and fringed with glaciers.[1] These five mountains belong to the line of the great Western Cordillera which runs, apparently along the line of a volcanic fissure, all the way north to Ecuador and Colombia.

This was our first view of the Andes, a view to which few parts of the Old World furnish anything similar, for nowhere else, except in Iceland, and in Tibet and Turkistan, do snow mountains rise out of waterless deserts. Yet this contrast was only a part of the strange weirdness of the landscape, a landscape unlike Alps or Pyrenees or Apennines, unlike the Caucasus or the Himalaya, unlike the Rocky Mountains and Sierra Nevada of North America. The foreground of wandering sand and black stones, the sense of solitude and of boundless space, a space useless to man and a solitude

[1] Since our visit Coropuna has been ascended by my friend Professor Hiram Bingham of Yale University (U. S. A.). The average of his observations gives it a height of 21,700 feet. A very interesting account of his long and difficult snow climb may be found in *Harper's Magazine* for March, 1912.

he can never people, the grimness of these bare walls of
rock and pinnacles of untrodden snow rising out of a
land with neither house nor field nor flower nor animal
life, but only two lines of steel running across the desert
floor, would have been terrible were it not for the exquisite richness and variety of the colours. In the foreground the black rocks and the myriad glitter of sand
crystals were sharp and clear. The tints were more delicate on the red hills beyond, and the stern severity of
the precipices in the far background was softened into
tenderness by distance. The sunlight that burned upon
these lines of iron and danced in waves of heat upon the
rocks, seemed to bring out on all the nearer hills and
all the distant crags varieties of hue, sometimes contrasted, sometimes blending into one another, for which
one could find no names, for pink melted into lilac and
violet into purple. Two months later, in the forests
of Brazil, we were to see what the sun of the tropics
does in stimulating an exuberant life : here we saw what
beauty he can give to sterility.

This "Pampa," or flat stretch of ground over which
the railroad runs, is the first step eastward and upward
from the sea on to the great inner plateau of Peru,
and has a height of from four to five or six thousand feet. Its surface is generally level, yet broken
by ridges and hummocks of rock, and dotted all over by
mounds of fine grey or brownish sand composed of mi-
nute shining crystals. These sand hills, called *médanos*,
are mostly crescent shaped, much like the moon in its
first quarter, steep on the convex side, and from ten

to fifteen or even twenty feet high. They drift from place to place under the south wind, which blows strongly and steadily during the heat of the day, the convex of the crescent always facing the wind. Sometimes they are swept on to and block the railway line; and when this is apprehended large stones are heaped up at the convex of the crescent and the movement is thus arrested or the sand dissipated. Such scanty vegetation as we had seen on the mist-covered hills toward the coast, has here quite disappeared under the fiery sun, — not even a cactus lifts its stiff stem. It is all sand and rocks, till the line, having run for some twenty miles across the Pampa, enters and begins to climb the second stairway of mountains to another and higher level, which forms the second terrace over which the way lies to the central plateau. The stairway is that line of red and grey mountains which were described as filling the middle distance in the view from Cachendo. Winding up through their hollows and along their faces the train enters a deep gorge or canyon, at the bottom of which, between vertical rock walls, is seen a foaming stream, and mounts along a ledge cut out in the side of the gorge. The canyon widens a little, and at its bottom are seen bright green patches of alfalfa, cultivated with patient toil by the Indians who water them by tiny rills drawn from the stream. At last the line emerges on open and nearly level ground. One has mounted the second step and reached the second terrace or shelf of the Peruvian tableland. Here on a gently rising slope, in a grand amphitheatre, the northeastern and eastern and southeastern sides of which are formed by the three great peaks, Chachani, El Misti, and Pichu Pichu stands Arequipa, the second city in Peru.

It is built on a gentle slope, on both sides of the river Chile, a torrent descending from distant snows in a broad, shallow and stony bed, and indeed owes its existence to this river, for it was the presence of water, enabling a little oasis in the desert to be cultivated, that caught the military eye of Francisco Pizarro. Discerning the need for a Spanish stronghold between the interior tableland and the coast, he chose this spot by the river at the foot of the pass that gives the easiest access to that tableland. It had already been a rest-house station, as its Quichua name implies, on one of the Inca tracks from Cuzco to the sea, along which a service of swift Indian runners is said to have been maintained by the Incas and to have carried up fresh fish to the monarch at Cuzco. It became the seat of a bishop, was soon well stocked with churches and convents, and has ever since held its head high, proud of its old families, and having escaped that occupation by the victorious Chilean army to which Lima succumbed. The air has the desert quality of purity and invigorating freshness. Although thin, for the height above the sea is over seven thousand feet,[1] it is not thin enough to affect the heart or lungs of most persons in ordinary health. The sun's heat is great and there is plenty of it, for here one is quite above the region of sea mists,

[1] The Harvard Observatory Report gives it as 7550.

but there is so little to do that no one needs to work in the hot hours, and for the matter of that, nobody, except the Indians, and the clerks of a few European firms, works at all. The nights are deliciously cool. Plenty of water for fields and gardens and fountains can be drawn from the river, and if the municipal authorities took pains to clean up the city by removing rubbish, and set themselves to make the outskirts neater and plant more trees, nothing would be wanting to render Arequipa, so far as externals go, a delightful place of residence. The clearness of the air has led to its being selected as the site of an astronomical observatory maintained by Harvard University for mapping out the stars of the Southern Hemisphere. Not even in Egypt or in the deserts of South Africa do the constellations shine with a more brilliant lustre. The Harvard observers placed and for a time maintained two meteorological stations on El Misti, one near the top, at a height of 19,200 feet, another at a point they called Mont Blanc (15,700 feet). Those who know how recent is the love of mountain climbing in Europe will be interested in hearing that the volcano was ascended as far back as A.D. 1677, on which occasion the crater was exorcised and sacred relics cast into it. The observers also constructed a mule path to the summit, for though the face turned to Arequipa is steep, there is no difficulty in ascending from the north by a circuitous track. There are two craters, a newer one with a diameter of 1500 feet inside a larger one, whose diameter is 2800 feet. I could find no record of any eruption of lava or ashes since the Spanish Conquest, but the vapours in the new crater, always thick, sometimes increase sufficiently to alarm the Arequipeños.

The line of perpetual snow is extremely high in this dry region, as it is in the equally dry peaks of northern Chile.   On some mountains of 19,000 feet the snow disappears in summer, except in sunless hollows.

I found myself wondering whether the fascination of the city, with views out over the furrowed desert to the west, where the sun goes down into the cloud bank that hangs over the Pacific, and views up to the tall peaks that guard it to the east, would retain its power when it had grown familiar, and wondering, also, whether, through the four centuries since Europeans came to dwell here, there were many who drew delight from the marvellous nature that surrounds it, and found in the contemplation of this extraordinary scenery some relief from the monotony of life in a society so small and so isolated.   The three great mountain masses that tower over the city, emblems of solid and unchanging strength in their form, are always changing in their aspect.   The snows creep down in the season of rains, and ascend again when the time of drought returns.   Sunrise and sunset bring perpetual miracles of loveliness in the varying play of colours upon snow and rocks.   Pichu Pichu, with its long, grey line of precipices, glows under the western sun in every tint of pink and crimson.   Chachani's black pinnacles turn to a dark violet, while the snows between them redden.   In the middle the broad-based cone of El Misti, with its dark lava flows and beds of brown or yellow ash, ranges from glowing orange to a purple deep as if the mountain were all colour to its core. Behind it, when twilight comes, there rises to the zenith a pale bank of pearly grey, faintly touched by the light that is dying in the west. No wonder that this solemn and majestic summit, traditions of whose outbursts of fire in days gone by still survive, has been personified and worshipped by the Indians, who, though nominally Christians, have, like other primitive races, retained a great deal of the ancient nature religion which sees spirits in all remarkable objects. The reverence for the mountain deities still lingers in secret among them, though it seldom takes form in sacrifices like those of the olden time, when, as tradition says, youths and maidens were flung into the crater to appease the wrath of the fire spirit. A Jesuit annalist relates how, in A.D. 1600, when the volcano of Omate, farther to the southeast, was in violent eruption, casting forth showers of ashes which fell round Arequipa, darkening the sky, while a glow of lurid light shone from the distant crater, the Indian wizards robed themselves in red and offered to Omate sacrifices of sheep and fowls, beseeching the mountain not to overwhelm them. Then he adds, "These wizards told the Indians that they talked to the Devil, who told them of the approaching catastrophe, and said that Omate had asked El Misti to join him in destroying all the Spaniards. But El Misti answered that he could not help Omate, because he had been made a Christian and had received the name of

San Francisco; so Omate was obliged to undertake the work alone." [1]

. Built far more solidly than Lima, with house walls five or six feet thick, and lying more out of the stream of modernizing conditions, Arequipa has retained an air of antiquity, and, it may be said, of dignity, superior to that of the capital. As one looks north-eastward from the lower part of the town up the rising ground, the numerous churches, with here and there a tall conventual pile, make a varied and effective skyline. The gardens on the higher northwestern bank of the river relieve the mass of houses, and the yellow-ish grey volcanic stone of which they are built, mellowed by the strong sun, shews well against the purple mass of Misti. There are some picturesque street vistas too, but one misses the bright colours of peasant dress which a city of Old Spain or Italy would shew. The women are largely in black. The black manta drawn over the head is absolutely prescribed for church; indeed, even a European visitor is not allowed to enter a church anywhere in these countries in hat or toque; she must cover her head with the manta.

The houses are low, for here, too, earthquakes are dreaded, and the streets roughly paved with large cobblestones of hard, smooth lava. Streams of water drawn from the river run down many of them, and other streams water the fields along the outskirts.

[1] Quoted in the learned notes to Mr. Bandelier's valuable book, *Islands of Titicaca and Koati*, p. 161, from a MS. in the National Archives at Lima. Omate is probably the volcano now usually known as Ubinas.

Here and there one sees a garden planted with dark green trees, which relieve the glare of light. The Plaza, less ample than that of Lima, is hardly less striking, with the great pile of the Cathedral occupying more than half of one side of it, arcades filled with shops bordering the other three sides, flowers and shrubs planted in the middle. Everything reminds one of the Asiatic or North African East, — the long, low, blank house walls which enclose the streets, walls into which few and small windows open, because the living rooms look into a central yard or *patio;* the concentration of the better sort of shops in arcades which represent the Eastern bazaar; the flat roofs on which people sit in the evenings; the deep and pungent dust; the absence of wheeled vehicles; for everybody rides, the richer on horses and the rest of the world on donkeys; the scantily dressed Indians, wild looking as Bedaween, though with reddish brown instead of yellowish brown skins. Instead of camels there are llamas, the one native beast of burden in Peru, much smaller than the camel and more handsome, but not unlike it in its large lustrous eyes, and in the poise of its long neck, with the small erect head slightly thrown back. It resembles the camel also in its firm resolve not to move except at its own fixed pace, and to bear no load heavier than that (of one hundred pounds) to which it is accustomed. The brilliant light, too, and the dry, keen air are like the light and air of the East. But no Eastern city has around it a mountain landscape like this. One must place Tunis or Trebizond in the valley of Zermatt to

F

get an impression of Arequipa as it stands, encircled by snow fields and majestic towers of rock.

The Oriental quality, which startles one in these Spanish-American cities of the Far West is perhaps not wholly due to the Moorish influences transmitted through their Spanish colonists. Climatic and social conditions resembling those of northern Africa and southern Spain have counted for a good deal. Sunlight and dryness prescribe certain ways of building, and the Peruvian Indian resembles the Arab or the Moor in his indifference to cleanliness and comfort. Here in Arequipa, one begins to realize that Peru is in respect of population still essentially a land of the aborigines. All the lower kinds of work are done by Indians, and the class next above is at least half Indian in blood, though not readily distinguishable from the man of Spanish stock, either in aspect or in character and manners. The negro who still abounds at Lima and Callao, though he is beginning to be absorbed into the mass of whites, is no longer seen at Arequipa, for he cannot stand this cold, thin, highland air; and even the zambo, a half-breed of Indian and negro, who is said to want the best qualities of both races, is a trifling element. Here and elsewhere in South America it is impossible to determine the proportion of perfectly pure Spanish families to the whole population. Probably it is small, not five per cent over the whole country, but in Arequipa it may be much larger.

In one respect the city, while thoroughly Spanish, is very unlike the East. It is, and always has been, steeped in ecclesiasticism. The Cathedral is a long and handsome pile, rebuilt after the earthquake of 1868, with two tall towers on the south façade, and an unusually spacious and unadorned interior. It contains a picture attributed to Van Dyck. There is only one other church of special interest, that called the "Compañia," *i.e.* church of the Company of Jesus. Everywhere in South America the Jesuits were numerous, wealthy, and powerful till their suppression in the middle of the eighteenth century ; and here, as in many Italian and Spanish towns, their churches are the most profusely decorated without and within. The north façade of this one, built of reddish grey sandstone, is a wonderfully rich and finely wrought piece of ornamentation, and the seventeenth century pictures and wood carvings of the interior are curious if not beautiful specimens of the taste of the time. There are scores of other churches and convents, far more than sufficient for a city of thirty-five thousand people. Their bells clang all day long, and clerical costumes are everywhere in the streets. What is still more remarkable, the men, as well as the women, are practising Catholics, and attend church regularly, a rare thing in most parts of Spanish America. The city was always an ecclesiastical stronghold, and during the long War of Independence, was accounted the most conservative place in Peru. Indeed, it is so still.

But if Arequipa seems old-fashioned and conservative to-day, when a railway connecting it with the coast brings it within three days of Lima, what must it have been two centuries ago, when probably one-third of the white population consisted of priests, monks, and nuns, and the Church ruled unquestioned?

One can imagine no spot more absolutely cut off than this was from the world outside. It was an oasis like Tadmor in the wilderness. Three days' journey across desolate wastes lay between it and the coast, a coast itself scarcely inhabited, and behind towards the north and east there were only mountain solitudes, over which pastoral Indians roved. The bishop and the head of the Jesuits were the real powers, even the governor, and beneath him the alcalde, bowing to them. Nowhere in the world to-day could one find anything like that uniformity of opinion and custom which reigned in this little, remote city in those colonial days which came down into the days of Hume and Bentham in England, of Voltaire and Rousseau in France, and indeed down almost to the memory of men still living. The vision of the Holy Office in the background at Lima was hardly needed to enforce absolute submission of word and thought in such a society. The traveller of to-day marvels at the stillness and stagnation of one of the smaller cities in the interior of Old Spain. Yet a Spanish city, however small or remote, is at least in Europe: there are other cities not far off, and men come and go. Here there were no breaks in the monotony of life, nothing but local interests of the most trivial sort to occupy men's minds. The only events were feast days and religious processions, with now and then an earthquake, and once, thirty years before

the War of Independence, the terror of an Indian insurrection far up in the plateau.

Yet life was not wholly monastic. There was some
learning, mostly theological. There was also a good deal
of verse making : Arequipa was even famous for its
poets. Upon what themes did their Muse employ
itself ? What sighs were there from nuns behind the
convent walls ? What sort of a human being was the
bishop who walked in solemn processions behind
chanting choristers to and from his Cathedral ? Must
there not have been even here the perpetual play of
human passion, and could any weight of conservatism
and convention extinguish the possibilities of romance ?
I heard from a trustworthy source a story which shews
that even in grave and rigid Arequipa love would have
its way and that the hearts of stately ecclesiastics
could melt in pity. I tell it in my informant's words.

In old colonial days there lived in Arequipa a powerful family owning large estates and rich mines which
they had inherited from their ancestors among the
Conquistadores. They wielded authority both in
Church and State. At the time when the incident to be
described happened the heads of the family were two
brothers, of whom the elder held the landed property and
the younger was bishop and ruled the Church. The
elder was a widower with two children, a son and a
daughter. The great convent of Nuestra Señora de los
Dolores, founded and richly endowed by this family,
always had one of its members as its Abbess, and at that
time the only sister of these two brothers held the post.

The family, being a power in Arequipa, sought to preserve their supremacy, and accordingly decided that the young daughter of the elder brother should enter the convent and eventually succeed her aunt as Abbess, while her brother should marry and inherit the estates. The girl had no vocation for a religious life and rebelled against the fate proposed for her, but the father and uncle were inexorable, and after a vain struggle she was forced to yield and take the veil. Her aunt felt sympathy for the poor child, having perhaps passed through a like experience herself, and she made the young sister's religious duties as light as possible, allowing her to lead the choir, as she possessed a fine voice, and giving her the business of the convent to attend to. Embroidery was one of the occupations of the nuns, especially fine work on linen, the designs for which were brought from Spain; and to supervise this work and to take care of it was one of the girl's chief pleasures. She always despatched it to the laundry herself and received it on its return, laying it carefully in the presses perfumed with jasmine flowers, and the laundress was the only person from the outside world (except her own family) with whom she had any communications. This laundress happened to be an alert and intelligent woman, and she gave the nun all the news she had of the world outside the convent walls. After the young sister had been about five years in the convent the Abbess fell ill, and all the old-fashioned remedies known to the nuns failed to help her. She grew steadily worse and they were beginning to think of administering the last offices of the Church when the laundress suggested to the niece of the Abbess that the clever Scotch physician who had lately come to Arequipa should be consulted. To consult a man and a heretic horrified the nuns, but the laundress pressed her advice, and finally the bishop was appealed to and was induced, since his sister's life was at stake, to give his consent. The patient, however, even then refused to see the doctor in person, but the niece, closely veiled, was to be allowed to have an interview with him and to describe the symptoms. Although the doctor was aware that an opinion given under such circumstances was of little use, he consented to this arrangement. Accordingly, at the appointed time he presented himself at the convent gate, under the guidance of. the laundress, and was taken to the antechamber of the Abbess's apartment, for a lady of such high rank as the Abbess did not occupy a cell. There the niece received him, closely veiled, and described her aunt's condition. On his asking her if she could count the pulse, she replied, "No, I have never tried." "If you will place your fingers on my wrist, I will teach you," he said. Timidly she did as he bade her, and counted the beats; and, thrilled as he was by the musical softness of her voice, it is possible that he prolonged the lesson, for at length she said, "I understand perfectly, and will now go and count my aunt's pulse," and returned presently with a written report. During her absence the doctor had made enquiries of the laundress in regard to the Abbess's symptoms, and had decided that the old lady was suffering from cancer and had not long to live. But the young sister had made too profound an impression on him to let him give up the case at once, and he prescribed some soothing remedies and offered to return in the morning. These visits continued for several days, and at last he succeeded in seeing the sister's beautiful face and counting her pulse. The laundress could not always be in attendance, and the narcotics administered to the Abbess dulled her vigilance. Realising that his patient's days were numbered and that his work would soon be over, he saw there was no time to lose. The scruples of the young sister were finally overcome. Love won the day, and she promised to fly with her lover after the death of her aunt. With the help of the laundress he devised a plan for escape. The convent was built of stone and the sisters' cells were solidly arched like casemates, the only wood about them being the doors. Obtaining a skeleton from the hospital, the doctor took it to the house of the laundress and she conveyed it in a large linen basket to the convent the day after the funeral of the Abbess, and concealed it in the young sister's bed. That night the girl set fire to her bed, and in the confusion occasioned by the smoke and the alarm she escaped unnoticed into the street, where the laundress awaited her and took her to her house. The frightened nuns sought for her in vain, and when finally a few charred bones were found in her cell, which they imagined in their ignorance to be hers, they mourned her as dead, and buried the bones with all the honour due to her rank and station. Meanwhile the girl herself was in great danger, for had she been discovered she would have been tried for faithlessness to her vows, and she shuddered at the bare possibility of the old punishment of being walled up alive. It was impossible to stay long in the laundress's house, and the doctor implored her to fly with him to the coast, an arduous ride of seventy miles over the desert. Recoiling from such a step, she insisted on first trying to win the pardon and protection of her relatives, and she resolved to throw herself on the mercy of her uncle, the bishop, who had always shewn her much affection and was all-powerful with the rest of the family. Accordingly, just after twilight, and wrapped in her manta, which concealed her face and figure, she stole into the bishop's palace, where she found her uncle at evening prayer, and throwing herself on her knees before him, she implored his protection. He took her at first for her own ghost (for had he not performed the funeral service over her remains?), and when he discovered that it was really she, in flesh and blood, he was horrified and put her from him as he would a viper. But as she still clung to him, telling him her story and imploring his mercy and protection, he at last listened to her, and finally said, "wait a moment," and left the room, returning shortly with a bag containing money and family jewels, emeralds, which he thrust into her hand. "Take this," he whispered, "and fly with your lover to the coast. I will see that you are not followed." She found the doctor with horses at the city gate, and they rode away across the desert, never stopping except to change their mounts and to eat a little food, until they reached the coast, where by an extraordinary piece of luck they found an English frigate lying at anchor. Hurrying on board they told the captain their story, and he at once summoned the chaplain, who married them, and they were soon on their way to England.

Time passed, and the South American colonies became independent of Spain. Many years later, the brother of the nun went on a public mission to Europe. Before he left Peru his uncle, the bishop, told him the story of his sister's life, which had been kept secret until then, and after telling him where she was to be found (for through the Church he had watched over her), he desired her brother to communicate with her. This the nephew did in due course, and his sister was finally forgiven, and her descendants recognized and received by their Peruvian relatives. One of these descendants was seen by my informant wearing the emeralds that had been in the bishop's bag.

CHAPTER III

CUZCO AND THE LAND OF THE INCAS

NONE of the countries of South America, except Chile, has been demarcated by Nature from its neighbour; it is to historical events that they owe their present boundaries. This is eminently true of Peru, which is, save on her ocean side, marked off from the adjoining countries neither by river line nor by mountain line nor by desert. Her territory includes regions naturally very dissimilar, about each of which it is proper to say a few words here.

The western strip, bordering on the Andes and the Pacific, is nearly all pure desert, sterile and uninhabited, except where those river-valleys referred to in the last chapter descend to the sea. The eastern part, lying on the farther side of the Andes, and called by the people the Montaña, subsides from the mountains into an immense alluvial plain and is covered by a tropical forest, thick and trackless, unhealthy for Europeans, and inhabited, except where a few trading towns have been built on the rivers, only by Indian tribes, none of them much above savagery, and many still heathen. It is a region most of which was until lately virtually unexplored and thought not worth exploring. Within recent years, however, the demand for india rubber has brought in the agents of various trading companies, who have established camps and stations wherever the rivers give access to the forests and send the rubber down the Amazon to be shipped to Europe and North America. The harmless and timid Indians have in some places been seized and forced to work as slaves by ruffians supplying rubber to these companies, wretches apparently of mixed Spanish and native blood, who have been emboldened by the impunity which remoteness from regular governmental control promises to perpetrate hideous cruelties upon their helpless victims. It is a country of amazing natural wealth, for the spurs of the Andean range are full of minerals; there are superb timber trees in the forests, and the soil, wherever the trees and luxuriant undergrowths have been cleared off from it, has proved extremely fertile, fit for the growth of nearly every tropical product. Eastern Peru is physically a part, and not the largest part, of an immense region which includes the easternmost districts of Colombia and Ecuador upon the north and of Bolivia on the south, as well as a still larger area in western Brazil over which the same climatic conditions prevail — great heat and great humidity producing a vegetation so prolific that it is hard for man to hold his own against the forces of nature. This is indeed the reason why these tracts have been left until now a wilderness, suffering from the superabundance of that moisture, the want of which has made a wilderness of the lands along the Pacific coast. To this region, however, and to its future I shall return in a later chapter,[1] and men-

[1] Chapter XVI.

tion it here only because it is politically a part, and may hereafter become the most productive part, of the Peruvian Republic. The real Peru, the Peru of the ancient Indian civilization and of the Spanish colonial Empire, is the central region which lies along the Andes between these thinly settled, far eastern forests and the barren deserts of the Pacific coast.

Central Peru is altogether a mountain land, and is accordingly called by the people "the Sierra." It is traversed by two (more or less parallel) ranges of the Andes, the eastern and the western Cordilleras, which with their spurs and their branching ridges cover a large part of its area. It includes what is called the *Puno*, a comparatively level plateau, some seventy to one hundred miles wide and enclosed by these two main lines of the Cordilleras. Between the main ranges and their branches, there lie deep valleys formed by the courses of the four or five great rivers which, flowing in a northwesterly or northeasterly direction and ultimately turning eastward, unite to form the mighty Amazon. This Sierra region is, roughly speaking, about three hundred miles long (from northwest to southeast) and one to two hundred miles wide; but of this area only a small part is fit for settled human habitation. The average height of the plateau is from ten thousand to thirteen thousand feet above sea level, and that of the region fit for pasture on the slopes and tops of the ridges from ten thousand to fourteen thousand feet — the snow line varying from fifteen to nineteen thousand. As these slopes give pasture to llamas and alpacas and sheep, and in some favoured places to cattle, so in the less arid and less sandy tracts of the plateau there is some tillage. But the parts best suited for agriculture are to be found in the valleys, especially in so much of them as lies between ten thousand and four thousand feet above sea-level, for below five thousand feet their conditions become tropical and resemble those of the Amazonian forests. In these valleys the soil, especially where it is volcanic, is extremely fertile, but many of them are so narrow and their declivities so steep that cultivation is scarcely possible. No one accordingly who has studied the physical features of this country need be surprised to find that while the total area of Peru is about seven hundred thousand square miles, its population is estimated at only four million six hundred thousand. He may indeed be more surprised at the accounts which Spanish historians almost contemporary with the Conquest give of the far larger population, perhaps ten millions, that existed in the days of the Incas. The great falling off, if those accounts be correct, is explicable partly by the slaughter perpetrated by the first Spaniards and the oppressions practised by their successors during nearly three centuries, partly by the fact that districts near the coast which the remains of irrigation works shew to have been formerly cultivated are now sterile for want of water.

It was in the central highlands, at an altitude of from eight thousand feet and upwards that there arose such civilization as the ancient Peruvians developed:

and its origin here rather than elsewhere in South America may be mainly due to favourable climatic conditions. There was enough rain to provide grass for animals and make tillage possible, and enough warmth to enable men to live in health, yet not enough either of rain or of heat to make nature too strong for man and to enfeeble man's capacities for work.

Temperature and rainfall resembled generally those of the plateau of Mexico, a region somewhat lower, but farther from the Equator: and it was under similarly fortunate conditions of climate and agricultural possibilities that the races inhabiting those highlands had made, when Europeans arrived, some considerable advances in the arts of life. This central Peruvian area is to-day, with the exception of the irrigated banks of a few streams reaching the Pacific, the only part of the country where either an agricultural or a pastoral population can support itself. The rest of Peru depends upon its mines, chiefly of silver and copper, — a source of wealth uncertain at best. It is only in a few valleys, the most productive of which I am going to describe, that the agricultural population occupies any large continuous area. As a rule each community is confined to its own valley and cut off from the others either by mountains or by high, bare ridges on which only sheep can be kept, most of them too high and bleak even for pasture.[1]

There is no better way of conveying some notion

[1] *Paramo* is the name applied to these bleak regions between the valleys.

of the character of this central region, the true Peru, than by describing the country through which I passed by railway from Arequipa eastward to Lake Titicaca and thence northward to Cuzco, the ancient Inca capital. This railroad follows the line of the most important through route which war and commerce took in pre-Conquest times. It is the Southern Railroad of Peru, the main highway of the country. The section from Mollendo to the plateau at Juliaca was built many years ago, but the extension to Cuzco had been completed and opened less than a year before our visit. Both sections have been constructed by engineers from the United States, and the way in which the difficulties of extremely steep ascents and cuttings along precipitous slopes have been overcome reflects great credit on their skill. The gauge is the normal one. The line is owned by the Peruvian Corporation, a company registered in London, and under the energetic management of North American engineers it is doing a great deal to open up regions in which till some ten years ago there was not even a road fit for wheels. The passenger traffic is of course very small, and passenger trains run only once a day to Arequipa and thrice a week to Juliaca and Cuzco.

Quitting Arequipa on the south-western side, the line winds up to the north and then to the east across a rugged and dreary region of rocky hill slopes, pierced by deep gorges through some of which brooks come down, fed by snow beds far above. It follows the line of a canyon, and wherever there is level ground at the bottom, some bright green strips of cultivation appear on the margin of the stream, with a few Indian huts; so even these upper regions, cold and desolate as they are, are not so wholly desolate as the Pampa below. The view looking back over the city lying in its green oasis, with a stony desert all round, is superb. As we climb higher, the mass of Ampato and other giants of the western Cordillera deep with snow, rise in the northwest, while westward one sees beyond the reddish grey mountains through which we had mounted to Arequipa from the desert Pampa, the gleaming sands of that desert, and behind them again, just on the horizon, the long, low bank of clouds that covers the Coast Range. Here at nine or ten thousand feet, one looks over the white upper surface of these clouds. Resting on the western edge of the Pampa, they stretch far out over the Pacific and veil it from sight. Thus steadily mounting, and seeing below in a ravine the hamlet of Yura, where is a mineral spring whose pleasantly effervescent water is drunk all over Peru, the train winds round the northern flank of Chachani under its huge black precipices. Behind it and behind El Misti, which shews as a symmetrical cone on this side as well as on that turned towards Arequipa, we entered at a height of about eleven thousand feet a region typical of the Peruvian uplands. There was plenty of coarse grass, studded with alpine flowers, a few belonging to European genera. Llamas and alpacas were grazing on the slopes, herded by Indians: there were sheep, and a few cattle, and in

one place we thought we caught sight among low bushes
of a group of vicuñas.   This is a creature like the llama,
but smaller, and useless as a beast of burden, because
untameable.   It roams over the hills between eleven
thousand and fifteen thousand feet, and produces the
finest of all the South American wools, of a delicate
light brown tint, silky and soft as the fur of a chinchilla.

The scenery was strange and wild, not without a
certain sombre grandeur.   Below was the Chile River,
the same which passes Arequipa, and to which we had
returned after our circuit round Chachani.   It was
flowing in a deep channel which it had cut out for
itself between walls of black lava : and the wide bare
hollows beyond were filled with old lava streams and
scattered ridges and piles of rock.   To the southwest
El Misti and his two mighty neighbours shut in the
valley, and away to the south huge mountains,
among them one conspicuous volcanic cone, were dimly
seen, snowy summits mingled with the gathering clouds,
for at this height rain and snow showers are frequent.
The cone was probably Ubinas, the only active volcano
in this neighbourhood, about sixteen thousand feet
high.

Still mounting to the eastward, the line rose over
gentler slopes to a broad, bleak, and wind-swept ridge
where tiny rivulets welling up out of pools in the
yellowish grass were flowing west to the Pacific and
eastward to the inland basin of Lake Titicaca.   Large
white birds like wild geese were fluttering over us.

Here were a few huts of the Indian shepherds near the
buildings of the station ; and here a cross marked the
Cumbre or top of the pass, which is called the Crucero
Alto, 14,666 feet above sea level.   Higher ground cut
off the view to the north and clouds obscured the view to
the east, but to the south we could discern some of the
lofty summits of the western Cordillera on the watershed
of which we stood.   Thunderstorms were growling on
both sides, and out of black clouds far in the northwest
towards Coropuna came bright flashes of chain lightning.
At this height the country is comparatively open and the
valleys shallow, and this, along with the wonderful clearness of the air, enables the eye to range to a vast distance.
This northwestern thunderstorm which we were watching was possibly a hundred miles away.   We were awed
by the mere vastness of the landscape, in which we
looked over tracts it would take many days' journeys to
traverse, and saw mountains eighteen thousand feet
high separated by nameless valleys no one ever enters,
with hills and rocks tumbled about in chaotic confusion,
as though the work of world-shaping had here just begun.   Stepping out into the bitter wind, we walked
about awaiting signs of the *Soroche* or mountain sickness so much dreaded by Andean travellers, especially
when they come straight up from the coast to this vast
height, as high as the Matterhorn or the highest peaks
of the Rocky Mountains.   The air was very cold and
very thin, seeming not to fill the lungs.   But nothing
happened.

From the Crucero Alto the railway descends rapidly

for two thousand feet past two large lakes, embosomed in steep green hills — they reminded me of Loch Garve in Ross-shire — till it reaches a wide, bare, desolate flat, evidently part of the former bed of Lake Titicaca, which was once far larger than it is to-day. Here we were in that central plateau which the people call the *Puno* and which surrounds the lake, its lower part cultivated and peopled. At the large village of Juliaca, whence a branch line runs to the port of Puno on the lake farther to the southeast, the main line turns off to the north, still over the flat land which, where not too marshy, is under tillage. The inhabitants were all Indians, and only at Tirapata, which is a point of supply for the mines on the eastern slope of the mountains, were white people to be seen. Far to the northeast, perhaps one hundred miles away, could be discerned a serrated line of snowy mountains, part of the eastern Cordillera which divides the Titicaca basin from the Amazonian valleys. At last the hills begin to close in and the plain becomes a valley, narrowing as we travel farther north till, at a sharp bend in the valley which opens out a new landscape, we pass under a rock tower sixteen thousand feet high, like one of the aiguilles of Mont Blanc immensely magnified, and see in front of us a magnificent mountain mass streaming with glaciers. Two great peaks of from eighteen thousand to nineteen thousand feet are visible on this side, the easternmost one a long snow ridge resembling the Lyskamm above Zermatt; and behind it there appears a still loftier one which may approach or exceed twenty thousand feet. This is

the Sierra of Vilcanota, the central knot of the mountain system of Peru, as in it branches of the western
inosculate with those of the eastern Cordillera.   Though
very steep, the highest peaks seemed to me, surveying
them from a distance of fifteen or twenty miles, to offer
no great difficulties to an active and experienced climber,
apart of course from the rarity of the air at this immense
height, a difficulty which, while negligible by many, is
serious to some otherwise excellent mountaineers.   The
fact that the railroad passes close to these splendid
summits gives unusual facilities for an assault on them,
since the transportation of warm night coverings and of
food is one of the chief difficulties in a cold and thinly
peopled region.   As none of the tops seems to have been
yet scaled, they deserve the attention of aspiring alpin-
ists.

Above the village of Santa Rosa the valley is uninhabited, a deep, grassy hollow between the Vilcanota
group of peaks on the east and a lower though lofty
range on the west, with piles of stones at intervals, and
now and then we met or passed a string of llamas carrying their loads, for the railway has not wholly super-
seded the ancient modes of transportation.

Just at the very highest point of the col or pass of
La Raya 14,518 feet above sea-level, in which the valley
ends, the westernmost of these Vilcanota peaks is visible
on the east behind a deep gorge, the upper part of
which is filled by a glacier.   From this glacier there
descends a torrent which on the level top of the pass
spreads out into a small shallow marsh or lake which

the Peruvians held sacred as the source of the sacred
river Vilcamayu : and from this lake the water flows
partly south into Lake Titicaca, partly north into the
Amazon and the Atlantic.   Here indeed we were looking
upon one of the chief sources of that gigantic stream, for
of all the rivers that join to make the Amazon this is
among the longest.   During its course till it meets the
river Marañon, it is called first Vilcamayu, then Urubamba, and finally Ucayali.   The pass itself, a broad
smooth saddle not unlike, if one may compare great
things with small, the glen and watershed between
Dalnaspidal and Dalwhinnie which marks the summit
level of the Highland Railway in Scotland, has no small
historic interest, for it has been a highway for armies as
well as for commerce from the remotest times.   The ancient track from Cuzco to the southern boundary of the
Inca empire in Chile passed over it.   By it the Spanish
Conquistadores went backward and forward in their
campaign of subjugation and in the fierce struggles
among themselves which followed, nor was it less important in the War of Independence a century ago.
Till the railway was recently opened, thousands of
llamas bearing goods traversed it every year.   What
one now sees is nothing more than a fairly well-beaten
mule track, and I could neither discern any traces nor
learn that traces have been discovered either of the wall
which the Inca rulers are said to have built across it
as a defence from the Collao tribes to the south, or of
the paved road which, as the old writers say, they constructed to connect Cuzco with the southern provinces.

Were such a spot in Switzerland or Tyrol, its lonely beauty would be broken by a summer hotel for health-seeking tourists; nor could one imagine a keener and more delicious air than this, though people with weak hearts might find it trying. As soon as we had got a little way down from the top, the lungs began to feel easier, for the denser and warmer air of its lower levels comes up on the northerly wind which we met in descending. The valley, still smooth and grassy, sinks rapidly and in an hour or two we had entered a climate quite different from that of the Titicaca plateau to the south. After some six or eight miles a place is reached called Aguas Calientes (Hot Waters), from the numerous mineral springs which bubble up close together from the ground, most of them too hot to taste, and all impregnated with iron and sulphur. They are said to be valuable in various maladies, and in France or Switzerland an Établissement des Bains would doubtless have arisen to enclose and exploit them. As it is, the only sign that they are used is a wooden hut erected over one of the springs in which the station master cures himself of rheumatism. There are only two houses besides the station, but on the hill above mines of copper and antimony are worked by Indian labour.

Below this point the floor of the valley falls again. It is still narrow, but the now warmer climate permits tillage, and the patient toil of the Indians, turning every bit of ground to account, cultivates fields of grain and potatoes sloping at an angle so steep that ploughing or hoe-

ing seems almost impossible. When one asks how
this happens, the answer is that the rapacity of lawyers, ousting the Indian from the better lands below,
drives him to these less productive slopes. The hillsides are extraordinarily bare, but as fruit trees appear
round the cottages, this may be due not to the altitude,
but to the cutting down during many centuries of all
other trees for fuel. Never have I seen an inhabited
region — and in the case of this particular valley, a
thickly inhabited region — so absolutely devoid of wood
as is Peru. Even in Inca days, timber seems to have
been very scarce. There is plenty to be had from the
tropical forests lower down, but the cost of carrying
logs up from them upon mule-back is practically pro-
hibitive. A good, solid plank would be a load too
heavy for a llama.

Twenty miles below the pass of La Raya is the town
of Sicuani, which we were fortunate enough to see on
the market day — Sunday — when the Indians from
many miles round come to sell and buy and enjoy themselves. It is a good type of the well-to-do Peruvian
village, the surrounding country being fertile and populous. The better houses, a few of them two storied, are of
stone, the rest of sun-dried mud — that *adobe* which one
finds all over Spanish America from the pueblos of New
Mexico down to Patagonia. Their fronts are covered
with a wash of white or light blue, and this, with the
red-tiled roofs, gives a pleasant freshness and warmth
of tone. The two plazas whose joint area is about
equal to half of the whole town, are thronged with

Indians, all the men and many of the women wearing the characteristic poncho, a rough woollen or, less often, cotton cloak which comes below the waist, and is usually of some bright hue. To this the women add gaudy petticoats, red or purplish, blue or green or violet, so that there is even more colour in the crowd than on the houses. The greatest variety is in the hats. The women wear round felts or cloth-covered straws, some almost as wide as a cardinal's; many are square, set off by gilt or silvered bands like the academic cap of the English Universities, though the brim is larger. The man's hat is smaller; it is mostly of stiff white felt, and underneath it is a tight fitting cloth cap of some bright colour, usually red, with flaps at each side to protect the ear and cheek from the piercing winds. Strings of glittering beads complete the Sunday dress of the women, and we saw only a few with silver ornaments. Most of the trading seemed to be done by barter, country folk exchanging farm or garden produce with the town dealers for groceries or cloth. The cotton cloths were largely made from the Peruvian plant cultivated in the warm coast valleys, while some of the woollen goods, such as blankets or stuff for petticoats, had come from England, as I saw on them the names of Yorkshire firms. Besides maize and nuts and peppers, together with oranges carried up from the hot valley of Urubamba seventy miles to the north, the most noticeable articles of commerce were a sort of edible seaweed brought from the coast, and dried marine star-fishes, and, above all, small bags of coca leaves, the article which

is the one indispensable stimulant of the Indian, more
for him than tea or coffee or alcoholic drinks are for the
Asiatic or the European.   It is a subtropical shrub or
low tree which grows on the lower slopes of the Peruvian
and Bolivian Andes and is sold to the Indians in small
quantities, as indeed all the sales and purchases seemed
to be on a small scale, there being among the peasants
very little money though very little downright poverty.
South American countries are, for the traveller at least,
a land of high prices, but here we saw savoury messes
of hot stewed meat with chopped onions and potatoes
and a small glass of chicha (the common drink of the
country brewed from maize), thrown in, offered at the
price of five centavos, less than two English pence or
a United States five cent piece.   It was surprising
that in so thick and busy a crowd there should be,
instead of the chattering and clattering that one would
have heard in Europe, only a steady hum.   The Quichua
Indians are a comparatively silent race, quiet and well
mannered, and inoffensive except when they are drunk.
These Sicuani people were small in stature, few exceeding five feet six inches, their faces a reddish brown,
the features regular though seldom handsome, for while
the nose is often well formed, the mouth is ugly, with
no fineness of line in the lips, although these are far less
thick than a negro's.   Some have a slight moustache,
but beards are seen only on the mestizos (half breeds).
Among the many diversities of feature which suggest
that there has been an intermixture of races, perhaps
long ago, there are two prevailing types — the broad,

round, short face with full cheeks, and the longer face with an aquiline nose. All have dark brown or black eyes, and long, straight, black, rather coarse, hair, and in all there is a curiously stolid and impassive look as of men accustomed to centuries of monotony and submission. Impassiveness is the characteristic note of the Indian. The Kafir is like a grown-up child ; the Chinese have a curious quiet alertness and keenness of observation ; the Hindus (and most Orientals) are submissive though watchful as if trying to take the white man's measure : but the Indian is none of these things. In his obedience there is no servility : he is reserved, aloof, seemingly indifferent to the *Viracocha* [1] and to things in general. The most noticeable in the throng were the Indian village alcaldes, each carrying as the badge of his office a long, heavy staff or cane, with a spike at the bottom and a large round head, bound with silver bands and covered at the top with a silver casing. This dignitary, appointed by the local authority annually, exerts in his little community an undisputed sway, enforced by his power of imprisonment. The post is eagerly sought, so that the wealthier sort will offer money to obtain it. We saw them moving through the crowd, all making way for them. There were, however, no disturbances to quell : the bright sun shone on an orderly and good-humoured crowd. Some groups, drawn a little apart, were enjoying the strains of a guitar or an ac-

[1] This is the term of respect by which an Indian usually addresses a white man of superior station. The word was in Inca mythology the name of a divine or half-divine hero — it was also the name of one of the Inca sovereigns.

cordion or those of the true national instrument, the Pandean pipe made of hollow reeds unequal in length, while above, on the hillside, the donkeys on which the wealthier peasants had ridden in and the llamas that had carried their produce stood patiently awaiting the declining light that should turn them homeward.

The only point of interest in Sicuani is the church and the arched gateway beside it.   It is like any other village church, the architecture dull, the interior gloomy.   But it was in this church that in 1782 Andres the nephew of Tupac Amaru, half of Spanish Biscayan, half of Inca blood, received episcopal absolution for his share in the great insurrection of the Indians under that chieftain, an absolution to be shortly followed by his murder at the hands of perfidious Spaniards; and it was on this arch (if the story we heard be true) that some of the limbs of the unfortunate Tupac Amaru himself were exposed after he had been torn in pieces by four horses in the great square of Cuzco.

The valley of the Vilcamayu River below Sicuani unfolds scene after scene of varied beauty.   It is indeed even more bare of wood than those valleys of the central Apennines, of which, allowing for the difference of scale, it sometimes reminds one.   The only tall tree is the Australian Eucalyptus, which though only recently introduced, is now common in the subtropical parts of South America, and already makes a figure in the landscape, for it is a fast grower.   These Australian gum trees have now overspread the world.   They are all over South Africa and on the Mediterranean coasts, as well as in

Mexico and on the Nilghiri hills of southern India, where they have replaced the more beautiful native groves.

In the wider and more level stretches of the valley, populous villages lie near together, for the irrigated flats of the valley floor flourish with abundant crops, and the rich red soil makes the hillsides worth cultivating even without irrigation. Although stained by the blood of battles more than is any other part of Peru, the land has an air of peace and comfort. The mountains on each side seemed to be composed of igneous rocks, but only in one place could I discover evidences of recent volcanic action. About fifteen miles below Sicuani six or seven small craters are seen near together, most of them on the northeast side of the valley, the highest some twelve hundred feet above it; and the lava flows which have issued from two or three of these are so fresh, the surface still so rugged and of so deep a black, that one may conclude that not many centuries have elapsed since the last eruption. The higher ranges that enclose the valley, crags above and curving lines of singular beauty below, evidently belong to a more remote geological age. Their contrasts of dark rock and red soil, with the flat smiling valley between and the noble snow peaks of the Vilcanota group filling the southern distance, make landscapes comparable in their warmth of colour and variety of form to those of the Italian Alps. They are doubly delightful to the traveller who has been passing through the savage solitudes that lie between this and the Pacific coast. Here at last he seems to get a notion of what Peru may have been like before the invaders came, and when a peaceful and industrious people laboured in the service of the Inca and the Sun God. Now, to be sure, there is a railway, and the station houses are roofed with corrugated iron. Yet the aspect of the land can have changed but little. The inhabitants are almost all Indian, and live and cultivate much as they did four centuries ago; their villages are of the same mud-built, grass-roofed cottages. They walk behind their llamas along the track, playing a rustic pipe as they go; and the women wash clothes in the brook swollen by last night's rain ; and up the side glens which descend from the untrodden snowy range behind, one catches glimpses of high, steep pastures, where perhaps hardly even a plundering Spaniard ever set his foot and where no extortionate curate preyed upon his flock.

Swinging down the long canyon of the Vilcamayu — it is long, indeed, for there are four hundred miles more of it before it opens on the great Amazonian plain — and rattling through deep rock cuttings and round sharp curves above the foaming torrent, the line at last turns suddenly to the northwest towards Cuzco, and we bid farewell to the river. Gladly would we have followed it down the valley into scenery even more beautiful than that of its upper levels, where luxuriant forests along the stream contrast with the snowy summits of the Eastern Cordillera towering above. But from this point on there are only mule paths, and travel is so slow that a week would have been needed to reach the finest part of this scenery.[1] Renunciation is the hardest part of travelling.

Our way to Cuzco lay up a wide lateral valley, enclosed by green hills, well cultivated and studded with populous villages, near one of which can be descried the ruins of a large ancient building which tradition attributes to the Inca Viracocha. The vale has an air of peace and primitive quiet, secluded and remote, as of a peaceful land where nothing had ever happened. At last, as the mountains begin to close in, the end of the journey comes in sight; and here, under steep hills enclosing a basin-shaped hollow — what in Peru is called a *Bolson* — lies Cuzco, the sacred City of the Sun.

Cuzco belongs to that class of historic cities which have once been capitals of kingdoms and retain traces of their ancient glory, a class which includes Moscow and Krakau, Throndhjem and Upsala, Dublin and Edinburgh and Winchester, Aix la Chapelle and Bagdad and Toledo and Granada, a class from which imperial Delhi has now just emerged to recover its former rank. And Cuzco was the capital of an empire vaster than was ruled from any of those famous seats of power, the centre of a religion and a dominion which stretched southward from the Equator for two thousand miles and embraced nearly all that there was of whatever approached civilization in the South American Continent.

Every traveller is familiar with the experience of finding that the reality of some spot on which his imag-

---

[1] Above this valley, nearly a hundred miles away to the northeast, rises the splendid peak of Salcantay, whose height, said to approach 22,000 feet, will some day attract an aspiring mountain climber.

ination has dwelt is unlike what it had pictured. I
had fancied a walled city visible from afar on a high
plain, with a solitary citadel hill towering above it.
But Cuzco lies inconspicuous, with its houses huddled
close in its *bolson* at a point where three narrow glens
descend from the tableland above, their torrents meeting
in it or just below it; and no buildings are seen, except
a few square church towers, till you are at its gates.
It stands on a gentle slope, the streets straight, except
where the course of a torrent forces them to curve, and
many of them too narrow for vehicles to pass one another, but vehicles are so few that this does not matter.
They are paved with cobble stones so large and rough
that the bed of many a mountain brook is smoother,
and in the middle there is an open gutter into which
every kind of filth is thrown, so that the city from end
to end is filled with smells too horrible for description.
Cologne, as Coleridge described it a century ago, and
the most fetid cities of Southern Italy are fragrant in
comparison. The houses, solidly built of stone, are enclosed in small, square court yards surrounded by rude
wooden galleries. Many have two stories, with balconies also of wood in front, and a few shew handsome
gateways, with the arms of some Spanish family carved
on the lintel stone. One such bears the effigies of the
four Pizarro brothers, and is supposed to have been
inhabited by the terrible Francisco himself when he
lived here. But the impressive features of the city are its
squares. The great Plaza, a part of the immense open
space which occupied the centre of the ancient Inca town,
wants the trees and flower beds of the squares of Lima

and Arequipa. But its ample proportions, with three remarkable churches occupying two sides of it, and the fortress hill of Sacsahuaman frowning over it, give it an air of dignity. The two smaller plazas, that called Cusipata and that of San Francisco, are less regular, but rudely picturesque, with arcades on two sides of them, and quaint old houses of varying heights, painted in blue, and bearing in front balconies frail with age. The older Spanish colonial towns, inferior as they are in refinements of architectural detail to the ancient cities of Italy and Spain, have nevertheless for us a certain charm of strangeness, intensified, in the case of Cuzco, by the sense of all the changes they have witnessed.

The cathedral, if not beautiful, is stately, with its two solid towers and its spacious and solemn interior. One is shewn a picture attributed to Van Dyck — be it his or not it is a good picture — and an altar at which Pizarro communicated, and a curious painting representing ceremonies observed on the admission of monks and nuns in the seventeenth century. But what interested me most was a portrait in the sacristy, among those of other bishops of Cuzco, of the first bishop, Fray Vicente de Valverde. It may be merely a "stock" picture, made to order at a later time like those of the early Popes in the basilica of St. Paul at Rome. But one willingly supposed it taken from the life, because the hard, square face with pitiless eyes answered to the character of the man, one of the most remarkable persons in the history of the Spanish Conquest, because he is as perfect an illustration as history presents of a minister of Christ in whom every lineament of Christian character,

H

except devotion to his faith, had been effaced.[1]   He was the friar who accompanied Pizarro on his expedition and stood by the leader's side in the square at Caxamarca when he was welcoming as a friend the Inca Atahuallpa.   When Atahuallpa declined the summons of Valverde to accept baptism and recognize Charles the Fifth as sovereign, Pizarro, whose men were fully armed, and had already been instructed to seize the unsuspecting Inca and massacre his followers, hesitated or affected for a moment to hesitate, and turned to Valverde for advice.   "I absolve you," answered the friar.   "Fall on, Castilians, I absolve you."   With this the slaughter of the astonished crowd began : and thousands perished in the city square before night descended on the butchery.

When Cuzco was taken, Valverde was made bishop of the new see, the first bishopric of Peru.   Verily he had his reward.   He did not long enjoy it.   A few years later he was shipwrecked, while voyaging to Panama, on the coast near Tumbez, captured by the wild Indians of those parts, and (according to the story) devoured.

Of the other churches, the most externally handsome is that of the Compañia (the Jesuits), with its florid north façade of red sandstone, a piece of cunningly conceived and finely executed ornamentation superior even to that of the church of the same Order at Arequipa. Internally there is most to admire in the church of

---

[1] It is fair to say that when the conquest was once accomplished, Valverde seems to have protested against the reduction of the Indians to slavery.

Merced (Our Lady of Mercy, the patroness of Peru), for it has richly decorated ceilings on both stories of its charming cloisters, and a fine staircase leading up to the choir. All the larger churches have silver altars, some of them very well chiselled. But by far the most remarkable piece of work in the city is the pulpit of the old and now scarcely used church of San Blas. It is said to be all of one piece, the glory of an Indian craftsman, and is a marvel of delicate carving, worthy of the best executive skill of Italy or Spain. My scanty knowledge does not qualify me to express an opinion, but it was hard not to fancy that in this pulpit and in the fine ornamentation of the façades of the Jesuit churches I have described, there may be discovered marks of a distinctive type of artistic invention which was not Spanish, but rather Peruvian, and gave evidence of a gift which might, if cultivated, have reflected credit upon the Indian race.

It has seemed worth while to dwell upon the ecclesiastical buildings of these three Peruvian cities just because there is so very little to attract the student of art in South America, less even than in Mexico. Though the two greatest Spanish painters lived after the days of Pizarro, one may say, broadly speaking, that the best days of Spanish architecture and of taste in works of art were passing away before these American countries were settled, and it was seldom that anything of high excellence was either brought from Europe or produced in South America, produced even in Peru, the wealthiest of all the colonial dominions of Spain.

Before I turn from Spanish Cuzco to the ancient city a word may be said as to its merits as a place of residence. Its height (11,100 feet) and its latitude give it a climate free from extremes of heat or cold, and, for those who have capacious lungs and sound hearts, pretty healthful throughout the year. We found the air cool and bracing in the end of September. Disgusting as are the dirt and the smells, they do not seem to breed much disease; foul gases are probably less noxious when discharged into the open air than when they ooze out into houses from closed drains.[1] The country round is beautiful, bold heights surrounding a green and fertile vale, though there are so few trees that shade is wanting. Many places of great antiquarian interest are within reach, of course accessible by riding only, for there is only one tolerable road, that which leads down the valley to the Vilcamayu. Society, though small and old-fashioned, unfriendly to new ideas and tinged with ecclesiasticism, is simple mannered and kindly. No people can be more polite and agreeable than the Peruvians, whether of pure Spanish extraction, or mixed, as the great majority here are, with Indian blood. Though Cuzco is deemed, not less than Arequipa, a stronghold of conservatism and clericalism, modern tendencies can make themselves felt. Shortly before my visit there had been a revolt of the students of the University against a rector deemed "unpro-

[1] While these pages are passing through the press (April, 1912), I am informed that a serious effort is about to be made to lay drains in and generally to clean up Cuzco.

gressive" : and there had been chosen as his successor a young North American professor who had been living in Peru for a few years only, employed in some government work when he was appointed here. He seemed to be on good terms with both officials and pupils.

The university is an old one, founded in 1598, but its revenues and the attendance of students are not worthy of its antiquity. Those who come seek instruction in professional subjects, especially law and medicine. Nearly everywhere in South America the demand for teaching in philosophy, letters, or science is scanty indeed. The clergy, it need hardly be said, are not educated in these lay institutions.

Though essentially a Spanish city in its edifices, Cuzco is predominantly Indian in its people. The Quichua language is that commonly spoken, and it is the Indian aborigines who give to the aspect of its streets and squares the picturesqueness which half atones for squalor. They set up their little booths, sometimes covered with canvas, along the arcades and in the plazas, and loaf about in their bright-coloured ponchos and broad, flat, straw hats, the dry-weather side of the straw covered with a sort of velveteen adorned with tinsel, and the wet-weather side with red flannel. Women lean over the rough wooden balconies on the first floors of the houses, and talk to the loungers in the plaza below. Strings of llamas bearing their burdens pass along, the only creatures, besides the tiny mules, who do any work. There are scarcely any wheeled vehicles, for those not forced by poverty to walk, ride mostly on donkeys; and the only events are saints' days, with their processions, occurring so frequently that the habit of laziness has unequalled opportunities for confirming itself. Though the Quichuas were under the Incas a most industrious race, and still give assiduous labour to their fields, the atmosphere of the city is one of easy idleness, nothing to do, and plenty of time to do it. The only manufactory we came across was a German brewery, — there is no place, however remote, where one does not find the enterprising German. Neither is there any trade, except that of supplying a few cheap goods to the surrounding country folk. By far the best general warehouse is kept by an Italian gentleman who has got together an interesting collection of antiquities.

Now let us turn from the Cuzco of the last three and a half centuries back to the olden time and see what remains of the ancient city of the Sun and of the Incas, his children. It is worth while to do so, for here, more than anywhere else in South America, there is something that helps the traveller to recall a society and a religion so unlike the present that it seems half mythic. Whoever has read, as most of us did in our boyhood, of the marvels of the Peruvian Empire which Pizarro destroyed, brings an ardent curiosity to the central seat of that Empire, and expects to find many a monument of its glories.

The reality is disappointing, yet it is impressive. One learns more from a little seeing than from reading many books. As our expectations had been unduly raised, it is right to give this reality with some little exactness of detail. The interest of the remains lies entirely in what they tell us about their builders, for there is nothing beautiful, nothing truly artistic to describe. The traces of the Incas[1] to be seen in Cuzco, and, indeed, anywhere in Peru, are all of one kind only. They are Walls. No statue, no painting. No remains of a complete roofed building, either temple or palace; nothing but ruins, and mostly fragmentary ruins. The besom of Spanish destruction swept clean. Everything connected with the old religion had to perish : priests and friars took care of that. As for other buildings, it did not occur to anybody to spare them. Even in Italy, not long before Pizarro's day, a man so cultivated as Pope Julius the Second knocked about the incomparably more beautiful and remarkable buildings of ancient Rome when they interfered with his plans of building.

But the walls at Cuzco are remarkable. They are unique memorials, not only of power and persistence, but in a certain way of skill also, not in decorative art, for of that there is scarcely a trace left, but of a high degree of expertness in the cutting and fitting together of enormous blocks. Most of the streets of the modern city follow the lines of ancient pre-Conquest streets, and in many of these there are

[1] The name " Inca " properly belongs to the ruling family or clan in the Peruvian monarchy, of whose ethnic relations to its subjects we know very little, but I use it here to denote not only the dynasty, but the epoch of their rule, which apparently covered two centuries (possibly more) before the arrival of Pizarro. The expression " The Inca " means the reigning monarch.

long stretches of wall from six or eight to sixteen
or eighteen feet in height so entirely unlike Spanish
buildings that their Inca origin is unquestionable.
They are of various types, each of which probably
belongs to an epoch of its own. The most frequent,
and apparently the latest type, shews very large
blocks of a dark grey rock, a syenite or trachyte,
cut to a uniform rectangular oblong form, the outer
faces, which are nearly smooth and slightly convex,
being cut in towards the joinings of the other stones.
The blocks are fitted together with the utmost care,
so close to one another that it is no exaggeration to say
that a knife can seldom be inserted between them. The
walls which they make slope very slightly backward,
and, in most cases, the stones are smaller in the upper
layers than in the lower. Two such walls enclose a
long and narrow street which runs southeastward from
the great Plaza. They are in perfect preservation, and
sustain in some places the weight of modern houses
built upon them. There are very few apertures for
doors or windows, but one high gateway furnishes a
good specimen of the Inca door and is surmounted by a
long slab on which are carved in relief, quite rudely,
the figures of two serpents. In other places one finds
walls of the same character, but with smaller blocks
and less perfect workmanship. Of a third type the
wall of the so-called Palace of the Inca Roca is the
best instance. It is what we call in Europe a Cyclopean building, the blocks enormous and of various
shapes, but each carefully cut and adjusted to the in-

equalities of outline in the adjoining blocks, so that all fit perfectly together. One famous stone shews twelve angles into which the stones above, below, and at each side of it have been made to fit. This type seems older, perhaps by centuries, than that first described. In none of the walls is any mortar or any other kind of cementing material used : their strength consists in their weight and in the exactness with which they are compacted together. The most beautifully finished piece of all is to be seen in the remains of the great Temple of the Sun on whose site and out of whose ruins have been built the church and convent of St. Dominick. Here, at the west end of the church, there is what was evidently the external wall of the end of the temple. It is rounded, and each of the large squared stones is so cut as to conform perfectly to the curve of the whole. None of the single stones has the convexity which appears in the walls first described, because the surfaces of all have been levelled and polished so that they form one uniformly smooth and uniformly curved surface, as if they were all one block. A more exquisitely finished piece of work cannot be imagined. It is at least as good as anything of the same kind in Egypt, and stands as perfect now as it was when the Spaniards destroyed the superstructure of the temple.

The city is full of these fragments of wall. I discovered in out-of-the-way corners some that were supporting little terraced garden beds, others in backyards, or even in pigsties, and it seemed to me that there were four or five distinct styles or types of stone cutting and stone fitting,

belonging to different ages.[1] If all the buildings erected
since 1540 could be removed without disturbing the older
buildings beneath them, that which was left would be sufficient to give a fairly complete ground plan of the Inca
city and enable us to form some idea of its character.
But we should not then be much nearer to knowing
what was the actual aspect of the great palaces and
temples before the work of destruction began. The
Incas built immense covered halls, we are told of one
two hundred paces long by fifty wide, but it does
not appear how they were roofed over, for the arch
was, of course, unknown. Apparently there was little
or nothing of that advanced form of art in pattern ornamentation and in figures of men and animals which
we admire in the ruins of Copan (in Honduras) or
Palenque (in Mexico) and other places in Central
America. Perhaps the intractable nature of the
volcanic and other hard igneous stone used by the
Incas compared with the comparatively soft lime-
stones of Palenque and Mitla discouraged attempts at
elaborate mural decoration. Perhaps the artistic talent
of the Peruvians did not go far. Their pottery,
whether plain or made to represent the forms of living creatures, is generally rude, and the paintings on
wooden vessels shew only mediocre power of drawing,
though they do shew that fine sense of colour which is

---

[1] A patient archæologist might be able by examining and photo-
graphing specimens of each style to determine their chronological
succession and thus throw some light on the history of the city. The
oldest type appeared to be that of the Inca Roca wall, very similar
to that of the Sacsahuaman walls to be presently described.

present in most of the art work of the aboriginal Americans.

Cuzco has no public museum, but there are two or three small private collections. In one of these the most interesting objects shewn us were the pictures on wood representing combats between Peruvian warriors and their enemies, the savage tribes of the eastern forests. The former fight with the spear and have the sling for their missile weapon, the latter use the bow, as do their descendants to this day. In this collection there were also bows taller than a man, with arrows of corresponding size, formidable weapons, which some of the natives of the forest, placing them flat on the ground, draw with their feet and with which they are said to kill fish in the rivers as well as land game. These, and the beautiful feather plumes, and the rude heads of pumas, wild cats, and birds of prey, had all a flavour of barbarism, and were far inferior to the remains of Egyptian or Assyrian art.[1] The Peruvian mummies, specimens of which we also saw, are not laid out at full length, like those of Egypt, but have the knees pressed to the chin.

Grand as are the walls inside Cuzco, they seem insignificant when one examines the more stupendous ramparts of the prehistoric fortress on Sacsahuaman Hill, which rises immediately above the city to a height of about six hundred and fifty feet. I describe them the more fully because much study has been of late

[1] Good specimens of all these things may be seen in the American Museum of Natural History of New York.

years bestowed upon the (so-called) Cyclopean and other ancient walls of Europe, such as those of Tarragona in Spain, of Greek cities, like Tiryns and Naxos (near Taormina), and of the Volscian and Latin cities round Rome, so that an account of the more imposing Peruvian structures may be of interest to some readers. The hill, nearly halfway up which, on a terrace, are the remains of its palace attributed to the Inca Manco Capac, is in its upper part extremely steep, in places even precipitous, and commands a wonderful view over the mass of red-roofed houses, the long, straight streets in some of which the dark lines of Inca wall can just be discerned, the three broad plazas with Indians and their llamas creeping about like ants, the sunny vale below, and the snow-clad summits of the Nevado (snow mountain) of Ausungate, piercing the sky in the far distance. Stone ramparts ran all round the upper part of the hill, and parts of them still remain on this southern face. What with their height and solidity and with the natural strength of the ground, the fortress must have been on this side impregnable before the invention of gunpowder. But on the other, or northerly side, that turned away from Cuzco, the hill is not only less steep, but has also much less rise, for it is less than a hundred feet above the ground behind it. Here, therefore, since nature had done less, there was more for art to do; and here we find fortress walls on a scale of incomparable grandeur.

They are built in three parallel lines, one behind the other, and both their length, nearly one third of a mile, and the massiveness of their construction, and the enormous size of many of the individual stones make this fortress one of the most impressive monuments of prehistoric times that the world contains.   It shews that those who raised it had a boldness of conception and a persistent energy in carrying out that conception amazing in a primitive people,[1] for the work seems to belong to a very early time, long anterior to those historic Incas whom the Spaniards overthrew.

Hardly less wonderful than the gigantic proportions of these fortifications is the military skill shewn in their construction.   Their line is not straight, as in most of the walls of ancient Greek and Italian and early mediæval cities, but consists of a series of salient and re-entering angles, so that from each salient angle and each inner angle the whole space outside and below the wall as far as the next projecting angle could be commanded by the garrison.   This arrangement, which, while it increased the length of the work and required more labour to complete it, increased immensely its defensive efficiency, indicates a skill hardly to be expected in a race comparatively pacific, and more eminent in the arts of government than in those of war. Yet perhaps it was just because they were not first-

---

[1] There is reason to think that Cuzco must have been inhabited from remote times.   Traces of human habitation and handiwork have both inside and outside the city been discovered at depths so much below the present surface as to indicate that there must have been a considerable population long before the city, possibly before the fortress of Sacsahuaman, was built.   An account of these will be found in a book expected to appear in 1913 in which Mr. Hiram Bingham is to describe the results of the explorations of the Yale expeditions of 1911 and 1912.

class fighting men like the Aztecs or the Iroquois that the Quichuas were successful in devising expedients for defence. Sparta was the only considerable Greek city that did not surround herself with walls, because the valour of her people was deemed sufficient protection.

On the top of the hill behind these lines of ramparts there are remains of ancient buildings, though none with such enormous stones. It is hard to make out what these edifices were, for every bit of ground built upon has been ransacked over and over again for hidden treasure. Peru is full of stories about fabulous quantities of Inca gold hidden away to save it from the rapacity of the conquerors, and some of the tales may be true, though hardly any such treasures have been found for more than a century past. But the story that there is a secret passage cut in the rock from the Inca castle at the top of the hill down through it and into Cuzco where it opens to the Temple of the Sun is too much for any but native credulity. These beliefs in long subterranean passages recur everywhere in the world. It was — perhaps still is — believed in Oxford that there is such an one from the church of St. Peter in the city to the ruined nunnery on the river at Godstow (Fair Rosamond's place of confinement) two miles distant. It is believed in Kerwan (in Tunisia) that the most sacred of the wells in that most sacred of all African cities communicates underground with the well Zem Zem in Mecca two thousand miles away and on the other side of the Red Sea. The most persistent treasure hunt carried on by the Peruvians has been that for the golden chain made by the Inca Huayna Capac, which was long enough to be stretched all round the great square of Cuzco, and was thrown into the lake of Urcos lest it should fall into the hands of the Spaniards. Everybody believes it to be still at the bottom of the lake, which is very deep.

Opposite the great walls and about a third of a mile away is a rocky eminence called, from a curious convex mass of extremely hard igneous rock upon it, the Rodadero. The rock is polished smooth and has two projecting ridges on its surface. How much of this peculiar slope down which many generations of Peruvian boys have rejoiced to slide — they were doing so in the days of Garcilaso, soon after the Conquest — is due to nature, how much to art improving nature, has been matter for controversy. But far more curious are the seats carved in the hard rock all over the top and slopes of the hill, the cutting done with exquisite care and finish, the angles perfectly sharp, the flat parts perfectly smooth. The most remarkable is a set of thirteen seats, one in the centre and highest, nine others declining from it on the left and three on the right. This is called the Seat of the Inca, but there is no record, nor any authentic tradition, of the purpose for which, or the persons by whom, it was constructed, nor of the purpose of the many other seats, and small staircases, and niches, and basins similarly chiselled out of the rock which are scattered here and there all round. In one place two great and finely cut blocks look like fragments of a doorway shattered by an earthquake, and not far off there are singular passages hewn through the rock, and now in parts closed, which have the appearance of a sort of labyrinth. Looking at the Inca's Seat, one's first conjecture would be that it was a bench for judges to sit upon. Other seats look more like shrines meant for images; but no fragments of images are found. All these strange cuttings and polishings seem so inexplicable that one would conjecture the mere caprice of a whimsical ruler, but for the immense pains that must have been taken in doing such perfect work in such hard material. No Spanish writer of Conquest days gives us any light. It is a riddle, the key to which is lost, and lost irrecoverably, because there are no inscriptions and no traditions.

Reverting to the fortress of Sacsahuaman, there is a current view that it was erected as an outwork to defend Cuzco from the attacks of the fierce tribes of the eastern and northern valleys whose raids the Incas frequently had to repel. It seems, however, superfluously huge as a defence against such enemies, not to add that they could easily have descended upon Cuzco from the other sides of the two ravines between which the fortress stands. More probably, therefore Sacsahuaman is a very ancient stronghold, probably much older than Cuzco, or at any rate than Cuzco's greatness. It may have been the earliest seat of some very early king or dynasty, and have been, in the flourishing days of the Inca monarchy, a citadel where the reigning sovereign kept his treasures and to which he could retire for safety in case of need.

I am not attempting to describe all the relics of antiquity that are to be seen in or near Cuzco. There are striking ruins not far off, such as those at Ollantay-tambo and Pisac, and lower down the Vilcamayu Valley at Machu Picchu and Rosas Pata, as well as others still more distant in the high country between here and Lima.[1] But what is true at Cuzco is true everywhere. The only ruins are of walls and gates of fortresses and palaces; in a few spots of temples, also. In these there are evidences of enormous labour and considerable mechanical skill, but only slight evidences of artistic talent. The walls, perfectly cut and polished, have seldom the smallest ornament, except niches. There are no domes, for the art of vaulting was unknown, and hardly ever columns. So far as we can tell, the great Sun Temple at Cuzco consisted only of lofty walls enclosing courts, with no decoration but plates of gold attached to the walls. True it is that the Spaniards destroyed all the religious and many of the secular edifices, yet if there had been temples covered with ornaments like those found in Southern Mexico and Central America, some traces must surely have remained.

[1] Such as that at Choqquequirau described by my friend Professor Bingham in his book entitled *Across South America*. He discovered, in 1911, an Inca building at a place on the river Pampaconas fifteen days' journey north of Cuzco and only two thousand feet above sea-level. It was not previously known that their power had extended so far in that direction.

I

Notwithstanding this want of decorative art, the Cuzco ruins leave upon the beholder a strong impression, the impression of immense energy and will in those who planned these works, of patient and highly trained labour in those who executed them. Only despotic rulers commanding like the Egyptian kings a host of obedient subjects, could have reared such a structure as the fortress of Sacsahuaman. The race that could erect such buildings and gather such treasures as the Temple of the Sun possessed, and could conquer and rule a dominion of fifty days' journey from north to south, must have been a strong and in its way a gifted race. It is hard to believe that it was the ancestor of those stolid and downtrodden Indians whom one sees to-day, peddling their rude wares in the market place of Cuzco. It is their old imperial town, but there is scarcely one among them above the rank of a labourer; and during the last three centuries few indeed have emerged from the abject condition to which the Conquest reduced them.

The sudden fall of a whole race is an event so rare in history that one seeks for explanations. It may be that not only the royal Inca family, but nearly the whole ruling class was destroyed in war, leaving only the peasants who had already been serfs under their native sovereigns. But one is disposed to believe that the tremendous catastrophe which befell them in the destruction at once of their dynasty, their empire, and their religion by fierce conquerors, incomparably superior in energy and knowledge, completely broke not only the spirit of the nation, but the self-respect of the individuals who composed it. They were already a docile and submissive people, and now ·under a new tyranny, far harsher than that of rulers of their own blood, they sank into hopeless apathy, and ceased even to remember what their forefathers had been. The intensity of their devotion to their sovereign and their deity made them helpless when both were overthrown, leaving them nothing to turn to, nothing to strive for. The Conquistadores were wise in their hateful way, when they put forth the resources of cruelty to outrage the feelings of the people and stamp terror in their hearts. One cannot stand in the great Plaza of Cuzco without recalling the scene of A.D. 1571, when one of the last of the Inca line, an innocent youth, seized and accused of rebellion by the Spanish viceroy Francisco de Toledo, was executed in the presence of a vast Indian crowd that filled it. When the executioner raised the sword of death, there rose such a wail of horror that he paused, and the leading Spanish churchmen hastened to the viceroy and begged him for mercy. Determined to make an example, Toledo was inexorable. The young Inca, Tupac Amaru, was beheaded and his head stuck on a pike, and placed beside the scaffold. At midnight a Spaniard, looking out of a window that commanded the Plaza was amazed to see it again filled with Indians, all silent and motionless, kneeling in veneration before the head of the last representative of the sacred line.

More than two hundred years later another more remote scion of the Incas, José Gabriel Condorcanqui, who had taken the same name of Tupac Amaru, — I have already referred to him on p. 92, — had been stirred to indignation by what he saw of the Indian population suffering from the exactions as well of the Spanish landowners who held them in serfdom as of the rapacious Spanish officials. After many vain complaints, he headed a movement to obtain redress by force, not rejecting the authority of the Spanish Crown, but trying to rouse the Indians by appeals to the faint memories of Inca greatness. The hope of relief from their miseries drew thousands of the aborigines to his standard. But they were ill armed and worse organized; the race had no longer any strength in it for a fight, and in some months the rising was quelled, after frightful slaughter, its leader betrayed to the Spaniards, his family seized, and all brought prisoners to Cuzco. There, by the sentence of the Spanish judge, a monster named Areche, the uncle and son-in-law and wife of Tupac Amaru, had their tongues cut out and were executed before his eyes, that death might be made more horrible to him by the sight of their agonies. He was then, after his own tongue had been cut out, torn in pieces by four horses attached to his four limbs. All this happened in 1781, within the memory of the grandfathers of men now living. Such atrocities were at once the evidence of what Spanish rule in Peru had been and a presage of its fall. Within twenty years thereafter began those first conspiracies against the authority of Spain which ushered in the War of Independence.

Many another scene of horror and strife has Cuzco seen. Wandering through its streets, one is possessed every moment by the sense of how much has happened in a place where nowadays nothing seems to happen. Perhaps it is because its annals are so tragic that this sense is so strong; but there are certainly few places where the very stones seem more saturated with history. More than three centuries ago the historian Garcilaso de la Vega compared Cuzco to ancient Rome. The two cities have little more in common than the fact that both were capitals of dominions long since departed, and the seats of faiths long since extinct. But in both this feeling of a vista stretching far back and filled with many spectres of the past is overpowering. The long, grey, mouldering streets and houses of Spanish Cuzco, the ancient walls of primitive Peruvian Cuzco, defying time better than the convents and the churches, each calling up contrasted races and civilizations, the plazas too vast for the shrunken population, the curious sense of two peoples living side by side in a place from which the old life has vanished and into which no new life has come, the sense of utter remoteness from the modern world, all these things give to Cuzco a strange and dreamy melancholy, a melancholy all the deeper because there was little in its past that one could wish restored. There were dark sides to the ancient civilization. But was it worth destroying in order to erect on its ruins what the Conquerors brought to Peru?

NOTE ON THE FORTRESS OF SACSAHUAMAN

The walls of Sacsahuaman are built in three parallel lines, the lowest of which stands on level ground, at the very base of the hill; the second about six yards behind the first, and therefore on the slope; the third still higher on the slope, three yards behind the second. The space behind each wall has been filled in and levelled, so as to be a nearly flat terrace, supported by the wall in front of it. These three lines of wall extend along and protect the whole northern face of the hill, nearly six hundred yards long, between the points where it falls abruptly into deep ravines to the east and the west, which give a natural defence. The outermost wall at the base of the hill is the highest, about twenty-six feet; the second is from eighteen to twenty feet; the third, the least perfectly preserved, is a little less high, perhaps fifteen feet. The stones in the outermost row are the largest. One is over twenty-five feet high, fourteen wide, and twelve thick. Not a few exceed fifteen feet in height and twelve in width. There were three openings or gateways in each wall, the largest of which is twelve feet high, and over each of these was laid a long flat slab. The blocks, which are of a hard, greyish limestone, are all or nearly all rudely square or oblong, though sometimes where the shape of one is irregular, the irregularity is cut into an entering angle and the next stone is made to fit into this with its projecting angle, thus knitting the structure together. The surface of each is slightly convex and bevelled down towards the outer lines, where it meets the blocks laid next. All are so carefully adjusted that even now there are virtually no interstices, though the fitting together may probably have been even more exact before earthquakes and time had begun to tell upon the fabric. Its strength, as there is no mortar, depends upon the massiveness of the stones and their cohesion. Each wall rises a little, perhaps a foot and a half, above the terrace immediately behind it, but the level of the terrace may probably have been originally somewhat lower, so that the bodies of those defending the fortress would be better covered by the wall in front of them against missiles from the enemy.

The stones of Sacsahuaman have been brought from a hill about three-quarters of a mile distant, where a huge mound of chips cut from them has been discovered by Mr. Bingham since the date of my visit. (Edition of 1913.)

CHAPTER IV

FROM Cuzco, the oldest of South American cities, with its mingled memories of an Indian and a Spanish past, I will ask the reader to follow me to a land of ancient silence where an aboriginal people, under the pressure of a stern nature, and almost untouched by all that modern civilization has brought, still lead the lives and cling to the beliefs that their ancestors led and held many centuries ago. This is the heart of the Andean plateau, where, in a country almost as purely Indian as it was when it submitted to Pizarro, lies Lake Titicaca.

Ever since as a boy I had read of a great inland sea lying between the two ranges of the Cordillera almost as high above the ocean as is the top of the Jungfrau, I had wondered what the scenery of such mountains and such a sea might be like, and had searched books and questioned travellers without getting from them what I sought. There are no other bodies of fresh water on the earth's surface nearly so lofty, except on the plateaux of Central Asia, and none of these, such as the Manasarowar lakes in Tibet [1] and Lake Sir-i-kul in the Pamirs is nearly so extensive as this lake in Peru. It fills the lower part of an immense shallow depression between the eastern and western Cordilleras; and the

[1] Dr. Sven Hedin gives the height of Tso Mavang as 15,098 feet above sea level.

land both to the north and to the south of it is for a great
distance so level that we may believe the area covered
by its waters to have been at one time far greater.   Its
present length is about one hundred and twenty miles,
its greatest width forty-one miles, and its area nearly
equal to that of Lake Erie.   The shape is extremely
irregular, for there are many deep bays, and many
far projecting promontories.   There are also many
islands, two of which, famous in Peruvian mythology,
I shall presently describe.

This central plateau of Peru is a singular region.
As its height is from twelve thousand to thirteen thousand feet above sea level, the climate is always cold,
except when one is actually exposed to the direct rays
of the sun, but it varies comparatively little from the
summer to the winter months ; and though snow often
falls, it soon disappears.   In so inclement an air, and
with a rather scanty rainfall, only a few hardy crops
can ripen, such as potatoes (the plant is a native of
South America, and there are many other species of
Solanum) barley, the Oca (*Oxalis tuberosa*, a sort of
wood sorrel), and the Quinoa (a kind of edible *Chenopodium*)[1] as well as maize, but this last only in the
warmer and more sheltered places.   There are few trees,
and these stunted; nowhere a wood.   Even the shrubs
are mere scrub, so fuel is scarce and the people use for

[1] In some parts of Mexico the Indians use the seeds of a species
of *Chenopodium* for food.   Civilized man has not yet troubled himself to enquire what possibilities of development there may be in
some of the plants which primitive or barbarous man turned to
account.

cooking purposes in the mountains the tufts of a large woody-rooted plant called *Yareta*, growing in the high mountains which, like the peat of Ireland, burns fiercely, but is soon burnt out, and, on the lower grounds, *taquia* (the droppings of the llama), as the droppings of the yak are similarly used in Tibet. Nobody thinks of lighting a fire for warmth : for while the natives seem not to feel the cold, white people shiver and put on more clothes. One is surprised that man should have continued to dwell in a land so ungenial when not far off to the east, on the other side of the eastern Cordillera, hot valleys and an abundant rainfall promise easier conditions of life.

This lofty tract, stretching from the snowy peaks of the Vilcanota as far as La Paz in Bolivia, a distance of more than two hundred miles, the northern and western parts of it in Peru, the eastern and southern in Bolivia, is really a pure Indian country, and is named the Collao. In ancient days it was one of the four divisions of the Inca Empire. The inhabitants speak a language called Aymará, allied to the Quichua spoken farther north. In Inca days there were apparently many small tribes, each with its own tongue, but their names and memories have perished with their languages, and with the trifling exception of a small and very primitive race called the Urus (to be mentioned later) all the aborigines of the High Andes are now classified as Quichuas and Aymarás. The modern distinction between Peru and Bolivia is purely arbitrary and political. Aymarás dwelling west of the lake in Peru are the same people as Aymarás dwelling east of it in Bolivia.

Like Tibet, which it most resembles in height and cold and dryness, this strange country produces no more than what its inhabitants consume and has nothing to export except alpaca wool and minerals, nor, at present, very much of these latter, for only few mines are now being worked. The population does not increase, but it holds its ground, and wherever the soil is fit for cultivation, that is to say, wherever it is not too stony or too swampy, it is cultivated by the Indians, who live here in the same rude fashion as their forefathers before the Conquest. Nor is it only on the flat bottoms of the valleys that one sees their little patches of potatoes and barley. The steep slopes of the hills that rise from the lake have also been terraced to make ground level for cultivation, and each strip of soil is supported by a wall of loose stones well fitted together. These *andenes*, as they are called, which are common all over the hilly grounds of Peru, remind one of the vine-bearing terraces of the Rhineland, and like them witness to centuries of patient toil. As there is no manure nor other fertilizer, the soil is allowed to rest by lying fallow from time to time, so the area under cultivation in any one year is less than the number of the terraces might suggest. Though all the tillers are Indians, most of the land belongs to large proprietors who seldom come to it for more than a couple of months in the year, the peasants paying them either in a share of the crops, or a certain number of days' labour on the proprietor's own special *hacienda* or *finca* (farm) which his steward manages, or perhaps in personal service for some weeks rendered to him in the town he inhabits.   Rude and harsh is the life of these peasants, though well above the fear of starvation and no more squalid than that of the agricultural peasantry in some parts of Europe.   Their houses are of mud baked hard in the sun — the usual *adobe* of Spanish America — or perhaps of large stones roughly set in the mud as a cement; animals often share the family bedroom, and the sleeping places are a sort of platform or divan of earth raised a little from the floor along the walls of the hut.   Furniture there is virtually none, for wood is scarce and costly so far from the coast on one side and the forests on the other, but some of them have scraped together a good deal of property, including rich dresses and ornaments fit to be displayed at festivals.   For clothing they have a shirt and drawers of coarse cotton, with a poncho of heavy woollen cloth; for food, potatoes frozen and squeezed dry, to enable them to be stored, and barley; their only luxury is *chicha* beer, or alcohol when they can get it; their diversions, church festivals with processions in the morning and orgiastic dances afterwards; or a fight with the inhabitants of the neighbouring village.   Yet with all this apparent poverty and squalor, they are in this region, and have been for many ages, more advanced in the arts of life than their neighbours, those half nomad tribes of the trans-Andean forests, who subsist on what their arrows or blow-pipes can kill, and live in terror of the jaguar and the anaconda and the still more dangerous packs of wild dogs and peccaries. Agriculture and settled life are always factors of material progress, and the Aymarás would probably have risen out of the sort of practical serfdom in which they lie and from which scarcely any of them emerge, if they had not fallen under the dominion of an alien and stronger race who had no sympathy with them and did nothing to help them upwards.

I return to the lake itself which fills the centre of this singular plateau. Its northern and northwestern coasts, lying in Peruvian territory, are low and the water shallow, while the eastern and southern, in Bolivia, are generally high and bold with many rocky promontories and isles lying off them. The greatest depth is about six hundred feet. Storms are frequent, and the short, heavy waves make navigation dangerous, all the more so because the water is so cold that, as is the case in Lake Superior also, a swimmer is so soon benumbed that his chance of reaching land is slight. Ice sometimes forms in the shallower bays, but seldom lasts. Many are the water birds, gulls and divers, and flamingoes, and a kind of heron, besides eagles and hawks, though the big so-called turkey buzzard of the lower country does not seem to come so high, and the huge condor is no longer frequent. There are plenty of fish, but apparently of two genera only, the species (eight are enumerated) being most of them known only in this lake and in Lake Poopo, into which it discharges. The scantiness both of fauna and flora is natural when the unfavourable climatic conditions are considered. Among the water plants the commonest is a sort of rush, apparently a species of, or allied to, the British and North American genus *Scirpus*, and called *Totora*. It grows in water two to six feet deep, rising several feet above the surface, and is the material out of which the Indians, having no wood, construct their vessels, plaiting it and tying bunches of it together, for it is tough as well as buoyant. In these apparently frail craft, propelled by sails of the same material, they traverse the lake, carrying in each two or three men and sometimes a pretty heavy load. These vessels which, having neither prow nor stern, though the ends are raised, resemble rafts rather than boats, are steered and, when wind fails, are moved forward by paddles. Their merit is that of being unsinkable, so that when a storm knocks them to pieces the mariner may support himself on any one of the rush bundles and drift to shore if he does not succumb to the cold. They soon become waterlogged and useless, but this does not matter, for the *totora* can be had for the gathering, and the supply exceeds the demand. This primitive kind of craft was known on the coast of Peru also : the first Spanish explorers met rafts of wood there carrying merchandise.

Nowadays four small steamers ply on the lake, one of them making a regular tri-weekly service from Puno, in Peru, the terminus of the Peruvian Southern railway, to Guaqui in Bolivia, whence a railway runs to La Paz. This is at present the quickest way from Panama and the coast of Peru to Central Bolivia.

The water of Titicaca is pure and exquisitely clear. Some have described it as brackish, but I could discover no saline taste whatever. Many streams enter it from the surrounding snow-clad mountains; and it discharges southward by a river called the Desaguadero, which flows with a gentle current across the Bolivian plateau for one hundred and twenty miles into the large, shallow lagoon of Poopo or Aullagas, itself once part of that great inland sea of which Titicaca is now the largest remnant. This lake of Poopo has no outlet to the sea. Part of its water is licked up by the fiery sun of the desert: the rest sinks into the sands and is lost.

We spent two days sailing on the lake, visiting the famous modern shrine of the Virgin of the Light at Copacavana on the mainland and the famous ancient shrine of the Rock of the Sun and the Wild Cat on the island of Titicaca which has given its name to the lake. When the grey clouds brood low upon the hills, stern and gloomy indeed must be the landscape in this bleak land. But our visit fell in the end of September, the spring of Peru, when such rains as there are had begun to refresh the land after the arid winter. The sun was bright. Only a few white clouds were hanging high in air or clinging to the slopes of the distant mountains; and the watery plain over which we moved was a sheet of dazzling blue. The blue of Titicaca is peculiar, not deep and dark, as that of the tropical ocean, nor opaque, like the blue-green of Lake Leman nor like that warm purple of the Ægean which Homer compares to dark red wine, but a clear, cold, crystalline blue, even as is that of the cold sky vaulted over it. Even in this blazing sunlight it had that sort of chilly glitter one sees in the crevasses of a glacier; and the wavelets sparkled like diamonds.

The Peruvian shore along which we were sailing was steep and bold, with promontories jutting out and rocky islets fringing them. Far away to the east across the shining waters the Bolivian coast rose in successive brown terraces, flat-topped hills where the land was tilled, and higher up bluish grey ridges passing into a soft lilac as they receded, and farther still, faint yet clear in the northeast, the serrated lines of the snowy Cordillera which divides the lake basin from the valleys that run down to the east and the Amazonian forests. There was something of mystery and romance in these far distant peaks, which few Europeans have ever approached, for they lie in a dry region almost uninhabited because hardly worth inhabiting, —

"a waste land where no man goes
Or hath gone, since the making of this world."

The nearer and higher range to the southeast of the lake, which the natives call the Cordillera Real, and geographers the range of Sorata, was almost hidden by the thick clouds which were by this time — for it was now ten o'clock, and the sun was raising vapours from the valleys — gathering on its snows, and not till the evening did its grand proportions stand disclosed. There were all sorts of colours in the landscape, bright green rushes filling the shallow bays, deep black lava flows from a volcanic peak on the west, and a wonderful variety of yellows, pinks, and violets melting into each other on the distant hills. But the predominant tone, which seems to embrace all the rest was a grey-blue of that peculiar pearly quality which the presence of a large body of smooth water gives. Views on a great lake can be more impressive than almost any ocean views, because on the ocean one sees only a little way around, whereas, where distant heights are visible beyond the expanse of a lake, the vastness of the landscape in all its parts is realized. Here we could see in two different directions mountain ranges a hundred miles away: and the immensity was solemn.

The village of Copacavana, to which we first turned our course, stands a little above the lake at the foot of rocky heights, beyond which rises a lofty volcano, said to have been active only a century ago. Traces of antiquity are found in the polished stone seats, two on each side of a higher one, called the Judgment Seat of the Inca, and in steps cut here and there, all in the hard rock, their form resembling that of those near Cuzco, described in the last chapter, and their purpose no less obscure.[1] Other ruins and abundant traditions prove that the place was a noted seat of worship in Inca days. There stood on it, say the early Spanish chroniclers, not only gilded and silvered figures of the Sun and

[1] Dr. Uhle has suggested that the so-called seats may have been places on which to set images. Mr. Bingham thinks they were more probably spots on which priests stood to salute the rising sun by wafting kisses with their hands, a Peruvian practice described by Calancha, who compares the book of Job, chap. xxxi, v. 27.

Moon, but also older idols, belonging to some older local religion, one in particular which is described as having a head like an egg with a limbless body, wreathed with snakes. When these figures and their shrines were demolished, a church was erected on the same spot, which presently became famous by the setting up in it of a sacred image of Our Lady. It is the Santissima Virgen de la Candelaria, carved by a scion of the Incas, Francisco Tito Yupanqui, in A.D. 1583. This image had been seen by a pious friar to send out rays of light around it: miracles followed, and an Augustinian monastery was founded and placed in charge of the sanctuary, which soon became the most frequented place of pilgrimage through all South Amerca. Even from Mexico and from Europe pilgrims come hoping for the cure of their diseases. The figure is about a yard high, and represents a face of the Indian type in features and colour, though less dark than the equally sacred figure of the Virgin of the Pillar at Saragosa in Spain. It wears a crown of gold, with a gold halo outside the crown, has a half moon under its feet, and is adorned with many superb gems. The church is spacious and stately. The Camarin or sacred chamber in which the image stands is behind the great altar and approached by two staircases, the stone steps much worn by the knees of the ascending worshippers. The Augustinian monks were turned out in 1826, after the revolutionary war, but recently a few Franciscans have been settled in a home too large for them, so the wide cloisters are melancholy,

K

and echo to few footfalls. Nevertheless great crowds of Indians still resort hither twice a year, on February 2, the feast of the Candelaria (Candlemas), and on August 5 and 6. Within the sacred enclosure which surrounds the church is a lofty cupola supported by columns, open at its sides so that the three tall crosses within it are visible, and roofed in a sort of Moorish style with bright green and yellow tiles, of the kind which North Africa has borrowed from the East. Round it are the accustomed pilgrimage "stations," and at the corners of the court, which is entered by a lofty gateway and planted with trees, are square brick buildings, wherein lie the bones of pilgrims. The shining tiles of this cupola, with the similarly decorated dome and tower of the church behind, make a striking group, whose half Moorish character looks strange in this far western land. The scene at the great festivals when the excited Indian crowd makes church and court resound with hymns in Aymará and when, after the Christian services of the day, the dances of primitive heathendom are kept up all through the darkness with wild shoutings and jumpings, till they end in a sort of jig, is described as strange and revolting. These dances come down from a time when this was a seat of Indian nature worship, and when images of the Sun and Moon were taken in pomp from the shrine here to the shrines upon the Sacred Isles.

To those isles we now bent our course. Delightful was the voyage along the southern shore of the lake, past shallow bays where the green water lapped softly in the rushes, across the openings of inlets that ran far in between walls of rock, with new islands coming into view and glimpses of new snowpeaks in the distance rising behind the nearer ranges, all flooded by a sunlight that had the brilliance without the sultry power of the tropics.

Koati or Koyata, the Island of the Moon, is said to take its name from Koya, the Quichua word for queen, the Moon being the wife of the Sun, whose worship the Incas established wherever their power extended. The isle is about two miles long, a steep ridge, covered in parts with low shrubs and grass; the rest cultivated, the slopes being carefully terraced to the top. The most interesting group of ruins stands in a beautiful situation some sixty feet above the shore, on the uppermost of four broad terraces, supported by walls. One of these walls is of the finished Cuzco style of stonework, the rectangular blocks well cut and neatly fitted to one another. It is probably of Inca date. That the large ruined edifice above has the same origin may be concluded from the niches which occur in the walls of its chambers. The purpose of such niches, frequent in the Cuzco walls, and indeed all over Peru, has never been explained. They are often too shallow for cupboards or wardrobes, and too high for images, yet it is hard to suppose them meant merely for ornament. This edifice, originally in two stories, is a mass of chambers, mostly small, which are connected by narrow passages. The large walled court which adjoins it is adorned by stuccoed niches. The walls are well preserved, but all the ceilings and roofs have gone. There are so few apertures for light that it is hard, as in most of the ancient Peruvian

houses to understand how light was admitted.   Probably light was sacrificed for the sake of warmth, for
the nights are extremely cold, even in summer.   Door-
ways are covered sometimes by a single slab, sometimes
by flat stones projecting each beyond the other, so as to
have the effect of an arch, but no true arch ever seems
to have been found in Peru or anywhere else in the
Western Hemisphere.   Sacrificial objects, dug up in
front of the building, confirm the legend that the place
was a shrine of the Moon Mother, but the name by which
it has been known is the Palace of the Virgins of the
Sun.   There may, therefore, have been in conjunction
with the shrine one of the numerous establishments in
which the Incas kept the women who were sent up to
them as a tribute from the provinces, and who, among
other things, wove fine fabrics and made various articles
needed for worship.   The early Spanish writers, with
their heads full of Christian nuns and Roman Vestals,
called them Virgins of the Sun, but the name was altogether inappropriate, for many of them were kept as
concubines for the reigning Inca.

Four miles from Koati and two from the mainland,
lies the larger and more sacred Island of the Sun.
It is ten miles long, nowhere more than a mile wide,
and very irregular in shape, being deeply indented
by bays.   A ridge of hills, rising in places to one
thousand feet or more, traverses it from end to end, and
much of the surface is too steep and rocky for tillage.
There are many groups of ruins on it, the origin and
character of some among which have given rise to con-

troversies into which I need not enter, proposing to describe two only. One of these is the so-called Fountain, or Bath and Garden of the Inca. Two buildings stand on the shore, evidently of a date anterior to the Conquest, and one was probably a royal residence. The most recent and most competent investigators divide them into two classes: those which the Indians call Chulpas, and are the work of an earlier race or races, and those which they ascribe to the Incas, the latter being larger and better built, and accompanied by pottery, weapons, and other relics, indicating a more advanced culture. Hard by a flight of low steps, rising from the water through a grove of trees, leads up to a spot where a rivulet, led in a channel from the hill above, pours itself into a receptacle hewed out of one piece of stone, whence it pursues its course in a murmuring rill to the lake below. The terraced garden on each side is planted with flowers, most of which are the same as those in European or North American gardens; but the brilliant red blossoms of the shrub called the *Flor del Inca* give a true local colour, and the view over the lake to the distant snows is unlike anything else in the world. How much of the beauty we now see was planned by the unknown monarch, who first made these terraces, and did the spot commend itself to him by the wonderful prospect it commands? Most of the so-called palaces of these isles occupy sites that look across the lake to the great snowy range, but a learned archæologist suggests that this was due not to admiration of their grandeur, but to veneration for them as potent

deities so that they might be more readily and frequently adored.

On this majestic range our eyes had been fixed all day
long. Its northernmost summit, Illampu, stands more
than twenty miles back from the eastern shore of the
lake, and more than thirty miles from the Island of the
Sun. Thence the chain trends southward, ending one
hundred miles away in the gigantic Illimani, which
looks down upon La Paz. All day long we had watched
the white clouds rise and gather, and swathe the great
peaks and rest in the glacier hollows between them, and
seem to dissolve or move away, leaving some top clear
for a moment, and then settle down again, just as one
sees the vapours that rise from the Lombard plain form
into clouds that float round and enwrap Monte Rosa
during the heats of a summer day. Evening was beginning to fall when our vessel, after coasting along
the island, anchored in the secluded bay of Challa,
where, behind a rocky cape, there is an Indian hamlet and
a garden and stone tank like that at the Bath of the
Inca. We landed and rambled through it, finding
its thick trees and rustling shade specially charming in this bare land. Just as we emerged from them
and regained the lake shore, the sun was setting,
and as the air cooled, the clouds that draped the mountains thinned and scattered and suddenly vanished, and
the majestic line of pinnacles stood out, glowing rosy red
in the level sunlight, and then turned in a few moments
to a ghostly white, doubly ghostly against a deep blue-
grey sky, as swift black night began to descend.

Early next morning we set off on foot along the track, well beaten by the feet of many generations of worshippers, which leads along the rocky slopes from Challa to the Sanctuary of the Rock. Here are no houses, for this end of the isle is rough and bare, giving only scanty pasture and a few aromatic flowers, but the little bays where the green water ripples on the sands, and the picturesque cliffs, and the vast stretch of lake beyond, made every step delightful. To our surprise we passed a spot where some enterprising stranger had bored for coal and found a bed, but not worth working. One could hardly be sorry, for though fuel is badly needed here, a colliery and its chimney would fit neither the landscape nor the associations. Less than three miles' walking brought us to a place where the remains of a wall cross the island, here scarcely a mile wide, and seem to mark off the sacred part which in Inca days was entered only for the purposes of worship. A little farther, two marks in the rock, resembling giant footprints, are, according to Indian tradition, the footprints of the Sun God and the Moon Goddess, when they appeared here. The marks are obviously natural and due to the form in which a softer bit of the sandstone rock has scaled off and left a whitish surface, while the harder part, probably containing a little more iron, as it is browner in hue, has been less affected by the elements. Then, after ascending a few low steps which seem to be ancient, we came out on a level space of grass in front of a ridge of rock about twenty-five feet high. This is Titi Kala, the Sacred Rock, the centre of the most ancient mythology of South America. Its face, which looks southwest over this space of grass, apparently artificially levelled, is on that side precipitous, presenting a not quite smooth face in which veins of slightly different colours of brown and yellowish grey are seen. At one point these veins so run as to present something like the head of a wild cat or puma ; and as Titi means a wild cat in Aymara, and Kala, or Kaka a rock, this is supposed to be the origin of the name Titi Kala, which has been extended from the rock to the island and from the island to the lake.[1]

The rock is composed of a light yellowish brown rather hard sandstone of carboniferous age, with a slaty cleavage. The back of the ridge is convex, and is easily climbed. From it the ground falls rapidly to the lake, about three hundred feet below. Except for what may possibly be an artificial incision at the top, the rock appears to be entirely in its natural state, the cave-like hollow at its base shewing no sign of man's handiwork. Neither does any existing building touch it. There are, however, traces of walls enclosing the space in front of it, especially on the north side, where there seems to have been a walled-in enclosure; and there are other ancient remains hard by. The only one of these sufficiently preserved to enable us to conjecture its purpose is a somewhat perplexing two-storied edifice, resembling, though less large and handsome, that which I have described as existing on the island

---

[1] Lake Titicaca was originally, it would seem, called the lake of Chucuito, from an ancient town on its western shore.

of Koati.   It is called the Chingana, or Labyrinth, and doubtless dates from Inca times, as it contains niches and other features characteristic of the architecture of that period.   The numerous rooms are small, scantily lighted, and connected by narrow passages.   A few flowers had rooted on the top of the walls, and I found tufts of maidenhair fern nestling in the moist, dark corners within.   All the roofs have perished.   There is nothing to suggest a place of worship, so probably the building contained the quarters provided for the various attendants on the religious rites performed here, and perhaps also for the women who were kept near many sanctuaries and palaces for the service of the Sun and the Incas.   None of the other ruins is identifiable as a temple, so we are left in doubt whether any temple that may have existed was destroyed by the zeal of the Spanish Conquerors, or whether the worship of the Sun and the local spirits was conducted in the open air in front of the Rock, whose surface was, according to some rather doubtful authorities, covered with plates of gold and silver.   In front of the Rock there lies a flat stone which it has been conjectured may have been used for sacrifices.   All our authorities agree that the place was most sacred.   Some say no one was allowed to touch it; and at it oracles were delivered, which the Spaniards accepted as real, while attributing them to devils who dwelt inside the rock.   Of the many legends relating to the place only two need be mentioned.   One is that here the Sun, pitying the barbarous and wretched condition of men, took his two children, Manco Capac

and Mama (mother) Occlo, and giving them a short staff
or wand of gold, directed them to go forward, till they
should find a place where the staff on being struck
against the ground entered and stuck fast.   They
travelled to the north for many days, and the wand
finally entered the earth at Cuzco, where they accordingly built a city and founded their dominion, Manco
being the first of the Inca dynasty.   The other tale is
that for a long, long time there was darkness over the
earth and great sorrow among men till at last the Sun
suddenly rose out of the Rock on Titicaca, which was
thenceforward sacred and a place of sacrifice and oracles.
Other traditions, more or less differing from these in
details, agree in making Titicaca the original home of
the Incas, and one of them curiously recalls a Mexican
story by placing on it a great foreign Teacher whom
the Spaniards identified with St. Thomas the Apostle.[1]
In these stories, some written down by Spanish explorers or treasure seekers at the time of the Conquest or collected subsequently by learned ecclesiastics, some still surviving, with grotesque variations,
in the minds of the peasantry, we may distinguish

[1] St. Thomas, according to an early legend, preached the Gospel
on the coast of Malabar, so the Spanish ecclesiastics when they
came to Mexico and Peru and heard tales of a wise deity or semi-
divine teacher who had long ago appeared among the natives, concluded this must have been the Apostle, the idea of the connection of
Eastern Asia with these new Western lands being still in their minds.
    In the ancient city of Tlascala in Mexico I have seen a picture
representing St. Thomas preaching to the natives in the guise of the
Mexican deity Quetzalcoatl, the Feathered Snake.   St. Thomas is
depicted as half serpent, half bird, but with a human head.

three salient points, — first, the veneration for the Rock as an object; secondly, its close relation to Sun worship ; and thirdly, its connection with the Inca rulers of Cuzco. It is a plausible view that from ancient pre-Inca times the Rock was a *Huaca* or sacred object (in fact a fetish, *i.e.* an object inhabited by a spirit) to the primitive tribes of the island and lake coasts, as the cleft rock of Delphi was to the Greeks, even as the Black Stone which they called the Mother of the gods was to the Phrygian worshippers of Cybele, as perhaps the Stone of Tara — perhaps even the Lia Fail or Coronation Stone of Scone and now of Westminster Abbey — was to our Celtic ancestors. When the Incas established their dominion over the region round the lake they made this spot a sanctuary of the sun, following their settled policy of superadding the imperial religion of Sun worship — the Sun being their celestial progenitor — to the primitive veneration and propitiation of local spirits which their subjects practised. It was thus that the Roman Emperors added the worship of the goddess of Rome to that of the local deities of Western Asia and Africa and set up to her great temples, like that at Pergamos, among and above the older shrines. If there be truth in the legend that the Incas were themselves originally a tribe of the Collas of the plateau who quitted their former seats to go northward to the conquest of Cuzco, it would be all the more natural for them to honour this sanctuary as an ancient home of their race.

The isle seems to have been abandoned and the worship forbidden soon after the Conquest. No Christian church was ever placed near it, as might have been done if it were deemed necessary to wean the people from rites still practised there. What the early Spanish chroniclers tell us of the devotion paid to it is amply confirmed by the religious ornaments and the numerous objects connected with worship which have been dug up near the Rock, including woollen ponchos of extraordinary fineness of workmanship and colour, and golden figures of men (or deities) and of llamas, the llama being a sacred animal like the bull in Egypt. The native Indians still approach the Rock with awe. Lightning and Thunder, as well as the Sun and the local spirits were worshipped, and human sacrifices, frequently of children, were offered. Standing on this lonely spot one thinks of what it may have witnessed in old days. What weird dances and wild uproar of drums and pipes before the Rock, and still wilder songs and cries of frenzied worshippers! What shrieks of victims from the Stone of Sacrifice! Now all is silence, and nothing, except the crumbling ruins of the Chingana, speaks of the past. No sound except the sighing of the breeze round the cliff and the splash of the wavelets as they break on the pebbly beach beneath. There is no habitation near. The green outlying islets, one of which is said to have run with the blood of human sacrifices, are all desolate. The villages on the Bolivian shore to the east and the Peruvian shore to the west are too distant to be visible, while to the north the vast expanse of glittering blue stretches out till the blue depths of heaven bend to meet it.

Bidding farewell to the Island of the Sun, we sailed southward through the Straits of Tiquina, only half a mile wide, which connect the principal lake with the shallower gulf at its southeastern end, called the Lake of Vinamarca. On each side of the channel between heights whose igneous rocks seemed to indicate volcanic action are picturesque little Indian villages, St. Paul on the southwestern, St. Peter on the northeastern shore. It was market day, and the balsas were carrying the peasants homeward. I have already referred to these raft-like boats, formed of bundles of *Totora* tied together, and equipped with a small mast carrying a sail also of the same kind of rush. There were only passengers upon these, but the rushes are so much lighter than water that they can support a considerable weight. Large blocks of building stone are often carried on them. The Indians were kneeling on them and paddling, one on each side. Progress was slow, but in this country time is no object; it is almost the only thing of which there is more than enough in Bolivia.

We had now got nearer to the great Cordillera Real, the range of unbroken snow and ice which runs southward from the village of Sorata nearly to the city of La Paz, and could better make out the several peaks and the passes which separate them and the splendid glaciers which stream down their hollows far below the line of perpetual snow. Eight or nine great masses can be distinguished, the loftiest and northernmost of which, Illampu, is nearly 22,000 feet high, the rest ranging from 19,000 to 21,000.

Illampu consists of two peaks and is the mountain which European travellers and maps call Sorata, from the town of that name near its northern base.   It consists of two peaks, the higher of snow, called by the natives, Hanko Uma,[1] and the slightly lower one, of rock, Illampu proper.   This, which is the loftiest of the range, and was sixty or seventy years ago believed to be the loftiest in the western hemisphere, was climbed by Sir Martin Conway, who has described his ascent and his other adventures in Bolivia, in a very interesting book,[2] but he found the last slope just below the top so unstable, owing to the powdery condition of the snow, that he was obliged to turn back.   So far as I know, no other summit of the range, unless Illimani is to be accounted a part of it, has ever been ascended. At the end of the chain the splendid pyramid of Kaka Aka, also called Huayna Potosi, seems to approach 21,000.   After it the range sinks a little till it rises again fifty miles farther south to over 21,000 feet in the snowy summit of Illimani.   The Aymaras seem to have no special names for most of these peaks, and when asked for one answer that it is Kunu Kollu (a snow height).[3] That is the case in many other mountainous countries. Neither in the White Mountains of North America nor in the Rockies and Cascades do the aborigines

[1] Sir M. Conway gives the height of the higher peak Ancohuma (Hanko Uma) at 21,490.   The loftiest summits in Peru seem to be Huascaran (some way N.N.E. of Lima), about 22,150 feet, and Coropuna (see p. 57), 21,700 feet.   Aconcagua in Chile is the culminating point of the Andes and the whole Western World (see p. 260).

[2] *Climbing and Exploration in the Bolivian Andes*, 1901.

[3] See Bandelier, *Islands of Titicaca and Koati*, ch. I, and notes.

seem to have had names for more than a few separate peaks. Names were not needed, for they seldom approached the great heights. On the other hand, in Scotland and Ireland every hill has its Gaelic name because the herdsmen had occasion to traverse them. In the Tatra Mountains of Northern Hungary almost the only names of peaks are those taken from villages near their foot. Here the tract at the foot of the range is desert; nobody, unless possibly a hunter now and then pursuing a vicuña, has any reason for approaching it.

The Cordillera Real is not of volcanic origin, though there may be recent eruptive rocks here and there in it. None of the great summits shew the forms characteristic of the volcano, and my friend Sir M. Conway tells me that all the rocks he saw seemed to be granite and gneiss or mica schist, or perhaps very old palæozoic strata. The region has been very little explored. There must be some superb glacier passes across it.

The scenery of this lake of Vinamarca, which we were now traversing, has a grand background in the Snowy Range, but the foreground is unlike that of Titicaca, for the shores are mostly low, shallow bays covered with water plants, over which flocks of lake fowl flutter, with the hills softer in outline than those of the great lake, though stranger and more varied in colour, for black masses of volcanic rock rise on the north and bare hills of a deep red on the south-west. Here is the point where the river Desaguadero flows out and a little to the east is the port of Guaqui whence runs the railway to La Paz. Here we halted for the night, a very cold one, and set off in a cold morning for the Bolivian capital. An open valley runs south between flat-topped stony ridges affording thin pasturage, past clusters of Indian huts; and after some few miles, we see huge blocks of stone scattered over a wide space of almost level ground. These are the last ruins I have to mention, and in some respects they form the most remarkable group of prehistoric structures not only in the Andean countries, but in the Western Hemisphere. I will not attempt to describe them, for they are too numerous and too chaotic, but only to convey some impression of the more significant objects. The place is Tiahuanaco, or Tihuamacu, as the Indians of the neighbourhood call it.

The configuration of the ground, and the remains of what seems to have been an ancient mole for the landing of boats, suggest that in remote ages the waters of the lake came close up to this spot, though it is now five miles distant. I have already remarked that the character of the western and northern shores of Titicaca, as well as Indian traditions that places now far from the shore were once approachable by water, seem to indicate that the lake has receded within historical times and may be still receding. The ruins are scattered over a very large area, but those of most interest are to be found within a space of about half a square mile, the rest being mostly detached and scattered blocks to which it is hard to assign any definite

plan or purpose. Within this space three deserve
special notice. One is a huge, oblong mound of earth,
about fifty feet high, with steep sides supported
by stone walls. It has been called the Fortress, but
there are now no traces of defensive ramparts, and it
may have been raised for a palace or, more probably, for
some religious purpose. That it was a natural hill seems
unlikely. There are no remains on it of any large and
solid building and in the middle there is now a hollow, its
bottom filled with water, which is said to have been dug
out by those who have excavated here, in old days for
treasure, and more recently for archæological purposes.
Its vast proportions and the fine cutting of the stones
which are placed along the edges are evidences of the
great amount of labour employed upon it.

A little below the mound are the remains of a broad
staircase of long, low steps of sandstone, well cut, standing
between two pillars of hard diorite rock. These led up
to a platform, on which a temple may have stood. The
proportions of the staircase and the pillars are good, and
the effect is not without stateliness. No fragments of the
supposed temple remain, but on the platform there are
many stone figures, some found on it, some brought from
the ground beneath and placed here, heads of animals,
condors and other birds, pumas and fishes, all forcibly,
though rudely, carved. Still more notable is a human
head surmounting a square pillar or pedestal. It is
much damaged, and no wonder, for the Bolivian soldiers
used it as a mark to shoot at; but though the execution
is stiff, the head has a certain dignity. Two other

L

human figures, sadly defaced, stand at the gate of the village churchyard, a mile away. The style of all these is said to bear some resemblance to the remarkable colossal figures found on Easter Island, which lies out in the Pacific, two thousand miles west of Chile, and which are evidently the work of some race that inhabited that isle in ages of which no record remains.

The most striking object, however, is the monolithic sculptured gateway, which now stands alone, the building of which it formed a part having perished. It is hewn out of one block of dark grey trachytic rock, is ten feet high, the doorway or aperture four and a half feet high from the ground and two feet nine inches wide. Its top has been broken, whether by lightning, as the Indians say, or by its fall, or by the Spanish extirpators of idolatry, is not known. Thirty years ago it was lying prostrate. The front is covered with elaborate carvings in low relief, executed with admirable exactness and delicacy, and owing their almost perfect preservation to the extreme hardness of the stone. They represent what may be either a divine or a royal head, surrounded by many small kneeling figures with animal heads, some human, some of the puma, some of the condor, these being the largest quadruped and the largest bird of prey in the Andes. The treatment is conventional and the symbolism obscure, for we have no clue to the religion of the people who built these monuments. The association of animal forms with deities is a familiar thing in many ancient mythologies, — human figures had animal heads in Egypt, and bulls and lions had human heads in

Assyria,—so one may guess at something of the kind in Peruvian mythology. But these sculptures are unlike anything else in South America, or in the Old World, and bear only a faint resemblance to some of the figures in Central American temples.[1] This sculptured portal, the unique record of a long-vanished art and worship, perhaps of a long-vanished race, makes an impression which remains fresh and clear in memory, because it appeals to one's imagination as the single and solitary voice from the darkness of a lost past.

All over the flat valley bottom there lie scattered huge hewn blocks, some of the sandstone which is here the underlying rock, some of andesite apparently brought on balsas from quarries many miles away (when perhaps the lake water came up this far. I measured one massive prostrate stone lying near the staircase and found it to be thirty-four feet long by five feet wide with one and one-half feet out of the ground. How much there was below ground could not be ascertained. Yet the stones that remain to-day scattered over a space more than a mile long are few compared to those which have during centuries past been carried away. The church and many of the houses in the village are built of them. The Cathedral and other edifices in La Paz have been built of them, and within the last ten years five hundred train-loads of them were carried off by the constructors of the railway to build bridges,

[1] They have some likeness to the carved stone found at Chavin in northern Peru, figured in Sir C. Markham's *The Incas of Peru,* p. 34. There was also found lately in a grave near Lima a textile fabric with a pattern resembling this.

station houses, and what not, along the line. It is pitiable to think that this destruction of the most remarkable prehistoric monument in the western world should have been consummated in our own days.

Whether there was ever a city at Tiahuanaco there is nothing to shew. The place may have been merely a sanctuary or, perhaps, a royal fortress and place of worship combined. If there was ever a population of the humble class, they lived in mud huts which would quickly disappear and leave no trace. The modern village is composed of such huts, with some of the stones of the ruins used as foundations. Nevertheless the size of the church and its unusually rich decoration, and its handsome silver altar, suggest that the place was formerly more important than it is today. Pottery and small ornaments are still found in the earth, though the treasures, if ever there were any, have been carried off long ago. An arrow point of obsidian, which an Indian shewed me, was interesting as evidence that the ancient inhabitants used bows and were not, as apparently were the Peruvians of Cuzco, content with slings as missile weapons.[1]

The valley is fertile, and much of it cultivated, but at this season, before the crops had begun to pierce the earth, it was very dreary. The brown hills all around are themselves bare and featureless, and they cut off the view of the snowy Cordillera and of the lake. The sight

[1] The arrow point may however have been brought from the northeastern shores of Titicaca. Mr. Bingham tells me that such obsidian tips are sometimes found in auriferous gravels there.

of this mass of ruins, where hardly one stone is left upon another in a place where thousands of men must have toiled and many thousands have worshipped, makes its melancholy landscape all the more doleful. It recalls the descriptions in the Hebrew prophets of the desolation coming upon Nineveh.

Aymará tradition, with its vague tales of giants who reared the mound and walls and of a deity who in displeasure turned the builders into stones and for a while darkened the world, has nothing more to tell us than the aspect of the place suggests, viz., that here dwelt a people possessed of great skill in stone work and obeying rulers who had a great command of labour, and that this race has vanished, leaving no other trace behind. Upon one point all observers and all students are agreed. When the first Spanish conquerors came hither, they were at once struck by the difference between these works and those of the Incas which they had seen at Cuzco and elsewhere in Peru. The Indians whom they questioned told them that the men who built these things had lived long, long before their own forefathers. Who the builders were, whence they came, how and when and whither they disappeared — of all this the Indians knew no more than the Spaniards themselves knew, or than we know now. The width of the interval between the greatness of Tiahuanaco and the Conquest appears also by the fact that the Inca sovereigns had not treated it as a sacred spot in the way they did the shrine at Copacavana or the islands in Titicaca, nor has it to-day any special sanctity to the Indians of the neighbourhood. To them it is only what the Pyramids are to a wandering Arab or Stonehenge to a Wiltshire peasant. The one thing which the walls have in common with those in and around Cuzco is the excellence of the stonework. The style of building is different, but the cutting itself is equally exact and regular. This art would seem to have arisen early among the races of the plateau, doubtless because the absence of wood turned artistic effort towards excellence in stone.

One receives the impression here, as in some other parts of Peru, that the semi-civilization, if we may call it so, of these regions is extremely ancient. We seem to look back upon a vista whose length it is impossible to conjecture, a vista of many ages, during which this has been the home of peoples already emerged from such mere savagery as that in which the natives of the Amazonian forests still lie. But how many ages the process of emergence occupied, and how many more followed down to the Spanish Conquest we may never come to know.

It is possible that immigrants may at some time, long subsequent to the colonization of America by way of Behring's Sea, have found their way hither across the waters of the Pacific. The similarity of the figures on Easter Island to the figures at Tiahuanaco has been thought to suggest such a possibility. Those figures are, I believe, unlike anything in any other Pacific island.

Archæological research, however, does not suggest, any more than does historical enquiry, the existence of any external influence affecting the South American races. We may reasonably assume that among them, as in Europe, the contact and intermixture of different stocks and types of character and culture made for advancement. But this great factor in the progress of mankind, which did so much for western Asia and Europe, and to the comparative absence of which the arrested civilization of China may be largely due, was far less conspicuously present in South America than on the Mediterranean coasts. Think what Europe owed not only to the mixture of stocks whence the Italo-Hellenic peoples sprang, but also to influences radiating out from Egypt and the West Asiatic nations. Think what Italy owed to Greece and afterwards to the East and of what modern European nations owe to the contact of racial types in literature, art, and ideas, such as the Celtic, the Iberian, the Teutonic, and the Slavonic. How different was the lot of the Peruvians, shut in between an impassable ocean on the west, a desert on the south, and the savage tribes of a forest wilderness on the east! No ideas came to them from without, nor from any of the inventions which Old World peoples had been making could they profit. They were out of contact even with the most advanced of the other American peoples, such as those of Bogotá and Yucatan, for there was a vast space between, many shadowy mountains and a resounding sea.

As after these ruins I saw no others in South America, for neither southern Bolivia nor Chile nor Argentina, nor Uruguay has any to shew, this seems the fittest place for such few thoughts on the ancient civilization of South America as are suggested to the traveller's mind by the remains of it which he sees and by what he reads in the books of historians and archæologists.   A large part of the interest which Peru and Bolivia have for the modern world is the interest which this ancient civilization awakens.   It is a unique chapter in the history of mankind.

The most distinct and constantly recurring impressions made by the remains is this: that the time when man began to rise out of mere savagery must, in these countries, be carried very far into the past.   Our data for any estimate either of the duration of the process by which he attained a sort of civilization or of the several steps in it, are extremely scanty.   In the Old World the early use of writing by a few of its peoples enables us to go a long way back.   The records which Egypt and Babylon and China have been made to yield are of some service for perhaps three or even four thousand years — some would say more — before the Christian era, and from those of Egypt and Babylon we get at least glimpses of the races that lived in Asia Minor and along the Mediterranean coast.   But none of the American peoples advanced as far as the invention of even the rudest form of writing, though in Mexico and Yucatan pictures were to some slight extent used to preserve the memory of events.   Here, in South America, where neither writing nor pictures aid us, our only data for what may be called prehistoric history, are first, the remains of buildings, whether fortresses or palaces or temples, and, secondly, works of art, such as carvings, ornaments, or religious objects, utensils of wood or earthenware and paintings on them, weapons of war, woollen or cotton fabrics, such as ponchos or mummy-cloths. All such relics are more abundant in Peru than anywhere else in the Western world, except that in Yucatan and some parts of Central America the ruined temples have been preserved better than here. The Peruvian relics are found not only in the Andean plateau, but also in those parts near the coast of northern Peru where cultivation was rendered possible by rivers. There, at the ruins of the Chimu city, near Truxillo, and farther south at Pachacamac, near Lima, a great deal has been obtained by excavation in ancient cemeteries and temples; and much more would have been obtained but for the damage wrought by generations of treasure seekers who melted down all the gold they found and destroyed nearly everything else.

The objects found on the coast differ in style from those found on the high Andean regions, and among these latter there are also marked differences between things found at Cuzco, and generally in northern Peru, and things found in the tombs and graves in the Titicaca regions. All, however, have a certain family resemblance and form a distinct archæological group somewhat nearer to Mexican and Central American art than to anything in the Old World. Specimens of all can be just as well studied in the museums of Europe and North America as here on the spot, where

the collections are neither numerous nor well arranged.
There is, perhaps, more fertility of invention, more freedom of treatment and more humour in the objects found
on the coast at Chimu and Pachacamac than in any
others; but the most impressive of all are the sculptures
of Tiahuanaco.

Considerable skill had been attained in weaving.
Handsome woollen ponchos, apparently designed for
use as religious vestments, have been found, the colour
patterns harmonious and the wool exquisitely fine. The
Chimu tapestries and embroideries shew taste as well as
technical skill. Copper, the metal chiefly used in Peru,
was mined and smelted in large quantities; and the
reduction of silver ores was also understood, yet the
age of stone implements was not past, either for peaceful or for warlike purposes. As no cementing material
had been discovered, walls were rendered exceptionally
strong either by carefully fitting their stones into one
another or fly clamping them together by metal. Of
this latter method there are examples at Tiahuanaco.

Taking Peruvian art as a whole, as it appears in
pottery and pictures and carvings, it is inferior in grace
of form and refinement of execution both to Egyptian
and to early Greek work, such as that of the Mycenæan
period. Neither is there anything that shews such a
power of drawing the human figure and of designing
ornament as the ruined temples of Yucatan display.

The most signal excellence the Peruvians attained
seems to have been in building. The absence of wood
turned their efforts towards stone, and gave birth to

works which deserve to be compared with those of Egypt, and far surpass in solidity any to be found in North America. Of the temples, too little remains to enable a judgment to be formed, either of their general design or of their adornment. But the stonework is wonderful, indicating not only a high degree of manual expertness, but the maintenance of a severe standard of efficiency through every part, while the skill shewn in the planning of fortifications so as to strengthen every defensive line and turn to account the natural features of the ground would have done credit to the military engineering of fifteenth-century Europeans.

But the race was also in some ways strangely inept. Both the Quichua tribes and the subjects of the Chimu sovereign on the Pacific coast seem to have shewn no higher invention than the Aymarás, who launched their rush. balsas on Lake Titicaca, for the Spaniards found them using nothing but small canoes on the rivers and clumsy rafts for creeping along the shore with the help of a rude sail, though the Caribs of Venezuela, otherwise far less advanced, carried on a brisk trade in large sea-going canoes all the way along the line of the Antilles from the mouth of the Orinoco to the peninsula of Yucatan.

The few songs that have been preserved do not commemorate events or achievements like the ballads of Europe, but are mostly simple ditties, connected with nature and agriculture. There were, however, dramas which used to be acted, and among them one considerable work which, long preserved by oral recitations, was written down in the seventeenth century by Dr. Valdez, a Spaniard, the priest of Sicuani, and generally held to be in the main of native authorship, though perhaps touched up by Spanish taste. This is the so-called drama of Ollantay. It has a fresh simplicity and a sort of romantic flavour which suggest that there was something more than prosaic industry in this people.

In the absence of literature, one seeks in the mythology of a race a test of its imaginative quality; and in its religion, an indication of its power of abstract thinking. In both respects, the Peruvians seem to have stood as much below the primitive Celts and Teutons, as they stood above the negro races, with their naïve animism and childish though often humorous fables. Whether the Spanish ecclesiastics were right in finding in the worship of the earth god Pachacamac a belief in a supreme deity, creator of the world, may be doubted. But that the worship of Sun, Moon, and Stars should have coexisted with ancestor worship, and with a sort of fetichism which revered and feared spirits in all objects, need excite no surprise. Such a mixture, or rather such a coexistence without real intermixture, of different strata of religious ideas, finds plenty of analogies in the ancient Helleno-Italic world as it does to-day in China and other parts of the East. There was a worship of the ghosts of the progenitors of the family and the tribe, a worship of various more or less remarkable natural objects, or rather of the spirits that dwelt in them, a worship of animals such as the strongest beast and largest bird of prey, the puma and the condor, and of the supremely useful llama (a devotion which was compatible with the sacrificing of the animal), a worship of plants, and especially of the maize and of the power which bade it grow, the Maize Mother. Above all these forms, congenial to the humbler classes, rose the worship of the Sun, Moon, and Stars (especially the Pleiades), representing a higher range of ideas, yet connected with the more primitive nature superstitions by the sense that the Sun evoked life from the earth and by the finding, in the constellations, the shapes of the animals that were sacred on the earth. Nor were these the only points in which we discover resemblances to Old World religions. Peru rivalled Egypt in the care taken to preserve the bodies of the dead as mummies,[1] and these, so skilfully dried as not to offend the senses, were sometimes placed in their dwellings. The Quichuas practised divination by the flight of birds (like the Dyaks of Borneo), and by the inspection of the entrails of victims, as the Romans did down to the end of the Republic. They had oracles delivered from rocks or rivers, like the Greeks, and the *Huillca* through whom the spirit spoke could, like the Delphic Pythia, sometimes be guided towards the answer desired. Men, and especially children, were sacrificed (though to a far smaller extent than in Mexico or among the Phœnicians). If cannibalism existed on the Plateau, it was rare, though it still remains among some of the wildest of the Amazonian tribes.

---

[1] The primitive inhabitants of the Canary Isles, who were apparently of Berber stock, also preserved their dead as mummies.

That there is nothing of which men are so tenacious as their superstitions may perhaps be ascribed to the fact that life is ruled more by emotion and habit than by reason. The Peruvians made no fight for their religion, which, to be sure, was not necessarily inconsistent with such Christian rites as the friars demanded. They submitted to baptism with that singular passivity which marks nearly all the South American races. They threw into the lakes or hid in the ground all the temple gold that could be got away before the Spanish plunderers fell upon them, but made little attempt to defend their sacred places or images. Nevertheless under a nominal, not to say a debased, Christianity, they long continued to practise the ancient rites, and to this day wizardry and the devotion to the local *huacas* (sacred places or objects) are strong among the people. These primeval superstitions, which existed long before the Inca Sun worship had been established, have long survived it. If all the people who now speak Spanish were to depart from Peru and Bolivia, and these regions were to be cut off from the world and left to themselves, pagan worship, mixed with some few Christian words and usages, might probably again become, within some twenty generations, the religion of the Andean countries, just as tribes in the Caucasus which were converted to Christianity in the days when the Roman Empire reached as far east as Tiflis were found to have retained of it, after twelve centuries, nothing but the practice of fasting in Lent and the use of the sign of the cross. Nature worship still holds its ground, though no doubt in a highly extenuated form, in every country of Europe.[1] Habit and emotion are the most universal and the deepest-down things in human nature, present where reason is feeble, and gripping the soul tighter than do any intellectual convictions. Religious sentiment may hold men to old beliefs and practices long after the origin and grounds of the belief have been forgotten.

Comparing the Indians of the Andes with those of the plateau of Anahuac, and especially with the Aztecs, the former appear a less vigorous and forceful people, and distinctly inferior as fighting men. The North Americans generally, including not only the Mexicans, but such tribes as the Sioux, the Comanches, and the Iroquois, loved war, and were as brave and fierce in it as any race the world has seen. The South Americans, except of course the Araucanians of Chile, the Charruas of Uruguay, and perhaps also the Caras of Quito, were altogether softer. They still make sturdy soldiers when well led, and do not fear death. But they shewed little of the spirit and tenacity of the Red Men of the North. Even allowing for the terror and amazement inspired by the horses, the firearms, the armour, and the superior physical strength of the Spanish invaders, who were picked men, some of them veterans from Italian wars,

[1] Abundant evidence on this subject may be found in Mr. J. G. Frazer's *Golden Bough*. In Cornwall and Ireland sacred wells still receive offerings. I once met a French peasant who believed in were-wolves and knew one ; and I remember as a boy to have been warned by the peasants in the Glens of Antrim to beware of the water spirit who (under the form of a bull) infested the river in which I was fishing.

the resistance of the Peruvians was strangely feeble. They were also mentally inferior. The Spaniards thought the Mexicans far more intelligent. Neither race had made the great discovery of alphabetic writing, but those of Anahuac had come much nearer to it with their quasi-hieroglyphic pictures than had the Peruvians with their *Quipus*, knotted strings of various colours. On the other hand the rule of the Incas and their more pacific type of civilization represent a more fully developed and better settled system of administration than the military organization of those allied pueblos which were led by the Aztecs of Tenochtitlan (Mexico City). These latter did no more than exact tribute and require contingents in war from the tribes who dwelt round them on the Mexican plateau and between the plateau and the Gulf, while the Incas not only exercised undisputed suzerainty for a thousand miles to the south of Cuzco and nearly another thousand to the north, but had devised, in their own domain of central Peru, a scheme of government whose elaboration witnesses to the political capacity of the rulers. Even if we discount a good deal of the description given by the early writers of the "State Socialism" established by the Incas, it seems probable that more was done in the way of regulating the productive activities of the subjects than in any other primitive people, either of the ancient or of the modern world. Public officials, it is said, regulated the distribution and cultivation of the land, its produce being allotted, partly to the Inca, partly to the service of the Sun, his temples and ministers, partly to the cultivator or the clan to which he belonged. Thus State Socialism was strengthened by its association with a State Church, and as everybody was free to worship his local *huacas* as well as the Sun there was nothing to fear from heresy or non-conformity. The Incas maintained roads, some of which are said to have been paved,[1] and tambos or rest-houses along the roads, together with a service of swift messengers whose feats of running excited the admiration of the Spaniards. They made plans in relief of their cities, and some accounts declare that they adorned their walls with pictures of former sovereigns. By the general testimony of the early Spanish writers, the country was peaceful and orderly. Other vices, including that of drunkenness, are charged upon them, but theft and violence were extremely rare. Indeed, the habit of obedience was cultivated only too successfully, for it made them yield, after a few scattered outbursts of resistance, to a handful of invaders.

The political astuteness of the Incas, visible in their practice of moving conquered tribes, as did the Assyrian kings, to new abodes and replacing these by colonists of more assured loyalty, was perhaps most conspicuous in the success that attended their scheme of basing imperial power upon national Sun worship, making the sovereign play on earth the part which the great luminary held in the sky, and surrounding his commands

[1] It is, however, probable that the early Spanish accounts of the excellence of the roads were exaggerated, for few traces of them can be discerned to-day.

M

and his person with an almost equal sanctity. The Inca was more to his subjects than any European or Asiatic monarch has ever been to his, more than was the Mikado in Japan or the Czar to the peasantry of Russia a century ago.

When the Spanish invasion broke like a tornado upon Peru, it was natural that the Inca throne should be uprooted and the ancient Sun worship with it. But the Conquerors also therewith destroyed, in the thoughtless insolence of force and greed, the whole system of society and government. Some of them, writing twenty or thirty years later, expressed their regret.[1] Wretchedness had replaced prosperity; such virtues as the people had possessed were disappearing, their spirit was irretrievably broken. The serfdom to which the peasantry were by the Conquest subjected was not paternal, as that of the Incas had been, and was harsher, because the new master was a stranger without sympathy or compassion. There was no one to befriend the Indian, save now and then a compassionate churchman; and even if he could get the ear of the Viceroy or bring his appeal to the Council of the Indies in Spain, the oppressor on the spot was always able to frustrate such benevolent efforts. How far the people died out under these new conditions is matter of controversy, but it seems clear that the coast valleys (already declining as the result of frequent wars) were soon almost depopulated; and in place of the eight millions whom the Viceroy Toledo's enumeration reported in

[1] See note III at end of book.

1575,[1] there were in 1794 only 608,000 Indians and 244,000 mestizos within the seven Intendancies of Peru (excluding what is now Bolivia).

It is the extraordinary interest of the subject,—a religion and a polity resembling in so many points those of Old World countries, yet itself altogether independently developed—that has drawn me into this digression, for all that I had intended was to describe the impression which the existing ruins make, and what it is that they seem to tell us about the capacities of the race that has left them as its monument. They are far scantier than are the remains of the Egyptian and Assyrian civilizations, and they are as inferior in material grandeur and artistic quality to those remains as the race was intellectually inferior not only to the Greeks, but also to our own early Celtic and Teutonic ancestors of the first five Christian centuries who produced few buildings and had not advanced in settled order and in wealth so far as the subjects of the Incas. Nevertheless, the Peruvian remains do bear witness to two elements of strength in the American race. One of these is a capacity for the concentration of effort upon any aim proposed and for a scrupulously exact and careful execution of any work undertaken. The other is a certain largeness and boldness of conception, finding expression not only in the

[1] It is not clear how much territory this enumeration covered and it was probably only a rough estimate ; still, the fact that the population was far larger in the middle of the sixteenth than it was in the eighteenth century seems beyond doubt.

plan of great buildings, but also in an administrative
system which secured obedience over a vast area, which
diffused its language over many diverse tribes, and impressed upon them one worship and (to some extent at
least) one type of society. That a people who wanted so
many advantages possessed by the peoples of the Old
World should have effected these things shews the high
natural quality inherent in some at least of the aboriginal races of the Western Hemisphere.

Was this semicivilization of Peru — and one may
ask the same question regarding that of Mexico — still
advancing when it was suddenly and irretrievably swept
away by the Spanish Conquest? Did it possess such
further possibilities of development as might have
enabled it, had it been spared, to have made some substantial contribution, whether in art, or in industry, or in
the way of intellectual creation, to the general progress
of mankind? Or had it already reached the full measure of its stature, as the civilization of Egypt seems
to have done some time before the Persians conquered
that country, or as that of China did many centuries
ago? This is a question which the knowledge so far
attained regarding the pre-Conquest ages of Peru does
not enable us to answer.[1] Could the voyage of Columbus have been postponed for four or five hundred years,
Peruvians and Mexicans might have risen nearer to an

[1] A vast deal still remains to be done both in Mexico and Peru,
perhaps even more in the latter than in the former, to examine
thoroughly both the accounts given by the early Spanish writers and
the existing remains of buildings and graves and the objects found
in or near them, so as to lay a foundation for some systematic account of the ancient native civilizations.

equality of intelligence with the European peoples, however inferior they had remained for the purposes of war. But America once discovered, the invasion of Mexico and Peru was certain to follow ; and so soon as the Old-World races with their enormous superiority poured in among those of the New World, the weaker civilization could not but be submerged, submerged so utterly that little or nothing of it remained to be taken up into and incorporated with that of the invaders.

It is this complete submersion that strikes one so forcibly in Peru and Mexico ; perhaps even more forcibly in the former than in the latter. The aborigines went under at once. In Peru and Bolivia they constitute the majority of the population. But to the moral, intellectual, and political life of Peru and Bolivia they have made no contribution. Even to its art and its industries they supplied nothing except painstaking artificers, retaining the old talent for stonework, which they did at the bidding of Spanish masters. Negatively and harmfully, they have affected politics by preventing the growth of a white agricultural class and by furnishing recruits to the armies raised by military adventurers. The break between the old Peru of the Incas and the newer Peru of colonial times was as complete as it was sudden. The earlier has passed on nothing to the later, because the spirit of the race was too hopelessly broken to enable it to give anything. There remains only the submissiveness of a downtrodden peasantry and its pathetic fidelity to its primitive superstitions. Some old evils passed away, some new evils appeared. Human sacrifices ended, and the burning of heretics began.

CHAPTER V

BOLIVIA was for two centuries after the Spanish Conquest a part of Peru and has neither natural boundaries nor any distinctive physical character to mark it off from its neighbours, Peru on the northwest and Argentina on the southeast. It is an artificial creation, whose separate national existence is due to two events. After the Jesuits had, by the king of Spain's decree in 1769, been forced out of Paraguay, which they had ruled with considerable success for many years, the Spanish government found that it was more and more difficult to administer from Lima their vast southeastern dominions lying to the east of the Andes, since these were then becoming more and more exposed to contact with European nations, reaching them across the Atlantic. Accordingly, they created, in 1776, the viceroyalty of Buenos Aires and assigned to it all the River Plate countries, while for the southeastern parts of what had hitherto been upper Peru they set up a separate administrative authority with the seat of its *audiencia* at Chuquisaca. Then came the War of Independence. When that struggle ended with the decisive battle of Ayacucho, in 1824, and the surrender of Lima and Callao, the triumphant revolutionary leaders determined to maintain the political separation from Peru of this south-

166

ern region, which had been under the audiencia of
Chuquisaca, and to constitute a distinct republic lying
between Peru and Argentina.   To this new creation the
name of Bolivia was given in honour of Simon Bolivar,
the "Liberator," himself a Venezuelan.   Independent
it has since then remained, having, however, lost in an
unfortunate war with Chile a large slice of territory adjoining the Pacific.   It is now, except Paraguay, the
only entirely inland state in South America.   And just
as on no side has it anything that can be called a natural frontier, neither have its inhabitants any distinctive
quality or character to distinguish them sharply from
other peoples.   They differ but little from the Andean
Peruvians, being of similarly mixed Spanish and Indian
blood and living under similar physical conditions.

Bolivia includes several regions quite different in
their character.   Nearly all the western part is a desert,
with a few mining towns scattered here and there, a
desert enclosed by the two great almost parallel Cordilleras of the Andes.   The southeastern part is a plateau,
or rather succession of plateaux, lying on the eastern
side of the Eastern Cordillera, and gradually sinking
into those vast levels on the borders of Argentina, Paraguay, and Brazil, from which rivers flow northward into
the Amazon and southward to form the Paraná and Rio
de la Plata.   Much of this region is too dry or too rugged
for cultivation or even for ranching.   Yet much is also
valuable for one or other purpose, and capable of supporting an agricultural population as well as that which
lives off the mines.   The third or northeastern region

is a part of the great Amazonian low forest-covered country, — the so-called Selvas (woodlands), — which stretches out to the east from the declivities of the Eastern Cordillera, and is still, save for a few white settlements, inhabited only by wild Indians. Thus in the enormous total area of Bolivia, 605,000 square miles, there are only 2,000,000 people, and the large majority of these are Indians, uncivilized in the forests, semicivilized in the other regions. The white population, estimated at 200,000, most of whom, however, have some Indian blood, is virtually confined to a few towns, only one of which, La Paz, has more than 25,000 people. Santa Cruz (de la Sierra), far out in the eastern lowlands, and Chuquisaca, now called Sucre, Cochabamba, and Potosi, with its wonderful mountain of silver, have some families of Spanish blood. Oruro and Uyuni in the desert are mining towns with the mixed population that gathers in such places. La Paz, the largest city, and virtually, though not officially, the capital, has 50,000 inhabitants, the bulk of whom are Indians. These six towns are far apart, there are few inhabitants between them, and these are nearly all Indians. Till the railroad from Uyuni by Oruro to La Paz was made, communication was very slow and difficult. Anyone can see what obstacles to economic and political progress such conditions create.

The traveller who approaches La Paz from Lake Titicaca — and this has been the usual route from the coast — rises slowly through the bare hills amidst which Tiahuanaco stands till he emerges on an immense level, stretching south to a distant horizon, and bounded on the west by bare rolling mountains and on the east by the still loftier Eastern Cordillera.   Here in the bleakest spot imaginable, about 13,000 feet above sea-level, the railway from Guaqui, the port on Titicaca, meets the railway from Antofagasta, the Chilean port on the Pacific, four hundred miles away to the south, and this is the point to which a third railway is now converging, that which is being built to connect La Paz with Arica on the Pacific, one hundred miles to the west. From this point, called Viacha, the route turns eastward towards the Cordillera, the line climbing slowly in wide sweeps over the dusty and shrubless plateau on whose thin grass sheep are browsing.   There is not a house visible and the smooth slope seems to run right up against the mountain wall beyond.   Where can La Paz be? asks the traveller.   Presently, however, he perceives strings of llamas and donkeys and wayfarers on foot moving along the slope towards a point where they all suddenly vanish and are no more seen.   Then a spot is reached where the railway itself seems to end between a few sheds.   He gets out and walks a few yards to the east and then suddenly pulls up with a start on the edge of a yawning abyss.   Right beneath him, fifteen hundred feet below, a grey, red-roofed city fills the bottom of a gorge and climbs up its sides on both banks of the torrent that foams through it.   Every street and square, every yard and garden, is laid out under the eye as if on a map, and one almost seems to hear the rattle of vehicles over stony pavements coming faintly up through the thin air.

I had often heard La Paz described as lying in a
deep rift of volcanic origin, due to a sudden subsidence
in the course of an eruption, or perhaps to an earthquake.   Such a hypothesis seemed natural in a land
of earthquakes and volcanoes.   But there is no trace
here of any volcanic action, whether eruption or dis-
ruption.   This *barranca* — it is the Spanish name for
such a hollow — has evidently been scooped out by the
action of water.   The sloping plateau up which the
railway rises from Viacha is an immensely thick alluvial
or lacustrine deposit of earth and gravel, doubtless
formed in the days when the whole region between
the Eastern and Western Cordilleras formed part of
a far larger Lake Titicaca.   The torrent which comes
down from the snows of the Cordillera Real to the north
has cut its way down through this deposit and thus
formed the "gulch," to use the word which, in western
North America, is appropriated to gorges hollowed out
by streams.   The sides of the hollow are all of earth,
extremely hard, and in many places almost precipitous,
but there is no rock, certainly no igneous rock, visible
anywhere.

How did so strange a site come to be chosen?   Apparently in the first instance because gold had been found
in the earth along the river, and the Spaniards set
the Indians to wash it out for them.   This industry has
long been abandoned; but the spot, first settled in or
about 1548, when the civil wars among the Conquistadores were ended by capture and execution of Gonzalo
Pizarro, and called Our Lady of Peace, was recom-

mended for continued occupation by its having a copious and perennial stream, by its sheltered position, and by its standing at the opening of a deep ravine through which a track leads down along the banks of the river, into the forest country on the east. Through this ravine it is supposed that Lake Titicaca formerly sent its surplus waters to the Atlantic. No spot within many a mile is so well protected from the fierce winds that sweep over the plateau. Up there nothing will rise three feet from the ground. Down below flowers are grown and trees can be coaxed up to give shade and put forth branches in which birds can sing.

From the edge of the *barranca* — it is called the "Alto" — electric cars descend into the city by a track which doubles hither and thither in zigzags along the face of the almost precipitous declivity. The line has been skilfully laid out, and as the cars are light and fitted with powerful brakes, the descent is perfectly safe, steep as is the grade. Such a railway is, of course, not capable of carrying heavy goods traffic; but there is not, and may not for a long while be, any great quantity of heavy traffic to carry. The new line, which is to connect the city with the coast at Arica, is meant to have its terminal station at the southern end of the *barranca*, where descent from above is somewhat easier.

La Paz has the distinction of being the loftiest capital city in the world, as it stands 12,470 feet above sea-level, more than 2000 feet higher than Quito, and 5000 feet higher than Mexico. Lhasa in Tibet comes next to it at 11,830 feet. The mean annual temperature is

50 degrees Fahrenheit. The keen air which this elevation gives has a fine, bracing quality, yet there are disadvantages. One is never warm except when actually in the sunlight, and there are no fires, indeed, hardly any fireplaces, partly, no doubt, because there is nothing to burn, the country being treeless and coal far distant. The inhabitants get accustomed to these conditions and shiver in their ponchos, but the traveller is rather wretched after sunset, and feels how natural was Sun worship in such a country. So thin is the air that people with weak hearts or narrow chests cannot live here. An attack of pneumonia is rapidly fatal, because there is not enough oxygen to keep the lungs going under stress, and the only chance for the patient is to hurry him down to the coast by railway. Pressure on the breathing and palpitation of the heart are the commonest symptoms of the *soroche*, or *puna*, the so-called mountain sickness which prevails all over the plateau at heights exceeding 10,000 feet, many persons suffering from it at even lower levels. Less frequent symptoms are nausea and vomiting, violent headache, and general disturbance of the digestive organs. Some constitutions are, of course, much more liable to suffer than others are, but all who come from the lowlands experience a difficulty in any violent physical exertion, such as running uphill or lifting heavy weights. We enquired before leaving the coast whether any remedies or preventives could be applied, and were told that drugs were of little or no use, the best prophylactic being to abstain from smoking, from drinking, and from eating.

I observed only the second of these directions, but neither of us suffered in any way, not even at heights exceeding 15,000 feet, save that it proved desirable in climbing hills to walk more slowly than we were accustomed to do at home, and that, when lying down in bed at night, we found ourselves drawing a few very long and deep breaths before sleep came.   English and North American acquaintances in La Paz told us that to play single sets in lawn tennis was too hard work, because the effort of getting quickly to different corners of the court tried the lungs; and we heard of people who, having come here for business purposes, found, after a few months, that it was prudent to return to the coast for an interval of rest.   The native Indians, being to the manner born, seem to suffer from the thinness of the air no more than they do from the cold, and in the days of the Incas they performed extraordinary feats of swift running for long distances.

The causes which make elevation above the sea affect our organs more on some mountains than on others have never been fully ascertained.   Sir M. Conway thinks that the rarity of air is more felt in dry regions, as here in the central Andes and in Colorado, where I personally remember to have found it a greater hindrance to exertion at 8000 feet than on the Alps at 15,000 feet.   Others declare that it is more severe in moist and rainy weather than in clear weather.   One may venture to suggest that it is more felt on a plateau or wide mass of lofty mountains than on a narrow range where there is abundance of denser air just below, which rises from the valley. This would explain why climbers suffer so little from it in the Alps. Such experience as I have had on the Himalayas and in America as well as on the North American ranges and in Hawaii favours this view.

The lesson of slowing down one's pace in walking uphill is soon learnt in La Paz, for, as it stands on very irregular ground, sloping sharply on both sides to the stream which traverses it in a broad, stony channel, all the streets are steep, except those that run along the bottom of the valley parallel to the stream. All are very roughly paved, so driving is no great pleasure till you get outside the town upon one or two well-kept suburban avenues. Still less is riding, till one has learnt to trust the experienced local animal to keep his feet on the large, smooth cobblestones. In such a city, where there never were rich people and no church had any special sanctity, one cannot expect to find that charm, frequent in the old cities of Spain, which arises from the variety of architectural detail in the buildings. Few in La Paz bear an air of antiquity, few have anything picturesque in gables or doors or windows. The same thing is true of the churches also. Some have a more spacious interior than others, some a richer façade, some statelier towers, but all are of the invariable late sixteenth- and seventeenth-century type, with the same heavy and often tawdry ornament in the nave and choir. The churches of the friars have often more quality than the others; and here San Francisco with its handsome front and elaborate reredos pleased us better than the Cathedral. There are a few good houses, some of which tradition allots to former governors, with galleries built round the *patio* and gateways surmounted by armorial bearings, but the *patio* is cheerless, for it is apt to be a reservoir of chilled air. The central Plaza, where one usually looks to find the best that a town can do, is here quite small, but tastefully laid out. On one side of it are the government offices, on another the seat of the legislature, not a bad building, if it were not surmounted by a zinc spire. The markets are the most interesting places, because here, as in the open-air booths of the Plaza San Francisco and still more in the large covered passages of the principal Mercado (much like an Oriental bazaar or the Suk at Tunis), one sees not only the various fruits and roots and grains, the scanty produce of the plateau and of the nearest warmer valleys, together with such textile fabrics as native industry weaves or embroiders, but also the natives themselves in all their variety of costume. The Indian wears a felt hat, and the mestizo (half-breed), who belongs to a higher social stratum, a straw one. The former has always, the latter often, a woollen poncho, brightly coloured, over his rough and dirty cotton shirt and short, loose trousers. The white man, or the mestizo of the upper class who considers himself to be white, wears a European cloth coat, and usually for warmth's sake a cloak or overcoat above it; this is the distinctive note of social pretension. The native women are gorgeous in brilliantly coloured woollen petticoats, very heavy and very numerous.

Orange and pink are the favourite colours.   Strong and
solidly built as these Indian women are, one wonders
how their waists can support the weight of three, four,
or even five of these thick pieces of closely woven cloth.

Thus, though there is not much for the tourist to see
or do, nor for the art student to admire, still La Paz
is a picturesque place, with a character so peculiar that
it makes for itself a niche in the memory and stays
there, as being unlike any other place.   The strange irregularity of the steep, rough streets with cliffs of brown
earth standing up at the ends of them, the brawling
torrent, the wild-looking Indians in their particoloured
dresses, the flocks of graceful llamas with their long,
curved necks and liquid, wondering eyes, the extraordinary situation of the city in this deep pit, deep but not
dark, for the vertical sun blazes into it all day long ; and,
above all, the magnificent snowy mass of Illimani, towering into the sapphire blue sky with glaciers that seem to
hang over the city though they are forty miles away,
its three pinnacles of snow turning to a vivid rose
under the departing sun, — all these together make
La Paz a fascinating spot, one of those which flash
quickly and vividly before the mind when you think
of them.

The outskirts of the city, too bare and stern for beauty,
have a weird grimness which approaches grandeur.   A
pretty avenue between rows of *Eucalyptus*, the only tree
that seems to thrive here, and which stands the frost
better than it does in England, perhaps because Bolivia
has a dry air and a strong sun which more nearly repro-

duce the conditions of its Australian home, leads to a
public park whence a splendid view of the surrounding
heights and down the valley is obtained. The precipices
of hard earth that enclose it have been here and there
broken up into lofty earth pyramids like those which
one sees near Botzen in Tyrol, and have doubtless
been formed, like those, by the action of rain upon the
softer parts of the cliff. Behind the eastern earth wall
rise the spurs and buttresses of the Cordillera, wild,
bare glens running up to the watershed of the chain,
across the head of one of which is the pass which leads
down into the forest *Montaña*. It reminded me of some
of the recesses among the Noric Alps behind Gastein,
but was on a vaster scale, and more gloomy, as Andean
landscapes usually are. Quitting the city on another
side, I rode southward for some seven or eight miles
along the road which leads down the gorge, by a long
and devious course, through the heart of the Eastern
Cordillera under the southern flanks of Illimani, into the
land of gold and rubber, of alligators and jaguars. In the
sheltered nooks at the lower end of the town there were
gardens full of bamboos and flowering shrubs, and one
met strings of llamas, mules, and donkeys coming up the
road, laden with tropical fruits and other products of
the Yungas, as this region is called. Farther down
the scenery was stern and harsh, with great rock-
masses, crowning slopes that rose steeply three or four
thousand feet above the valley, but here and there
where there was room for cultivation beside the river,
a patch of bright green alfalfa relieved its monotony of

N

brown and black — a weird country, with these sharp contrasts of heat and cold, of verdure and sterility.   The air was already warm, and after thirty miles, one comes into the rains and the insects and the fevers of the tropics.

Within the city there is little for a visitor to do except wander through the market and buy rugs made of the deliciously soft and warm wool of the vicuña, the finest and costliest of Andean skins.   Neither is there much to see except the museum, which contains an interesting collection of minerals, specimens of woods, stuffed animals, and all sorts of curiosities, such as Indian weapons and various kinds of handiwork.   As the rooms are far too small for their contents, these are not seen to advantage.   The gentleman who seems to have the chief share in the management (Señor Ballivian) is a historical scholar and archæologist of high repute, belonging to one of the old families of La Paz.   Such accomplishments are not common in Bolivia, yet there are few countries which offer a wider and more attractive field to the naturalist and to the student of ethnology.

The legislature being in session, I was invited to be present at its sittings.   Both houses are small in number and are composed chiefly of lawyers, as, indeed, are most South American legislative bodies, law being the occupation which naturally leads to and comports with the profession of politics.   On this particular occasion the proceedings were unexciting and the speeches conversational in tone.   Members speak sitting, a practice which, though general in these republics, seems ill adapted for displays of that sonorous eloquence which belongs to the Spanish-American temperament. Among the eminent citizens whom it was my good fortune to meet none impressed me more than the veteran General Pando, who has been president of the republic and might have been so again, had not his patriotism made him prefer to devote his energies to the organization of the Bolivian army, the smallness of which makes its efficiency all the more needful. Nobody in the country is more widely respected and trusted.

There is a handful of foreign residents, German business men, English and North American railway men, a pleasant little society. The best school is said to be that conducted by a North American mission, which, however, devotes itself to education and not to proselytizing. Children of good Roman Catholic families attend it.

That the educated residents of Spanish stock should be few is not surprising when one realizes that La Paz is really an Indian city. Aymará is the language commonly spoken by three-fourths or more of its inhabitants. It has probably a larger aboriginal population than any other city in the New World, though the percentage of Indians may be somewhat greater in Asuncion, the capital of Paraguay. This may be a fitting place to give a brief account of their present condition, since of what they seem to have been before the Conquest something has been said in the last preceding chapter.

Though the bulk of the inhabitants of La Paz and Cuzco are Indians, the larger Andean towns are generally Spanish in appearance, and it is in the rural districts that the Indian is best seen and understood. He is essentially an agriculturist. Nearly all the land except in some coast plantations where a little Chinese or negro labour is employed is cultivated by the Indian, and all the llamas and sheep are herded by him. There is, indeed, no other industry by which a living can be made, except mining, for no factories on a large scale yet exist in these countries. Attached to the land, and dwelling usually in small villages which, save in fertile tracts like the Vilcamayu Valley, are seldom near together, the Indian has retained the beliefs and habits of his forefathers more than even the peasantry of Russia or the Turkish dominions. His primitive organization, the *ayllu* or clan, composed, like the Roman gens, or perhaps rather like a Greek phratry, of persons who traced their descent to a supposed common ancestor, still subsists in Bolivia, though it has of late years been interfered with by a new kind of grouping, that of the tenants or labourers on the same *finca* (landed estate). A number of *ayllus* made up a tribe, but this division has lost its importance since the *cacique* or chief of ancient times vanished. In every Indian agricultural community there are two officials. One is the *Ilacata*, whose functions are administrative, including the division of the land each year between the persons who are to till it and the receipt of the crops from common land, and the supervision of common labour. The other is the *Alcalde*, who combines executive and judicial powers, maintaining order, deciding petty disputes, and leading in fighting if the need for fighting should arise. The peasant, though legally free, practically goes with the estate, and though legally a voter, practically does not vote, the government being kind enough to relieve the rural citizens, and frequently the urban ones also, from a duty which few of them are qualified to discharge. They are in some places oppressed by the landowners, — that one must expect where there is a great difference of race and capacity, — yet much less than in colonial days, for there have been Indian risings, and firearms are more largely in their hands than formerly. They so preponderate in numbers that any movement which united them against the upper class might, could they find a leader, have serious consequences. Thus the fear of trouble restrains the excesses of power. Those who have land of their own are said to fare as ill at the hands of the lawyer and money-lender as any tenant could do at those of a landlord.

Scarcely any are educated. In Titicaca Island, with a population of about three hundred, there was a few years ago only one man who could read. In all Bolivia only 30,000 children were in the schools out of a population of 2,000,000. The sparseness of the population makes the provision of instruction difficult; nor do the aborigines seem to care for education, being so far satisfied with their lot as to have no notion of other pleasures than those which their fairs and festivals supply, and those derived from the use of alcohol at

these festivals, and at all times of the coca leaf, which
is for an Indian the first necessity of life. He is never
without his bag containing a bundle of leaves, which he
masticates (usually with a little clay) while walking or
working, finding in them a support which enables him
to endure fatigue without food for long periods. The
leaf when chewed is tasteless, and whether taken thus
or in a decoction produces no directly pleasurable feeling
of stimulus. I have experimented with it in both
forms without being able to discover any result except
that of arresting hunger. Taken by chewing the leaf, as
the Indians take it, it cannot have the highly deleterious
effects of cocaine, which is a concentrated essence ; indeed, if it had those effects, the aborigines of the plateau
must have been long ago ruined by it.[1] Possibly there is
something in the physical conditions of their life render-
ing it comparatively or altogether innocuous. It does
not seem to be much used by the whites, nor in the
lowlands by any class of the population. Perhaps,
therefore, it is "indicated" in the mild form of a chewed
leaf, as a stimulant suitable to those who take continuous exertion at great altitudes.

What has been said here refers generally to the aborigines of the high Andean regions, but there are two great
divisions of them, the characteristics of which are not
altogether the same. In very early times there were
probably many diverse tribes, and every valley spoke
a language, or at least a dialect, of its own. This

[1] Its habitual use may have contributed to give the Aymarás that
impassive dulness which characterizes the race.

is still the case in the Montaña region (the forests at the east foot of the Andes), where adjoining tribes are sometimes wholly unlike one another in speech and aspect. The conquests of the Incas, with their levelling and unifying rule, effaced most of these distinctions. There was a tongue called Mochica spoken by the coast people of Chimu, the race to whose artistic talent reference was made in last chapter, which seems to have been quite unlike the speech of the plateau. It is now extinct, but a grammar, made by a learned ecclesiastic, has fortunately survived. There is also another distinct tongue which remains among a half-savage tribe called the Urus, who dwell, now very few in number, among the rushy lagoons on the Desaguadero River, near the southwest end of Lake Titicaca. With these exceptions, the Spaniards seem to have found on their arrival only two forms of speech prevailing over Peru, corresponding to two racial divisions, the Quichuas to which the Incas apparently belonged, and the Aymarás. The latter held all the Collao, *i.e.* the country round Titicaca, and south of it round La Paz. The former occupied the northern valleys of Peru and the coast regions south of Lima, and a part of what is now southern Bolivia around Oruro and Uyuni. As these two languages are of the same type, it is generally held that the Quichua and Aymará races are cognate. Those who know both declare that the Quichuas are the gentler and the less forcible. The Aymarás, by the testimony of European as well as Peruvian observers, are ruder in manners, more sullen and vindictive in disposition.

Both races are alike secretive and suspicious of the whites, and for this sentiment they have had good reason. The impressions of a passing traveller are of no value, but it seemed to me, in noting the faces and deportment of the Indians whom we saw, that while both races had less intelligence and rather less look of personal dignity than the Indians of Mexico, the Aymarás seemed both a more dogged and a less cheerful race than the Quichuas. We might, perhaps, expect to find little buoyancy of spirit in those to whom Nature turns on this wind-swept roof of the world so stern a countenance. Yet the Icelander, whose far-distant isle is surrounded by a melancholy ocean, is of a lively and cheerful temper.

Both Quichuas and Aymarás have that remarkable impassiveness and detachment which belongs to all the American peoples and which in the Old World one finds only in some of the East Asiatic races. With plenty of stability, they lack initiative. They make steady soldiers, and fight well under white, or mestizo, leaders, but one seldom hears of a pure Indian accomplishing anything or rising either through war or politics, or in any profession, above the level of his class. The Mexican Juarez, the conqueror of Maximilian and of the priesthood, was a pure-blooded Indian. Since the days of the Araucanian chiefs Lautaro and Caupolican, South America has shewn no native quite equal to him. Curiosity and ambition are alike wanting to the race. Though one sees plenty of Indian blood in Peruvians and Bolivians of eminence, so that there must have been formerly much racial intermixture, and though there is practically no social distinction (except in three or four cities) between the white and the educated mestizo, intermarriage between pure Indians and pure Europeans is very uncommon.

The Indian of the plateau is still only a half-civilized man and less than half a Christian. He retains his primeval Nature worship, which groups together the spirits that dwell in mountains, rivers, and rocks with the spirits of ancestors, revering and propitiating all as *Achachilas*. In the same ceremony his medicine man invokes the Christian " *Dios* " to favour the building of a house, or whatever enterprise he undertakes, and simultaneously invokes the Achachilas, propitiating them also by offerings, the gift made to the Earth Spirit being buried in the soil.[1] Similarly he retains the ceremonial dances of heathendom and has secret dancing guilds, of whose mysteries the white man can learn nothing. His morality is what it was, in theory and practice, four centuries ago. He neither loves nor hates, but fears, the white man, and the white man neither loves nor hates, but despises him, there being some fear, at least in Bolivia, mingled with the contempt. They are held together neither by social relations nor by political, but by the need which the white landowner has for the Indian's labour and by the power of long habit which has made the Indian acquiesce in his subjection as a rent payer. Neither of them ever refers to the Conquest. The white man does not honour

---

[1] Mr. Bandelier (*Islands of Titicaca and Koati*) gives an interesting description of such a ceremony.

the memory of Pizarro ; to the Indian the story is too dim and distant to affect his mind.   Nor is it the least remarkable feature of the situation that the mestizo, or half-breed, forms no link between the races.   He prefers to speak Spanish which the Indian rarely understands. He is held to belong to the upper race, which is, for social and political purposes, though not by right of numbers, the Peruvian (or Bolivian) nation.

In no capital city have I felt so far removed from the great world, the European and Asiatic and North American parts of which are now so closely linked together, as here in La Paz.   There may probably be an equal sense of isolation in Quito and Bogotá, there can hardly be a stronger one.   To be enclosed between two lofty ranges and two deserts, to live at the bottom of a hole and yet be nearly as high above sea-level as the top of the Rocky Mountains or the Jungfrau are strange conditions for a dwelling place.   Nevertheless it was a place in which one might do much meditation, for new sensations awaken new thoughts, and solitude helps one to pursue them.   So it was with regret for everything except its climate that we quitted La Paz early one morning to resume our southward journey, bidding a long farewell to the *Achachila* [1] of the majestic Illimani, to which we had offered orisons of admiration in each dawning and each departing light.   After we had climbed to the rim of the *Barranca* in the electric car, an hour's run on the steam railroad carried us across the open plateau to Viacha, whence one route leads to Titicaca

[1] Mountain Spirit.

and over the lake to Mollendo, and another, now in construction, will in 1913 be ready to carry passengers down through the great Western Cordillera to the Pacific at Arica.[1] As this will be hereafter the most direct way of reaching La Paz from the coast, Viacha may some day be an important railroad centre, like Crewe or Chicago or Cologne. At present it is inexpressibly bleak and dreary, standing alone on a dusty and treeless waste. But the traveller of the future who has to wait here to "make his connections" will, while he paces up and down enquiring how much the incoming train is behind time, be able to feast his eyes on the incomparable view of the great Cordillera Real, piercing the northeastern sky, and here ending towards the south in the snowy pyramid of Huayna Potosi, round whose flanks gather the clouds that rise from the moist eastern forests sixteen thousand feet below.

At Viacha we entered the cars of the Antofagasta and Bolivia railroad, owned by an enterprising English company, and moved off to the south across a wide undulating plain which seemed an arid waste, but turned out to be pastured upon by flocks of sheep and llamas. Dry as the ground looked, — it was the end of September, when the summer showers were just beginning, — there was feed to be had and a few brooks here and there supplied drink. Some of those ancient round buildings of unmortared stone which the natives call *Chulpas* and which seem to have served as tombs rather than shrines were to be seen.   Here and there were villages, clusters of rude mud huts, sometimes with a bare,

---

[1] This line has now (December, 1912) been completed.

ugly church far too large for the place, and probably
owing its size to the zeal of some seventeenth-century
Jesuit or Augustinian.   At first low, brown mountains
cut off to the west the view of that Western Cordillera
through which the Arica line is making its difficult way,
but presently they subside, and one sees far off across
the plain a group of magnificent snowy peaks, apparently, from their shape and their isolation, ancient volcanoes.   Sahama, the highest, a pyramidal cone of
beautiful proportions, seemed, from the amount of snow
it carried, to be not less than 21,000 feet high.   It has
never yet been ascended.   In this western range the
snow line is higher than it is in the Eastern Cordillera
because the latter receives more moisture.   To the
northeast the great Cordillera Real which one admires
from Titicaca has now disappeared behind the low
ridges crossing the plain, and Illimani is seen only
now and then overtopping the nearer hills.   On the
east, however, farther south than Illimani, a new line
of snows comes into view, distant, perhaps, nearly a
hundred miles and doubtless forming part of the Eastern
Cordillera.   On each side there stretches out a wide
plain, but in one place the line runs for some miles
through a range of hills of black (apparently volcanic)
rock, following the course of a stream which presently
wanders off to the west and is there lost, swallowed
up in marshes.   Besides the tufts of coarse bunch grass
and a few low shrubs, there is still in the moister spots
some little pasture, — it is astonishing how llamas can
find something to eat on what seems bare ground, —

but the land grows more and more sterile as the line continues southward.   Presently the Indian villages cease; and great flats are seen to the west which are covered by water in the wet season.   At last a group of high, brown hills marks the site of Oruro, an old and famous mining town, one of whose mines, which has been worked for hundreds of years, formerly stood second only to Potosi in its output of silver.   Copper and tin as well as silver are worked in the hills, and on mining depends the prosperity of the town, which has now some twenty thousand inhabitants.   The long, straight streets of mean one-story adobe houses, covered with plaster, with only a few better residences where the business men and foreign mining people live, give little idea of the former importance of the place, but there is a large and rather handsome Plaza wherein stand the government buildings and a well-built arcade containing good shops.   Beside the big church are two enormous bells, of which the city has long been proud, but which have to stand on the ground because too heavy for the little erection on the church roof on which the bells in daily use are hung.   To the east, beyond a barren flat some eight or ten miles wide, a range of hills bounds the plateau, and beyond them the ground falls towards the Argentine frontier, so that within a day or two's riding one can get off this dry land of scorching days and freezing nights down into soft moist air and tall trees.

Oruro used to be the end of the railway which came up hither from the Pacific coast, and from here southward the gauge is of only two feet and a half. It is, however, to be widened, for traffic is increasing, and the company prosperous.

Next to the Germans, the most ubiquitous people in the world are the Aberdonians, so I was scarcely surprised to meet one here in the person of the principal doctor of the place, who, when we had talked about our friends on the banks of the far-distant Dee, gave me much information regarding the health conditions of Bolivia. He described Oruro as a more agreeable place of residence than its rather dreary externals promised. There was some agreeable society, for mining, which does not improve the quality of the working population, usually draws to a place a number of men of superior ability and sometimes of scientific attainments. Here, as elsewhere in Bolivia, foreigners, including some Chileans, own the mines, while business is chiefly in the hands of Germans. Manual labour is done by Indians (here speaking Quichua), whose number does not increase, because, although the families are large, the mortality among their children is very high, or else by half-breeds, here usually called *Cholos*, who would be good workers, were they not addicted to the use of the horrible spirits that are too easily procurable. There are, however, also some Chilean half-breeds and some English-speaking men, brought for the higher kinds of work.

About twenty miles away to the south is the great lagoon called Aullagas or Poopo, — the names are taken from villages on its shores, — which is fed by the river

Desaguadero.   This singular lake, which has the interest of a vanishing quantity, is fifty-three miles long by
twenty-four broad, is nowhere more than nine feet deep
and mostly less than five, is salt, turbid, with a bottom
of dark mud, and full of fish too small to be worth catching.   Like those of Titicaca they belong to species found
nowhere else.   Having so small a volume in proportion
to the surface area which it exposes to a strong sun
and an intensely dry air, it loses by evaporation all the
water it receives by the river from Titicaca and probably a little more, for it seems to be now shrinking.
When Titicaca, itself probably subsiding, has still less
to give, Poopo will disappear altogether, and this plain
will become a sheet of glittering salt.[1]

As one pursues the journey farther south, the country
becomes always more arid, and at Uyuni, the next town
of consequence, it is a veritable desert where only the
smallest stunted shrubs are seen among the sand and
stones.   This uninhabited region will soon be a converging point of railroads, for it is here that the existing
line from La Paz to the Pacific coast at Antofagasta
is to be joined by the new railway which is to be constructed to provide a quick through route from central
Bolivia to the Atlantic coast at Buenos Aires.   Its com-
pletion from Uyuni to Tupiza near the Argentine border is expected by 1916, and when the link has been
made, there will be a complete railway connection across
the Continent from the River Plate to the Pacific at

[1] I take these details from Dr. Romero's *Los Lagos de los
Altiplanos*, translated from the French of Dr. Neveu Lemaire.

Arica. Bolivia has hitherto suffered greatly from the want of communications, so when La Paz has been brought within twenty-four hours of the one ocean at Arica and within seventy-two or eighty hours of the other at Buenos Aires, a great impetus ought to be given to her export trade. This lofty and desert part of Bolivia finds its only source of wealth in minerals. The Western Cordillera is especially rich in copper and silver, the Eastern in gold and tin. One-third of all the world's production of tin now comes from Bolivia. Besides the silver found in various places, — the great silver mountain is still worked at Potosi, — the eastern spurs of the Peruvian and Bolivian Andes are believed to contain plenty of gold, which would be extracted from the gravels, perhaps from rock reefs also, much more extensively, but for the extreme difficulty of conveying mine machinery across the mountains down abrupt slopes and through trackless forests. It was from these East Andean regions that the Incas obtained those vast stores of gold which excited the cupidity of the Spaniards. Pizarro got from Atahuallpa a quantity roughly estimated at £3,000,000 ($15,000,000) on a promise that the Inca's life would be spared, — a promise broken as soon as most of the gold had been delivered. Yet the contemporary Spanish annalists declare that what the Spaniards laid their hands upon first and last in the days of the Conquest was much less than what the Indians buried or threw into the lakes when they could no longer guard it. Great, however, as is the mineral wealth of the Bolivian highlands, it is less on them, than on the development of the agricultural and pastoral resources of the eastern part of the republic that future prosperity must in the long run depend. Mines are a transitory source of wealth; they enrich the foreign capitalist rather than the nation itself; they do not help to build up an intelligent and settled body of responsible citizens.

It is not solely for the sake of industry and commerce that Bolivia may welcome the advent of railways. She is the least naturally cohesive and in some ways the least nationally united of South American states. Europeans and North Americans hear but little about her, and underestimate the difficulties she has had to contend with. Imagine a country as big as the German and Austrian dominions put together, with a population less than that of Denmark, four-fifths of it consisting of semicivilized or uncivilized Indians, and the few educated men of European or mixed stock scattered here and there in half a dozen towns, none of which has more than a small number of capable citizens of that stock. An energetic monarch with a small but efficient and mobile army might rule such a country, but it offers obvious difficulties to the smooth working of a republican government, for one of the essentials to such a government is that the minority of competent citizens, be they many or few, should be in easy communication with one another, capable of understanding one another and of creating a public opinion. This has hitherto been difficult, owing to the want of railways, for Santa Cruz, Cochabamba, and Sucre (Chuquisaca) have all been a many days' journey from one another and

o

from La Paz. These towns know little of one another and are mutually jealous. The old Spanish-colonial element in them regards with disfavour the larger but more Indian La Paz. Sucre is made the legal capital, but neither it nor any other city has both the size and the central position that would qualify to act as a unifying force. There is hardly any immigration, and little natural increase of population, so the vacant spaces do not fill up, even where they are habitable. Anything, therefore, that will help both to increase the material prosperity of Bolivia and to draw its people together will be a political benefit.

Besides the railway which is to run from Uyuni to Buenos Aires, five other lines through the High Andes are likely to be constructed. One is to connect Cuzco with the existing railway from Lima to Oroya, a wonderful line, which reaches a height of 15,600 feet. A second will continue that line eastward to the Ucayali River. A third is also to cross the Eastern Cordillera from Tirapata (north of Lake Titicaca) to the river Madre de Dios. A fourth will run from La Paz down the canyon of its torrent to the river Beni. A fifth will connect Potosi with a port upon the Paraguay River via Sucre and Santa Cruz. The opening of these communications must accelerate the development of Peru and Bolivia.

Uyuni is smaller than Oruro, and even less attractive. It has an enormous empty plaza and four wide streets of mud houses. Standing at 12,500 feet above sea-level, in a dry and cloudless air, where the radiation of heat is great the moment the sun goes down, we found the later hours of night so cold that the water froze inside our sleeping car, while the heat of the day, reflected from the desert floor, is no less intense. There is a famous mine at Pulucayo, in the eastern mountain range, — some ten miles distant from Uyuni and fifteen hundred feet above the town. We mounted to it by a little railway and were struck by the appearance of vegetation when we had risen some hundreds of feet above the torrid plain. Conspicuous was a cactus-like plant, with white, silky hairs, lifting its prickly fingers ten feet up, and ending in clusters of brilliant crimson blossoms. The staff of the French company who work the mine received us hospitably and explained the processes of extraction and the way in which electricity is applied to do the work. Silver, copper, zinc, lead, and iron are all found associated here; and shafts one thousand feet deep are sunk from the long galleries, driven far into the mountain, one of which goes right through to Huanchaca on the other side. A town of six or seven thousand people has grown up, to accommodate the labourers, all Indians or *Cholos*.[1] A church and school and tiny theatre have been built for them, and as their hardy frames can support the cold and the thin air, they seem cheerful and contented. The contrast between the refined appliances of modern science and the rudeness of semicivilized man never seemed sharper than when one saw this machinery and these labourers.

[1] The name *Cholo* properly means the offspring of a mestizo and an Indian, but it seems to be currently used to describe a peasant with a marked Indian strain.

From this height of about fourteen thousand feet one could look for more than a hundred miles over the desert, — and such a desert ! Many of us can remember the awe and mystery which the word Wilderness in the Old Testament used to call up in a child's mind. When a boy reads of the Desert of Sahara, he pictures it as terrible and deathful. After he has grown up and travelled outside Europe, the only continent that has no wildernesses, and has seen the deserts on either side of Egypt, or the Kalahari in South Africa, or the deserts of India, or Arizona, or Iceland, he comes to realize that a large part of the earth's surface is desert, and that deserts, if awful, can have also a beauty and even a charm of their own.[1] This may not seem to the practical mind to be a sufficient final cause for their existence, but that is a side issue, and philosophy has, since Bacon's time, ceased to enquire into final causes. Of the deserts I have named, those of northern Arizona are perhaps the most beautiful, but this high plateau of southern Bolivia, while very different, is not less impressive.

Right in the midst lay a sparkling plain of white. It was a huge salt marsh, on which the salt crystals shone like silver, for at this season it looks dry, though soft enough to engulf and entomb in its bottomless depths of mud any misguided wayfarer who may attempt to cross it. Beyond it to the northwest and north the waste of sand stretched out to the horizon,

---

[1] An admirable study of desert scenery may be found in a book by Mr. Van Dyke of Rutgers College (in New Jersey), entitled *The Desert*.

while southwest and south long ranges of serrated
mountains ran hither and thither across the vast expanse, as if they had been moulded on a relief map,
so sharp and so near did they seem to lie, though fifty
miles away.   Some were capped or streaked with snow,
indicating in this arid land a height of seventeen
thousand feet.

The splendour of such a view consists not only in the
sensuous pleasure which the eye derives from the range
of delicate tints and from the fine definition of mountain
forms, hardly less various in their lines than they are in
their colours, but even more in the impression which
is made on the imagination.   The immensity and com-
plexity of this nature speak of the vast scale on which
natural forces work and of the immense spaces of time
which their work has occupied.

Returning to the railway at Uyuni, we set off in the
afternoon on our southward way across the desert floor,
here perfectly flat and about 12,000 feet above the
sea.   A deep red soil promised fertility if water could be
brought to it, but there was not a tree nor a house, though
many a mirage shewed shining water pools and trees
around them.   Rocky hillocks rising here and there like
islands strengthened the impression that this had been
in some earlier age the bed of a great inland sea, larger
than Lake Superior in North America, stretching from
here all the way to the Vilcañota peaks north of Titicaca, and including, besides Titicaca itself, the salt lagoon
of Poopo and the white salt marsh we had seen from
the heights of Pulucayo.   Subterranean forces which, as

we know, have been recently at work all over these regions, may have altered the levels, and alterations of
level may, in their turn, have induced climatic changes,
which, by reducing rainfall, caused the inland sea to
dry up, as the Great Salt Lake of Utah and the Aral
Sea are drying up now.   Looking eastward, we could
see heavy clouds brooding over the eastern ranges,
which shewed that beyond it lay valleys, watered by the
rains which the trade-wind brings up from the far-
distant Atlantic. Presently the sweetest hour of the day
came as the grey sternness of the heights to the south
softened into lilac, and a pale yellow sunset, such as
only deserts see, flooded the plain with radiance.   The
night was intensely cold, and next morning, even at
eight o'clock, the earth was frozen hard in the deep,
dark hollow where the train had halted.

We were now just inside the Chilean frontier, in
the heart of the Western Cordillera, among some of
the loftiest volcanic mountains of the Continent.   On
one side a branch line of railway, the highest in the
world, begins its long climb to the Collahuasi copper
mine.   On the other side, there rose above us the huge
black mass of Ollague,[1] snow patches on its southern
side and steam rising in wreaths from a cleft not far
below the summit. We guessed the height at 19,000
feet.   The Collahuasi mine is nearly 16,000.   Beside us
was what seemed a frozen lake, which glittered white
when the welcome sun began to overtop the heights and
warm our shivering bodies.   Although the height is

[1] Pronounced Oyawe.

only 12,200 feet, this is a particularly cold spot, and the one place on the line which is liable to severe snowstorms. We had reached the smaller of the two famous lakes of borax, parts of which are water holding borax in solution, while the rest is mud covered with the valuable substance. They have neither influent nor outlet. This place, and a similar lake in Peru, not far from Arequipa, furnish the world with a large part of its supply, the rest coming from California and Siberia and Tibet, where the conditions of a rainlessness that keeps the deposit from being washed away out of the soil are somewhat similar. Presently we reached the larger lake, which is twelve miles long and two to five wide, and stopped to see the method of gathering and preparing the mineral. One end of the (so-called) lake is dry, a thin stratum of whitish earth covering the bed of borax, which is about three feet thick. When dug out, the mineral is spread out on the ground round the works to dry, and then calcined in furnaces, forming a white mass of crystals, which are packed in sacks and sent down to the coast to be shipped to Europe and there turned into the borax of commerce. A large number of labourers are employed in this lonely and cheerless spot fifty miles from the nearest village. When I asked what fuel was used for the furnaces, they pointed to a long wire cable stretched through the air from the works to a point high on the mountain side opposite Ollague. Down this rope small cars were travelling, containing masses of a kind of very hard, stiff plant with whitish flowers so inconspicuous that

it is usually taken for a sort of moss.[1]   It grows abun-
dantly on the slopes between eight and fourteen thousand feet, and its thick hard cushions have to be cut out
with a pickaxe.   Being very resinous, it burns with a
fierce flame, but so quickly that large masses must be
constantly thrown in to keep the fire going.   Hardly
anything else grows on the mountains, but they are
inhabited by the little chinchilla, whose light grey fur,
exquisitely soft, fetches a high price in Europe.

From this point onward the scenery is of incomparable grandeur.   I doubt if there be any other spot in the
Andes where the sternness and terror that surround the
volcano are equally felt.   The railway skirts the borax
lake and then rises slowly along a ledge above it,
whence one looks down on its still surface, where patches
of whitish green open water reflect the crags and snows
of the peaks that tower above.   The deep, dark valley
so winds and turns that it is in some places hard to
guess where the exit lies.   Above it stands a line of
volcanoes, seventeen to nineteen thousand feet high.
Their tops are of black rock, their faces, from which
here and there black crags project, are slopes of ash
and cinders, shewing those strange and gruesome contrasts of colour which are often seen in the mineral
world when vegetation and the atmosphere have not
had time to tell upon them.   In some of these peaks
one whole side of the crater seems to have been blown
out by an explosion, laying bare the farther wall of the

---

[1] It is called *Yareta*, and reminds one a little (though it is larger
and harder) of the *Cherleria sedoides* of the Scottish Highlands.

hollow, for the colours are just such as are seen in craters like those of Etna and Hekla, though here more vivid, because here there is so little rain to wash off their brightness.   One such breached crater, forming the face of what is called (from the variety of its tints) the Garden Mountain, displays almost every colour of the spectrum, bright yellow and orange, pink and purple, and a brick red passing into dark brown.   A ridge that stands out on its face shews on one declivity a yellowish white and on the other a brilliant crimson.   But the intensity of these colours heightens rather than reduces the sombre gloom of the landscape.   One seems admitted to view an abandoned laboratory of Nature, in which furnaces, now extinct or smouldering low, fused the lavas and generated the steam that raised them to the crater's edge and sent them forth in fiery streams.   Where there is now a deathlike silence, flames lit up the darkness of the clouds of ash that rose with the gushing steam, and masses of red-hot rock were hurled to heaven while explosions shook the earth beneath.

In the middle of this narrow pathway which leads through the purple depths of the Cordillera we reach at Ascotan the top of the pass, 13,000 feet above sea-level, whence the valley, turning to the northwest, begins to descend towards the Pacific.   The majestic portal through which one looks out into the western desert is guarded by two tall volcanoes standing side by side, St. Peter and St. Paul.   The latter has been long extinct, but San Pedro still smokes or steams from its summit.   A red hill near its foot has in quite recent times poured forth from its crater a vast lava stream through which the railway passes in a cutting, and which, splitting itself wherever it met a natural obstruction, has sent its long black tongues far down into the valley of the Loa River. For here, after hundreds of miles, one comes again upon a river. Behind the mass of San Pedro fountains fed by its snow break forth from the ground and come down into a clear green stream which has cut its way through the rock in a splendid cañon, across which the line is carried. The river has been turned to account by building several large reservoirs, whence pipes have been laid to the coast, supplying not only the nitrate fields below (of which I shall speak presently), but also the seaports of Antofagasta and Megillones one hundred and forty miles away, all these regions being without brook or spring.

Here we emerged from the mountains into broad sunshine and saw in front of us long ridges falling away, one behind the other, towards the still distant Pacific. Rattling rapidly down the incline, past junctions whence branch lines climb to mines high among the hills, we came at last to Calama, the first Chilean village, where rivulets drawn from the Loa make an oasis of bright green corn and alfalfa and support a few shrubs that gladden the wilderness. Evening is always the pleasantest time in the tropics, and it is most so in a desert, when, instead of the hard afternoon glare, gentle lights begin to fall upon rocks and earth and make their dryness luminous. It was our fortune to have at this best hour of the day a distant view of the Andes, as lovely as the landscapes through which we had passed were awesome. We were now some way west of the chain, and could see it running in a long serrated line from San Pedro southward. This line is the Western Cordillera, which from here all the way to the Straits of Magellan is the main Andean axis, rising over, and apparently created by, the great telluric fissure along which the eruptive forces have acted. Nearest and grandest were the massive cones of San Pedro and San Pablo; and from them the line of snows could in this clear and lucent air be traced without a break, peak rising beyond peak, till ninety miles away it sank beneath the horizon.

Seen close at hand, as we saw Ollague and the other volcanoes that rose above the borax lake, these mountains would be grim and terrible as those were, their slopes a chaos of tumbled rocks and brown cinders and long slides of crumbling ash, telling of the ruthless forces of Nature that had been at work. But seen afar off they were perfect in their beauty, with an exquisite variety of graceful forms, their precipices purple, and their snow crowns rosy in the level light of sunset. So Time seems to soften the horrors and sorrows of the Past as it recedes, and things which to those who lived among them were terrible and to those who had lived through them were fit only to be forgotten, become romantic to men of later generations, a theme for poets or painters, and glories for orators to recall.

Just where the range is lost to sight in the far south

it forms the western wall of the great Desert of
Atacama, long a name of terror to the Spaniards.
Not often in these countries does one find natural objects associated with events important enough to figure
in history.   But it was in the dreary and waterless
wastes of this desert that Almagro, first the friend and
partner, then the rival and enemy, and at last the
victim, of Pizarro, lost half his men and nearly perished
himself in his march into Chile from Peru through
what is now northern Argentina.   The enterprise was
one amazing even in that age of adventure, for Almagro's
force was small, there was no possibility of succour, and
he went into a land utterly unknown, a land of deserts
and mountains.   But it was an unlucky enterprise.
The tribes of Chile were fiercer than those of Peru; he
had gone beyond the regions of civilization and of gold,
and returned an empty-handed conqueror.

CHAPTER VI

EXCEPT Egypt, there is not in the world a country so strangely formed as Chile. Egypt is seven hundred miles long and nowhere save in the Delta more than twelve miles wide. Chile is nearly three thousand miles in length, nowhere more than one hundred and thirty miles wide and for most of her length much narrower. Even Norway, whose shape and sea-front best resemble those of Chile, has but fifteen hundred miles of coast and has, in her south part, two hundred and fifty miles of width. Much of the Chilean territory is a barren desert; much that is not desert is in fact uninhabited. Over large tracts the population is extremely thin. Yet Chile is the most united and the most ardently national in sentiment among all the Spanish-American countries.

Nor is Chile any more singular in the shape of her territory than in her physical conditions also. On the east she is bounded all the way down to Magellan's Straits by the Cordillera of the Andes, the height of whose summits averages in the northern regions from fourteen to twenty thousand feet and in the southern from five to nine thousand, some few peaks exceeding these heights. Parallel to the Cordillera, and geologically much older, there runs along the coast a range averaging from two to three thousand feet, between the foot of which and the ocean there is practically no level ground.   The space between this coast range and the Cordillera is a long depression from twenty to thirty miles wide, sometimes hilly, sometimes spreading out into plains, yet everywhere so narrow that both the Coast Range on the one side and the spurs of the Andes on the other are within sight of the inhabitants who live between them.   This long and narrow central depression is Chile, just as the cultivable land on each side the Nile is Egypt; and in it all the people dwell, except those who are to be found in the few maritime towns.

It may seem strange that a country of this shape, three thousand miles long, and with only three million three hundred thousand people, should be conspicuously homogeneous, united, and patriotic.   When the difference between territorial Chile, the country of the map, and actual Chile dawns upon the traveller, his surprise disappears.   There are in the republic three distinct regions.   The northern, from latitude 18° south as far as Coquimbo in latitude 30° south, is arid desert ; some of it profitable nitrate desert, most of it, like Atacama, useless desert.   The south, from Puerto Montt in latitude 42° south down to latitude 54° south, is an archipelago of wooded isles with a narrow strip of wooded mountain on the mainland behind, both of them drenched by perpetual rains and inhabited only by a few wandering Indians, with here and there a trading post of white men.   It is the central part alone that is compactly peopled, a narrow tract about seven hundred miles long, most of it mountainous, but the valleys generally fertile, and the climate excellent. This central part is the real Chile, the home of the nation.

To central Chile I shall return presently. Meantime a few pages may be given to the northern section, which, though a desert, has an enormous economic value, and is, indeed, one of the chief sources of natural wealth in the two American continents. It is the region which supplies the agriculturists of the whole world with their nitrates, and the nitrates are here because the country is absolutely rainless. Rains would have washed the precious mineral out of the soil long ago and swept it down into the Pacific.

One enters the nitrate fields in two or three hours after leaving the Bolivian plateau and passing through the Western Cordillera described in the last preceding chapter. They are unmitigated desert, a region of low stony hills, dry and barren, not a shrub, not a blade of grass. Sources of fertility to other countries, they remain themselves forever sterile. All the water is brought down in pipes from the upper course of the Loa, the stream which rises on the flanks of the volcano of San Pedro already mentioned. One can just descry in the far distance its snow-streaked summit. But the desert is all alive. Everywhere there are narrow-gauge lines of rails running hither and thither, with long rows of trucks passing down them, carrying lumps of rock. Groups of men are at work with pickaxes breaking the ground or loading the trucks. Puffs of smoke and dust are rising from places where the rock is being blasted

with dynamite.   Here and there buildings with machinery and tall iron pipes shew the *oficinas* where the
rock is ground to powder, then washed and boiled, the
liquid mass run off and drained and dried into a whitish
powder, which is packed into sacks and sent down
to the coast for shipment.   The mineral occurs in a
stratum which lies about a foot below the surface, and
averages three feet in thickness.   It is brownish grey
in colour and very hard.   There is a considerable by-
product of iodine, which is separated and sent off for sale.
The demand for it is said to be less than the supply.

Each *oficina* — that is the name given to the places
for the reduction and preparation of the mineral — is
the centre of a larger or smaller nitrate estate, and
the larger and more modern ones are equipped with
houses for the managers and workpeople, each being
a sort of village where the company supplies everything to the workpeople, who are mostly Chilean *rotos*,
sturdy peasants of half-Indian blood.   In South America
one sees plenty of isolated mining villages in deserts,
but here a whole wide region unable to support human
life is alive with an industrious population.

The air being dry and pure (except for the dust) at
this considerable elevation, averaging from three to five
thousand feet, the climate ought to be healthy.   But
it is impossible to imagine a more dismal place to inhabit, and those parts of the surface from which the
mineral has been removed are at once forsaken.

These nitrate fields cover a very large area in the
northern provinces of Chile, but some districts in

which the mineral is believed to exist are still imperfectly explored, and many in which it does exist shew a comparatively poor stratum, so that it is not possible to estimate how much remains to be developed and the length of time it will take, at the present rate of production, to exhaust that amount. We were told, however, that, so far as can be conjectured, the fields might (at the present rate) last nearly two centuries, before the end of which period much may happen in the field of scientific agriculture. The export duty or royalty which the Chilean government levies produces a large annual revenue, and is, indeed, the mainstay of the finance of the republic, enabling taxation to be fixed at a low figure.[1] There are those who say that this is no unmixed benefit, because it reduces the motives for economical administration. The guano deposits of Peru proved to be the source of more evil than good, for by pouring into her treasury sums which excited the cupidity of military adventurers, they made revolutions more frequent. No such danger need be feared in Chile; yet there are always temptations incident to the possession of wealth which a man or a nation has not earned by effort. As the nitrates are part of the capital of the country which will some day come to an end, it would seem prudent to expend what they produce upon permanent improvements which will add to the nation's permanent wealth, such, for instance, as railroads and harbours. A good deal is, in fact, being spent on rail-

[1] In the thirty years from 1880 to 1909 the Chilean treasury received £82,637,000 (about $412,000,000) in export duties on nitrates.

P

road construction, and a good deal on the creation of a naval stronghold and docks at Talcahuano.

Between the nitrate fields and the sea there lies a strip of wholly unprofitable desert, traversed by that range of hills which rises from the coast all the way along the west side of Chile and Peru. Its scenery is bold and in places striking, but the utter bareness and brownness deprive it of all charm except that which the morning and evening sunlight gives, bringing out delicate tints on distant slopes. Here the railway line forks, sending one branch to the port of Antofagasta, and the other to the smaller town but better sheltered roadstead of Megillones. We went to the latter. Local interests of a self-ish kind have here, as elsewhere along the coast, caused the selection of Antofagasta as the principal terminus of the line; and though it is now admitted that Megillones would have been a fitter spot, so much capital has been sunk in buildings at the former that it is deemed too late to make a change. The bay of Megillones, guarded by a lofty promontory on the south, and commanding a view of ridge after ridge of mountains stretching out to the north, has a beautiful sweep, and is enlivened by the abundance of seals and sea-lions, who wallow and bark to one another in the long, slow rollers of the Pacific. The beach is excellent for bathing, but the water so cold that only in the hotter part of the year do the Englishmen, who manage the railway and its machine works and who retain here the national love of salt water, find it suitable for anything more than a plunge in and out again. Though rain is extremely rare, one may conclude from the gullies in the hills down which torrents seem to have swept either that violent storms come occasionally or that the climate has altered since hills and valleys took their present form.

Antofagasta, where we landed on the southward voyage down the coast, is a much busier place than Megillones, but a less attractive one, for it has no such sweep of sand and space of level ground behind, being crushed in between the dreary, dusty hills and the rocky shore. Landing in the surf is often difficult and sometimes dangerous, but as the chief port of the southern nitrate country it receives a good deal of shipping, and has a pleasant little native society, besides an English and a German colony.

Nearly five hundred miles further south are the towns of La Serena and Coquimbo, the former a quiet old Spanish city, placed back from the coast to be out of the way of the English and Dutch marauders, who were frequent and formidable visitors in these seas, after Sir Francis Drake had led the way in his famous voyage in 1578, when he sailed up and down the coast plundering towns and capturing ships. Coquimbo is a newer place, with a fairly good harbour, and thrives on the trade which the mines in its neighbourhood assure to it. It is an arid land, yet here there begins to be some rain, and here, therefore, we felt that we were bidding farewell to the desert, which we had first struck at Payta, fifteen hundred miles further north. Nevertheless there was little green upon the hills until

we reached, next day, a far more important port, the
commercial capital not only of Chile, but of all western
South America, and now the terminus of the trans-
continental railway to Buenos Aires.

This is Valparaiso, where the wanderer who has been
musing among prehistoric ruins and Bolivian volcanoes
finds himself again in the busy modern world. The
harbour is full of vessels from all quarters, — coasting
steamers that ply to Callao and Panama, sailing ships as
well as steamers from San Francisco and others from Australia, mostly with cargoes of coal, besides vessels that
have come from Europe round Cape Horn or through
the Straits of Magellan. The so-called harbour is really
an open roadstead, for there is no shelter to the north,
and when, as often happens, the dreaded gale from that
quarter breaks, vessels that have not had time to run
out under steam are in danger of drifting ashore, for
the water deepens so quickly from the land that they
cannot anchor far out. Why not build a breakwater?
Because the water is so deep that the cost of a break-
water long enough to give effective protection would be
enormous. There is a more sheltered haven some miles
to the north, but as all the business offices and warehouses are here, not to speak of the labouring population and their houses, the idea of moving the city and
railway terminus has not been seriously considered.

Seen from the sea, Valparaiso is picturesque, and has
a marked character of its own, though the dryness of
the hills and the clearness of the light make it faintly
recall one of those Spanish or Italian towns which glitter

on the steep shores of the Mediterranean. It resembles Messina in Sicily in being very long and very narrow, for here, as there, the heights, rising abruptly from the shore, leave little space for houses, and the lower part of the town has less than a quarter of a mile in breadth. On this narrow strip are all the places of business, banks, shipping offices, and shops, as well as the dwellings of most of the poorer class. On the hills above, rising steeply two hundred feet or more, stands the upper town, which consists chiefly of the residences of the richer people. Their villas, interspersed with gardens, have a pretty effect seen from below, and in rambling along the lanes that run up to heights behind one gets charming views over the long line of coast to the north. Communication between the lower and upper towns is carried on chiefly by elevators (lifts) or trolley cars worked on the cog-wheel system.

At the time of my visit, the city was half in ruins, rebuilding itself after a terrible earthquake. The lower town had suffered most, for here, as at Messina and at San Francisco, buildings erected on soft alluvial ground were overthrown more frequently and completely than those that stood on a rocky foundation. The opportunity was being taken to widen and straighten the principal thoroughfares, and to open up some of the overcrowded poorer districts. The irregularities of the site between a sinuous coastline and spurs projecting from the hills make the city plan less uniform and rectangular than in most Spanish-American cities, and though nothing is old and there is little architectural variety, still the bright colours of the houses washed in blue or white, the glimpses of rocky heights seen at the eastern end of all the cross streets and of the sea glittering at the western give a quality of its own to the lower town, while the upper town has its steep gardens and tree clumps and wide prospects over the bay and the jutting capes beyond.

But Valparaiso is perhaps most picturesque when seen from a steamer anchored in the bay, especially when its white houses and hills, green for a few weeks in spring, meet the eyes of one who comes from the barren deserts of Bolivia and the nitrate region. In front are the ocean steamers and the tall spars of Australian clippers; nearer shore the smaller craft are tossing on the ocean swell; the upper town is seen rising on its cliffs behind the lower, with high pastures and rocky hummocks still further back. Far away in the northeast the snowy mass of Aconcagua, loftiest of all American summits, floats like a white cloud on the horizon.

A few miles north of Valparaiso is the pretty residential suburb of Viña del Mar, beyond which the rocks come down to the sea, here and there enclosing stretches of sandy beach on which the great green rollers break. The dark yellow Californian poppy (*Eschscholtzia*) which covers the fields in such masses round San Francisco is equally common here. Woody glens come down from the hills; and in the bottom of one of these the principal sporting club has laid out a race-course and polo ground, where we saw the fashionable world gathered for these diversions, just as popular here as in Europe. (South America has not yet given any game of its own to the world as the North American Indians gave La Crosse and the East Indies polo.) Everything looked very pretty in the fresh green of October, but everybody shivered; for though the summers are extremely hot, the spring was less genial than one expected in this latitude. Valparaiso has winds equally chilling whether they come down from the snowy Andes on the east or up from the Antarctic current on the west. It is a windy place and in summer a very dusty one, but in comparison with the dismal barrenness of Mollendo and Anto-fagasta it deserves its name of Valley of Paradise.

Despite earthquakes and northern gales, Valparaiso continues to be the most flourishing seat of world trade on the western side of its Continent, the only South American rival of San Francisco, Seattle, and Vancouver. It is also the centre of the coast trade of the Chileans, the only Spanish-American people who have shewn taste or talent for seafaring. We felt ourselves back in the modern world when we saw a Stock Exchange, having since we left New York passed near no city possessing that familiar appliance of civilization. Apart from stocks, abundant opportunities are supplied for speculation by the sudden and violent fluctuations in exchange upon Europe. The commercial houses are chiefly English and German, and among the Chilean firms there are some that bear English names. The Europeans of former days soon made themselves at home here, and their descendants in the third or even the second generation are patriotic Chileans. Some of the heads of British firms told me that the young men who come out to them to-day from England, are not, as a rule, equal either to those of thirty years ago or to the young Germans who are sent to serve German houses. "They care less for their work,"—so my informants declared,— and "they do it less thoroughly ; their interests at school in England have lain chiefly in playing, or in reading about, cricket and football, not in any pursuit needing mental exertion, and here where cricket and football are not to be had, they become listless and will not, like the young Germans, spend their evenings in mastering the language and the business conditions of the country." What truth there is in this I had no means of testing, but Valparaiso is not the only foreign port in which one hears such things said.

Fifty miles inland, as the crow flies, but much farther by railway, is Santiago, the capital of Chile, and in population the fourth city in South America.[1] Except Rio de Janeiro, no capital in the world has a more striking position. Standing in the great central valley of Chile, it looks out on one side over a fertile plain to the wooded slopes of the Coast Range, and on the other looks up to the gigantic chain of the Cordillera, rising nineteen thousand feet above it, furrowed by deep glens into which glaciers pour down, with snowy wastes behind. At Santiago, as at Innsbruck, one sees the vista of a long, straight street closed by towering mountains that crown it with white as the sea crowns with blue the streets of Venice. But here the moun-

[1] Buenos Aires, Rio, and São Paulo are the three larger cities.

tains are more than twice as high as those of the Tyrolean city and they never put off their snowy vesture. Wherever one walks or drives through the city in the beautiful public park and on the large open grounds of the race-course, these fields of ice are always before the eye, whether wreathed with cloud or glittering against an ardent sky.

The interior of the city does not offer very much to the traveller. There is one long, broad and handsome thoroughfare, the Alameda, adorned with statues and with four rows of trees, as well as several plazas, small compared to those of Lima and Arequipa, but very tastefully planted. There is a cathedral of the familiar type, spacious and well proportioned, with the usual two west towers and the usual silver altar. There are handsome government offices, and a fine building for the legislature. The streets are narrow, the houses seldom high, for here also earthquakes have to be considered. Everything looks new, as might be expected in a place which was small and poor till the end of the eighteenth century, and which has grown rapidly within the last sixty years with the prosperity of the country. Prosperity and confidence are in the air. Great, indeed, is the contrast between old-fashioned Lima and still more ancient Cuzco, or between La Paz, nestling in its *Barranca* under the mountains like an owl in the desert, and this brisk, eager, active, modern city, where crowded electric cars pass along crowded streets and men hurry to their business or their politics even as they do in western Europe or North America.

Santiago is a real capital, the heart of a real nation, the place in which all the political energy of the nation is focussed, commercial energy being shared with Valparaiso. Here are no loitering negroes, nor impassive Indians, for the population is all Chilean, though close inspection discovers a difference between the purer and the less pure European stock. A great deal of native blood flows in the veins of the Chilean *roto*.

There is little of historical or archæological interest in Santiago, no skeleton of its founder (as of Pizarro in Lima), for Pedro de Valdivia was taken prisoner and killed by the Araucanian Indians hundreds of miles away; no palace of the Inquisition, for Santiago was in the seventeenth century too small a place to need the elaborate machinery of the Holy Office for the protection of its orthodoxy. Till the War of Independence it was a remote provincial town. But Nature has given it one spot to which historical associations can attach. When Valdivia, one of the ablest and boldest of the lieutenants of Pizarro, was sent down hither to complete the conquest of that southernmost part of the Inca dominion from which Almagro had returned disappointed in the quest for gold, his soldierly eye lit upon and marked a steep rock that rose out of the plain on the banks of a torrent descending from the Andes. On this rock he planted (in 1541) a rude fort and, after receiving the submission of the neighbouring Indians, marched on still further south, into regions which the Incas had never conquered. After some successes, a sudden rising of the natives chased him back and he had to take refuge in the fort upon this rock, now called Santa Lucia. Besieged for many weeks and reduced to the utmost extremity of famine, he held out here with that desperate tenacity of which the men of Spain have given so many examples from the days of Saguntum to those of Cortes at Mexico and from those of Cortes to those of Palafox at Saragossa. The Indians had, however, no notion of how to conduct siege operations and at last Valdivia was relieved. The fort remained, and beneath it there grew up in course of time the city.

The ancient Acropolis or Hill Fortress is a familiar sight in India, in Greece, and Italy, and in western Europe also. Gwalior and Trichinopoly, Acrocorinthus and Taormina, and in England, Old Sarum, Durham, Exeter, Shrewsbury, London itself, are instances, and the Fortress has often as in the last four cases, been the germ of a city. But so far as I know Santa Lucia, below which Santiago has grown up, is the only conspicuous instance in the two Americas of any such stronghold built by Europeans. The hill, a little over two hundred feet high, is much lower than are the Castle Hills of Edinburgh and Stirling, and the space on it smaller. It is lower even than the Castle Rock of Dumbarton, which it more resembles. Like those three, it is a mass of hard igneous rock, so irregular in form as to suggest that it may be a detached fragment of an old lava flow, and most of its sides are so precipitous as to be easily defensible. The buildings which had defaced it having been nearly all removed, it is now laid out as a pleasure ground, and planted with trees. Walks have been made round it, with a footpath to the craggy summit, and there is a statue of Pedro de Valdivia, the only monument to any one of the Conquistadores which I can remember to have seen in Spanish America, for the men of that famous group are not much honoured by their colonial descendants. Every evening we walked to the top to enjoy the wonderful view over the valley, and the last rays of the sun reddening the Andean snows. A still more extended view is obtained from the summit, surmounted by a colossal statue of the Virgin, of the hill of San Cristobal, whose base is half a mile from the town.

Chile, like the rest of South America, is a country of large estates, the early conquerors having received grants of land, many of which have not since been broken up into smaller properties; so there exists a landed aristocracy something like that of England in the eighteenth century, with peasants cultivating the soil as tenants or labourers, while the small middle class consists of shopkeepers or skilled artisans in the towns. The leading landowners spend the summers in their country houses and the winter and spring in Santiago, which has thus a pleasant society, with plenty of talent and talk among the men, of gaiety and talk among the women, a society more enlightened and abreast of the modern world than are those of the more northern republics, and with a more stimulating atmosphere. Santiago has always been the centre and heart of Chile both politically and socially and has in this way con- tributed to give unity to the nation and to create a

Chilean type of character. The jealousy felt by the country folk against the capital which has been the source of so much strife in other states was generally less marked here. Santiago leads ; Santiago's influence forbids any attempts at federalizing the republic. Though learning and science have not quite kept pace with conquest and prosperity, there is a thriving university, and a fine museum, placed beside the zoological and botanical gardens. The last and the present generation have produced some gifted writers and among the too few students of to-day is one of the most accomplished historians and bibliographers in Spanish America, Señor José Toribio Medina. The bent of Chilean genius has, however, been on the whole towards war and politics. The material development of the country by railways, the opening of mines and the extension of agriculture, important as these are, do not absorb men's thoughts here so much as they do in Argentina and indeed in most new countries. Politics hold the field just as politics held it all through the nineteenth century in England and in Hungary, perhaps the most intensely political countries of the Old World.[1]

The mention of these two countries suggests another point of resemblance. The Chileans, a race of riders, are extremely fond of horse-racing. The races at Santiago rouse immense interest and are the occasion of a great deal of betting, not only in the city, but also at Valparaiso, for such of the Valparaiso sportsmen as cannot come to the capital gather in their clubhouse

[1] It is sometimes said that one hundred families rule Chile.

and carry on their betting during the progress of each race, every detail of which is reported from moment to moment by telephone, the bets coming as thick and fast as if the horses were in sight upon the course.

Chile is the only country in South America which can boast to have had no revolution within the memory of any living man. In 1890 there was a civil war, but that conflict differed materially from the familiar military revolutions of the other republics. President Balmaceda had quarrelled with the legislature, claiming that he could levy taxes without its consent, and was overcome, after a fierce struggle, the navy supporting the Congress, and the command of the sea proving decisive in a country with so long a coast line. So scrupulously regardful were the Chileans of their financial credit, that both Balmaceda and his congressional antagonists, each claiming to be the lawful government, tendered to the foreign bondholders payment of the interest on the same public debt while the struggle was going on.

There were, at the time of my visit, five political parties or divisions of the Liberal party, besides the Conservatives. The President had died suddenly while travelling in Europe, and the Liberal sections, holding the majority in Congress, met to select the candidate whom they should put forward as his successor. The discussions and the votings in their gatherings went on for several weeks, but force was never threatened; and the Chileans told their visitors with justifiable pride that although twelve thousand soldiers were in or near the capital, no party feared that any other would endeavour to call in the help of the army. Chile is also the only South American state which takes so enlightened an interest in its electoral machinery as to have devised and applied a good while ago a system of proportional representation which seems to give satisfaction, and certainly deserves the study of scientific students in other countries. I saw an election proceeding under it in Santiago. The result was foreknown, because there had been an arrangement between Liberal sections which ensured the victory of the candidates they had agreed upon, so there was little excitement. Everything seemed to work smoothly.

What I had seen of the aspects of nature round Santiago increased the desire to know something of southern Chile, a region little visited by travellers, but reported to be full of those beauties which make the scenery of temperate regions more attractive, at least to persons born in the temperate zone, than all the grandeurs of the tropics. Accordingly we set off for the south, the Chilean government having kindly provided special facilities along their railways.[1] All the lines, except that which crosses the Andes into Argentina, are the property of the state. From Santiago to the strait which separates the large island of Chiloe from the mainland, a distance of 650 miles, there stretches that long depression mentioned at the beginning of this chapter, the northern part of which contains nearly all of the population as

[1] A distinguished Chilean officer whose presence added greatly to the pleasure of the trip was detailed to accompany us.

well as most of the cultivable area of the republic. The
railway that traverses it from end to end is the main
highway of the country sending off branches which run
westward to the towns that lie on or near the coast, and
as it keeps generally in the middle of the valley, one
gets admirable views toward the Andes on one side and
the Coast Range on the other.

Travelling south, one observes four changes in physical
conditions. The rainfall steadily increases. At Santiago
it is only about fifteen inches in the year; at Valdivia,
440 miles to the south, it is seven times as great. With
this abundant rainfall, the streams are fuller, the
landscape greener, the grass richer, the trees taller.
The mountains sink in height, and not the Andes only,
but the average height of the Coast Range also. The
snow line also sinks. Near Santiago it is about 14,000
feet above sea-level ; at Valdivia it is rather under 6000.
These four things completely alter the character of the
scenery. It is less grand, for one sees no such mighty
peaks and wide snowfields as rise over Santiago, but
it is more approachable, with a softer air and more
profuse vegetation. As compared with the desert
regions of northern Chile, the difference is as great
as that between the verdure of Ireland and the sterility
of the Sahara.

From Santiago to Osorno, the southern limit of our
journey, there was beauty everywhere, beauty in the
fields and meadows which the railway traverses, beauty
in the wild *quebradas* (narrow glens) that descend from
the Andes, beauty in the glimpses of the snow mountains

where a break in the nearer hills reveals them. But I must be content to speak of a few points only.

The long depression between the Andes and the Coast Range, which forms the best part of Chile, is crossed by a series of large and rapid rivers descending from the Andean snows and forcing their way through the clefts in the Coast Range to the sea. The first of these is the Maule, which was the southernmost limit of the conquests of the Inca monarchs. Next to it, as one goes south, is the still larger Biobio, on whose banks the Spaniards strove for nearly a century with the fierce Araucanian tribes, till at last, despairing of success, they desisted and allowed it to be the boundary of their power. It is the greatest of all Chilean streams, with a broad and strong current, but is too shallow for navigation, and the commercial city of Concepcion, which lies a little above its mouth, uses the harbour of Talcahuano as its port.

Here, one is already in a well-watered land, but before I describe the scenery of this delightful region something may be said of the coast towns, which are quite unlike those of northern Chile and Peru. Concepcion, founded by Valdivia to bridle the Indians, is an attractive little city, with a large plaza and wide streets, which are tidy and well kept. Indeed, as compared with those of Spain and Italy, the larger cities of South America are as superior in cleanliness as they are inferior in architectural interest. Cuzco stands almost alone in its offensiveness to sight and smell. The cheerful airiness and brightness of the place are enhanced by the beauty of the wide river on whose north side it

Q

stands, and along whose shores, backed by wooded hills, there are many pretty villas with gardens, most of them the property of the British and German colonies who live here in social good will and active business competition. The former have laid out an excellent golf course a few miles away towards the Ocean and have infected some Chileans with their passion for the Scottish game. Though not now so large as Valparaiso, the city has played a more important part in Chilean history, for it was the military capital of the southern frontier on the side of Araucania and the centre of the energetic and fighting population of that region. The leading families formed the only aristocratic group that was capable of resisting, as, after independence had been achieved, they did occasionally resist, the larger aristocratic group of Santiago. There was not enough wealth in those days to build stately churches or mansions, but the place has a look of dignity and is more Chilean and less cosmopolitan than Valparaiso.

Talcahuano, possessing the finest natural harbour in central Chile, has been made the principal naval stronghold of this country which sets store upon the strength of its navy, deemed essential to protect its immensely long coast line. An enemy possessing a more powerful fleet would, it is thought, have Chile at its mercy until the longitudinal railway is completed which is to run the whole length of the country parallel to the coast. A naval harbour has been formed and docks built and batteries erected to command the approaches. From the heights one sees across the ample bay the site of an old Spanish town, abandoned because exposed to the English and Dutch sea-rovers of the sixteenth and seventeenth centuries. Since this time no hostile European vessels[1] have appeared in these waters, though they have seen plenty of sea-fights in the days of the Revolution and in those of the great war between Chile and Peru, and again in the civil war between Balmaceda and the Congress.

Two other places on the Chilean coast are worth mentioning. From Concepcion a railroad, crossing the Biobio by a bridge three-quarters of a mile long, runs southward to the ports of Coronel and Lota. The shore, sometimes rocky, sometimes bordered by thickets or grassy flats behind sand beaches, is extremely picturesque ; and were it in the populous parts of Europe or North America, it would be lined by summer cottages and alive with children. But its vegetation and general aspect are curiously unlike those of the Atlantic coasts of either of those two continents, and remind one rather of California. At Lota, the hills rise boldly from the sea and a large island lying some way out gives variety to the ocean view. Here, on an eminence behind the town, is a garden of singular interest and beauty which I had especially wished to see because it had excited the admiration of my friend, the late Mr. John Ball, the distinguished botanist and traveller, who has described it in his *Notes of a Naturalist in South America,* published in 1887. It occupies the top of a

---

[1] Except when Spanish ships of war bombarded Valparaiso in 1866.

hill which breaks down almost precipitously to the shore, and was formed by a wealthy Chilean, the owner of a coal mine and copper smelting works close by, who built a handsome villa, and assisted by an energetic Irish gardener, laid out a park with admirable taste, gathering and planting a great variety of trees and shrubs and so disposing the walks as to give delightful views along the coast and out into the ocean. There are few things in the course of journeys which one recalls with more pleasure than parks and gardens which combine opportunities for studying the flora of a new country with the enjoyment of natural beauty. This place had the peculiar interest of showing how, in a mild and humid climate, trees and shrubs from sub-tropical regions may flourish side by side with those of the temperate zone. Its profuse variety of trees, many of them seen by us for the first time, lives in my recollection with the gardens of the Scilly Isles and those on Valentia Island on the coast of Kerry, and the famous park at Cintra (near Lisbon), the two former of these possessing similarly favourable climatic conditions. The landscape at Lota is more beautiful than at any of those spots, and though it is marred by the smoke of the smelting works placed here to take advantage of the coal mine, one must remember that without the coal mine and the smelting works their owner would not have had the money to expend on the park and gardens.

About two hundred miles to the south of Concepcion a large river finds its way to the sea through a comparatively wide and open valley and meets the tide of the ocean at a point where Valdivia, the lieutenant of Pizarro, whom I have already mentioned as the first Spaniard to penetrate into these wild regions, built a small fort and called it by his own name. His fort was thenceforth the chief and sometimes the only seat of Spanish power in this whole stretch of country, constantly besieged and reduced to dire extremity by the warlike Indians, but almost always saved because it was accessible by sea from the ports of Peru. No trace now remains of the ancient stronghold, nor, indeed, are there any old houses, for in this well-wooded part of Chile houses are built of timber and fires are proportionately numerous and destructive. A terrible one had swept away half the town in 1909. They were busy rebuilding and improving it, for the country all round is being brought into cultivation, and trade is brisk. The phenomena remind one of western North America, though the pace at which population grows and natural resources are developed is far slower. There is a German colony, of course with a large brewery, the chief manufacturing industry of the spot, and a somewhat smaller British mercantile colony. The town stretches along both banks of the broad stream, on which light steamers ply to the seaport of Corral, some twelve miles below. Here, also, the resources of the land are being exploited. A French company has erected large works for the smelting of copper, which is brought by sea from the ports of northern Chile. All the most recent metallurgical appliances have been introduced, and a considerable population has been drawn to the

place. It is, however, an indigenous population.
That inrush of immigrants from Europe, which is the
conspicuous feature in North America, wherever railways or other large works are being executed, or new
industries set up, is here wanting. It has not yet been
worth while to tempt Italian or Slavonic labour from
Europe. Here at Corral, one touches an interesting
bit of history. There are on both sides of the port
ancient forts which command not only the harbour
and the passage out to sea, but lovely views over the
smiling land and wooded mountains. In their present
form they seem to date from the late seventeenth
or early eighteenth century. They stand now as
mouldering and grass-grown monuments of a vanished
empire. Erected to protect the colonists from British
and Dutch attacks, they succumbed long afterwards
to a later British adventurer leading those colonists
themselves against the power of Spain. Less than a
century ago (in 1817) they saw one of the most brilliant
achievements of Lord Cochrane, then fighting for the
Chilean revolutionaries, when with the crews of his
few ships he stormed these forts, chasing the Spaniards
away to Valdivia and received next day the surrender
of that town, their last stronghold on the Chilean mainland. The services of this Scotchman are gratefully
remembered here along with those of two men of Irish
stock, O'Higgins and Lynch. All three have won a
fame not unlike that of Lafayette and Rochambeau in
the United States.

In these seaports we saw the commercial side of

Chilean town life, a side in which the foreigner plays **a** considerable part, whether he manages metal works for European capitalists or represents some great English or German trading firm.   Temuco, situated in a purely agricultural district, supplying its wants and serving as a market for its produce, is of a different type and gave one a notion of what corresponds in Chile to the smaller country town of England or North America. It is a new place, for this region was almost purely Indian till thirty years ago, covers a great deal of ground, and reminds one more of an Hungarian or Russian town than of the North American West, for the wide and generally unpaved streets were not planted with trees and the one story houses were mostly thatched.   The air was soft and humid, rich green meadows stretched out on every side and though there were evident signs of growth and comfort, nobody was in a hurry.   The country is lovely.   To the west are picturesque wooded hills, outliers of the Coast Range, and on the east, there opens a view of the Andes twenty or thirty miles distant, their snow-peaks rising behind a mass of dark green forest.   We were entertained to dinner by the officers of the regiment quartered here, the commandant, who was also governor of the district, presiding, and met a large and agreeable company composed of the officers and their wives, a few officials, and some of the chief business men.   Here, as everywhere in Chile, educated society is more modern and less ecclesiastical in sentiment than what the traveller finds in the more northerly republics. In listening to the graceful and well-phrased speech in which the commandant toasted the guests, we had fresh occasion to admire the resources of the Castilian tongue, which like the Italian, perhaps even more than the Italian, seems to lend itself more naturally than English or German to oratory of an ornamental kind.

While in Peru and Bolivia the great mass of the aboriginal population remained distinct from their Spanish masters, in Chile the fusion began early and went steadily on until, except in one district, the two races were blended. A certain number of families, including most of the aristocracy, have remained pure white; but many more intermarried with the natives, and the peasants of to-day belong to this mixed race. As elsewhere in Spanish America, the man of mixed blood deems himself white, and does so the more easily here, because over most of the country there are no longer any pure Indians. The aborigines of this region were less advanced in the arts of life than those of Peru, but they were better fighters and of a bolder spirit. They have made a good blend with the whites; the Chilean *roto* is a hardy and vigorous man.[1]

The one district in which a pure Indian race has remained is that in which Temuco stands, for this is the land of those Araucanian Indians to whom I have already referred, a race deservedly famous as the only aboriginal people of the Western hemisphere that suc-

---

[1] The word *roto* seems originally to have been a term of disparagement; it meant 'a broken man.' Now it merely denotes one of the poorer class, and is opposed to *pelucon*, one of the upper class (literally a wig wearer).

cessfully resisted the European intruders.[1] I had imagined this people dwelling in the recesses of forest-covered mountains, and themselves tall and stalwart men like the Patagonian giants whom Magellan encountered on the other side of the Andes. But the Mapoche[2]—that is the name by which the Araucanians call themselves — are, in fact, short men, though sturdy and muscular, with broad faces, not unlike some East Asiatic types. Their country is part of that long and wide depression which constitutes the Central Valley of Chile, a fertile land which, though doubtless once more thickly wooded than it now is, was probably, even in the days of Valdivia's invasion, partly open savannah. There is, and apparently there always has been, so little game that the natives must have lived chiefly by tillage, for they had, of course, neither sheep nor cattle. Although less civilized than were the tribes dwelling north of them, who had received some of the material culture of the Inca empire, they had risen above the savage state, and were at least as far advanced as were the Algonquins or Dakotas of North America. They had organized a sort of fighting confederacy of four tribes, resembling the "Long House" of the Iroquois Five Nations. Each tribe had its leading family in which the chieftainship was hereditary, but if the eldest son were not equal to the place, a sec-

[1] The Yaquis of Sonora in Northwestern Mexico have never been subdued, but they are a small tribe dwelling in mountain fastnesses difficult of access.

[2] This is the form of the name that was given to me at Temuco. Others call them Moluche or Maluche.

ond or other son might be selected by the tribe in his stead. For war, they chose leaders of special bravery or talent, as Tacitus tells us that the Germans of his time did. Their weapons were the lance, probably a sort of assegai, and the axe or tomahawk of stone, and a club of wood, sometimes with a stone head fastened to it. When Valdivia, having overcome the more northerly tribes, and having strengthened his force by contingents from them, crossed the Biobio into the Araucanian country, the chiefs of the confederacy summoned a general assembly of all the fighting men — a sort of Homeric *agora* — and after three days' debate, resolved on resistance. In the first encounters they suffered terribly from the firearms and the horses of the Spaniards. Valdivia defeated them and marched through their country as far as the place where he built (as already mentioned) the town which still bears his name. After a few years, he returned with a stronger force hoping to complete his conquest. A hundred miles south of the Biobio the Araucanians attacked him. Their furious charge could not be stopped by musketry — gunshot range was very short in those days — the invading force was destroyed, and Valdivia, flying from the field, was captured. While he was attempting to save his life by a promise to withdraw altogether from Chile, an old chief smote him down with a club.

From this time on the warfare lasted with occasional intermissions for more than sixty years. The Araucanians discovered by degrees tactics fitted to reduce the advantages which firearms gave to the Spaniards. They obtained horses, and, like the Comanches in Arizona and the Basutos of South Africa, learnt to use them in war. They produced leaders like Lautaro and Caupolican of talents equal to their bravery. When they found themselves unable to stem a Spanish invasion they retired into their woods, and as soon as the enemy had retired, they fell upon the forts and raided across the border. Weary of this incessant and apparently hopeless strife, the Spaniards at last agreed to a treaty by which the Biobio was fixed as the boundary. During his daring cruise in the Pacific in 1578 Sir Francis Drake had occasion to land on the Chilean coast. The Araucanians, seeing white men come in a ship, assumed them to be Spaniards, and attacked them. Had they realized that Drake's crew, being the enemies of their own enemies, would gladly have been their friends, an alliance profitable to both parties could have been struck, and it might have been serviceable to Drake's English and Dutch successors. Fearing such a contingency, the Spaniards made it a part of their treaty with the Araucanians that they should give no help to the maritime foes of Spain. Fresh wars from time to time broke out, but they always ended in the same way, so Araucania continued independent down till, and long after, the revolt of Chile from Spain.

By the middle of the nineteenth century the nation had begun to lose its old fighting habits. Diseases contracted from the whites had reduced its numbers and sapped its strength, while peaceful intercourse with the colonists had mitigated the ancient animosity. Accordingly, when Chile, about 1881, asserted her authority, and the town of Temuco was founded in the middle of the Araucanian country, the idea of resistance which some of the chiefs entertained was dropped on the advice of others who saw that it would be hopeless under conditions so different from those of the seventeenth century. Thus it may still be said of this gallant race that though they have consented to become Chileans, they remain the one unconquered native people of the continent. Though there has not been much intermarriage between them and the Spanish colonists, the long conflict had a marked effect upon the character of the latter, giving to the Chileans a rude force and aptitude for war not unlike that which the constant strife with the Moors gave to the Spaniards in the Middle Ages. The earlier part of the conflict had the rare honour of being made the theme of an epic poem which ranks high among those of modern Europe, the *Araucana*[1] of Alonzo de Ercilla, who himself fought against Caupolican. No ill feeling seems to exist now between the Mapoche and the Chileans. Educated men among the latter feel a certain pride, as do the Araucanians themselves, in their romantic history, each race remembering that its ancestors fought well.

How large the Mapoche nation was when the Spaniards first came is quite uncertain. The estimate of 400,000 seems excessive for a people who had no cattle, and did not till the soil on a large scale. Even now

[1] First part written in Chile, where he was fighting, in 1558, and published in 1569.

while some put the present population as high as 140,-000, others put it as low as 50,000. There is, unfortunately, no doubt that they are diminishing through diseases, especially tubercular diseases, which have spread among them from the whites, and are now transmitted from parents to offspring. Laws have been passed for their benefit, and a functionary entitled the Protector of the Indians appointed, but some of these laws, such as those restricting the sale of intoxicating liquors, are enforced quite as imperfectly as they are in other countries better known to us. The tribal system has almost vanished, but the local communities into which the people are now grouped respect the heads of the old families and often regret the days when a simple and speedy justice was administered by the chieftains.

Scattered over a wide area they dwell in villages of grass huts or frame houses, the latter far less favourable to health, and live by tillage or stock keeping, though a few go north to seek work and are deemed excellent labourers. The custom observed by the Kafir chiefs in South Africa, of allotting a separate hut to each wife, does not seem to hold here, but as the huts are large, each wife, if there are several, is allowed her own hearth and fire. Some families have considerable estates; some own large herds of cattle and sheep which at certain seasons are driven across the Andean passes to the pastures of Argentina.

While the wars lasted there was, of course, no question of converting the Araucanians to Christianity; and though in the intervals of peace friars sometimes went among them, they remained practically heathen till the establishment of Chilean authority in 1882. Their religion is a form of that spirit worship which one finds among nearly all primitive peoples. Its rites are intended to avert the displeasure of the spirits, to obtain from them fine weather or rain (as the case may be), and to expel a noxious demon from the body. The priesthood — if the name can be used — is not hereditary and is confined to females. The women who discharge the functions of wizards or medicine men are selected when young by the elder sorceresses and initiated with elaborate rites. A tree of a particularly sacred kind is chosen and a sort of ladder of steps cut in it, which the sorceress mounts to perform the ceremonies. When the tree dies, its trunk continues to be revered and is dressed up with fresh green boughs for ceremonial occasions. I could not find that any other natural objects, besides trees, receive veneration, nor is there anything to shew that the Inca worship of the sun and the host of heaven had ever spread so far to the south. The old beliefs and usages are now fast waning. Many Mapoche have become Christians, a considerable number Protestants, converted by the English South American mission, others Roman Catholics. They are described as a people of good intelligence, and easy to deal with when they are treated with justice, a valuable element in the population, and one which Chilean statesmen may well seek to preserve, if drink could be kept from them and the germs of hereditary disease rooted out.

The occupation by the Araucanians of a considerable part of the central Chilean valley accounts for the fact that the population of the region beyond them to the south has grown but slowly. It now contains no Indian tribes till one gets across the channel of Ancud to Chiloe and the other islands along the coast. Few settlers came to these parts from Europe until about the middle of last century the Chilean government encouraged an immigration from Germany which continued, on a moderate scale, for a good many years, but thereafter stopped altogether. Going southward from Valdivia one finds both in small towns and in rural districts round them a good many solid German farmers and artizans and tidy little German Fraus who might have come straight out of the Odenwald. We spent a night in Osorno, our furthest point toward the south, a neat and prosperous looking town, and dined with one of the leading German citizens, a man of wide reading, and especially devoted to Robert Burns, whose poems he recited to us, and to Thomas Moore, some of whose songs he had translated into German. Thereafter a group of the German residents hospitably took us to their club, where they have a concert hall and just such a Kegelbahn (skittle alley) as that in which I remember that we students used to play at Heidelberg in 1863, about the time when the parents of these worthy Germans were migrating to Chile. They gave us champagne, the unfailing accompaniment of every social function in South America; but it ought to have been Bavarian beer. This is the only part of western South America to which any considerable mass of settlers have come from Europe, for most of the English, Germans, French, and Spaniards one meets in the commercial and mining centres are passing business visitors. On the other side of the Andes it is different, for there the Italian immigration has been and still is very large.

Comparatively few immigrants enter Chile now, which would imply that the quantity of land available for agriculture, but not yet taken up, is supposed to be not very large. To me the country we traversed appeared to be far from fully occupied, though on such a matter the impressions of a passing traveller are of little value. Of all the parts of the New World I have seen there is none which struck me as fitter to attract a young man who loves country life, is not in a hurry to be rich, and can make himself at home in a land where English is not the language of the people. The soil of southern Chile is extremely fertile, fit both for stock-raising and for tillage. The climate is healthy and mild, without extremes either of heat or cold. Wet it certainly is, but not wetter than parts of our own western coasts.

The summer sun is strong yet not oppressive, the air both soft and invigorating, for Ocean sends up shrill blowing western breezes to refresh mankind.[1] There are no noxious beasts, no mosquitoes, no poisonous snakes, nor other venomous creatures, except a spider found in the cornfields whose bite, though disagreeable, is not dangerous. Intermittent fevers, the curse of most countries where new land is being brought under

---

[1] Ἀλλ' ἀεὶ Ζεφύροιο λιγυπνείοντας ἀήτας
Ὠκεανὸς ἀνίησιν ἀναψύχειν ἀνθρώπους.

— *Odyss.* IV.

cultivation, seem to be unknown. There are deer in the woods, and plenty of fish in the clear, rapid rivers. The Englishman who loves hunting will not want for foxes; the North American golfer will find grassy flats by the sea, waiting to be laid out as links. Remote, secluded, and tranquil as the country is, the settler should have little difficulty in procuring whatever Europe supplies, for even at Osorno he is only forty hours from Santiago, and Santiago is now only two days from Buenos Aires, and Buenos Aires only seventeen days from Europe.

Perhaps it is the charm of the Chilean scenery that prompts a view of the country, considered as a home for the emigrant, more favourable than might be taken by one to whom life would be just as enjoyable in the boundless levels of Manitoba as within view of a snowy range. Perhaps, also, this charm of southern Chile with its soft, green pastures and shaggy woods and flashing streams was enhanced to us by contrast with the dreary deserts of Peru and Bolivia, through which we had lately passed. Whoever has in his boyhood learnt to love the scenery of a temperate country never finds full satisfaction in that of the tropics, with all their glow of light and all their exuberance of vegetation. Such lands are splendid to visit, but not so good to live in, for exertion is less agreeable, the woods are impenetrable, and the mountains, therefore, less accessible, and the constant heat is enervating, not to add that insects are everywhere, and in many places one has to stand always on guard against fevers. Nothing could

R

be grander than the landscapes in the Andes which we had seen, nor more beautiful than the landscapes in Brazil which we were shortly to see. But of all the parts of South America that we visited, southern Chile stands out to me as the land where one would choose to make a home.

Two excursions, one to the sea, the other into the hills, gave us samples of two different kinds of scenery. Of the many brimming rivers that sweep down from the Andes across the Central Valley none is more beautiful in its lower course than is the Rio Bueno. It has in the course of ages cloven for itself through the hard rocks of the Coast Range a channel so deep that the tide comes up to the little town of Trumajo forty miles from the sea, and from that town small steamers can pass all the way to the bar at its mouth. In one of these little craft which a kind friend had procured we spent a long day in sailing down and back again. The hills on each side, sometimes hanging steeply over the stream, sometimes receding where a narrow glen opened, were clothed with the richest wood. It was a brilliant day in October, answering to our April, and the sun brought out an infinite variety of shades of green in the young foliage in these glens, the trees all new to us, and the spaces between them filled with climbing plants hanging in festoons from the boughs. Wild ducks and other water-birds fluttered over the water and rose in flocks as the little vessel moved onward, and green paroquets called from the thickets. As it nears the sea, the river spreads into a wide deep

pool under a crescent of bold cliffs, and at the end of
this is seen the bar, a stretch of sand on which the huge
rollers of the Pacific break in foam.   There is a lighthouse and a few houses near a flat stretch of meadow
by the banks, the grass as green and the flowers as abundant as in Ireland.   Specially vivid were the yellow
masses of gorse, apparently the same species as our
own, and, if possible, even more profuse in its blossoms
than on those Cornish shores of which it is the chief ornament.   I have seen few bits of coast more picturesque
than this meeting of the still, dark river and the flashing
spray of ocean under rocks clothed with feathery woods.

On our way back something went wrong with the
machinery and the vessel had more than once to moor
herself to the bank till things were set right.   This
gave opportunities for going ashore and exploring the
banks.   In some places the forest was too dense to
penetrate without a *machete* to hew a way through
the shrubs and climbers.   In other places where one
could creep under the trees or pull one's self up the cliffs
by the boughs, the effort was rewarded by finding an
endless variety of new flowers and ferns.   The latter
are in this damp atmosphere especially luxuriant; and
their tall fronds, dipping into the river, were often seven
or eight feet long.   It was a primeval forest, wild as it
had been from the beginning of things; for only in two
or three places had dwellings been planted on level
spots by the river and little clearings made; and the
hills are so high and rocky that it may remain un-
touched and lonely for many a year to come.

The other excursion was towards the Andes. There is along the railway no prettier spot than Collilelfu, where a rapid river, broad and bright like the Scottish Tay, but with clearer and greener water, sweeps down out of the foothills into the meadows of the Central Valley. Here a French company have constructed a little branch railway, partly to bring down timber, partly in the hope of continuing their line far up the valley and across a pass into Argentina, in order to carry cattle to and fro. The manager, a courteous Frenchman from the Basque land of Bearn, ran us up this line through a succession of lovely views along the river to a point where we got horses and rode for seven or eight miles further through the forest up and down low ridges to the shore of Lake Riñihue. The forest was in parts too thick to penetrate without cutting one's way through creeping and climbing plants, but in others it was open enough to give mysterious vistas between the tall stems, and delicious effects where the sunlight fell upon a glade. The trees were largely evergreen, but few or none of them coniferous, for in Chile it is only at higher levels that the characteristic conifers, such as the well-known *Araucaria*, flourish. Here at last we found that characteristic South American arboreal flora we had been looking forward to, a forest where all that we saw was new, unlike the woods of western North America and of Europe, not only because the variety of the trees was far greater than it is there, but also because so many bore brilliant flowers upon their higher boughs, where the sunlight reached them. We were told that in midsummer the flowers would be still more profuse, but those we saw were abundant and beautiful enough, some white, some crimson or scarlet, some yellow, very few blue. One climber lit up the shade with its red blossoms, and below there were long rows, standing up along the path, wherever it was fairly open to the light, of white and pink foxgloves, a species closely resembling our own, while a woody ragwort, eight to ten feet high, bore a spreading umbel of yellow. The *Calceolarias*, frequent in Peru, do not seem to come so far south as this. Most of the trees had small leaves, but two, one called the *lengue*, valued for its bark, and another resembling a laurel, had large, dark green, glossy foliage. It was a silent wood, except for the paroquets and the occasional coo of a wood-pigeon; nor did we see any four-footed creatures, except two large, reddish brown foxes scurrying across the path ahead of us. Wildcats are scarce, and the puma, the beast of prey that has the widest range over the Western Hemisphere, is here hardly ever seen. The woodscape was less grand and solemn than what one sees in the great redwood forests of California or in the sombre depths of those that cover the Cascade Range in Oregon and Washington, where the Douglas fir and the huge " cedar "[1] tower so high over the trails that one can scarce catch the light through their topmost branches. Nor can I say that the views were more beautiful than may still be had in the few remaining ancient forests of England with their ancestral oaks and spreading beeches. But there was

[1] *Thuja gigantea.*

here a peculiar feature, giving a sense of the exuberant vitality of nature, in the profusion of parasitic plants clothing the trunks of the trees, both the fallen and the living, some of them flowering plants, but more of them ferns and mosses, especially tender little filmy ferns such as one finds on the moist and shady rocks of western Scotland and among the mountains of Killarney.

We embarked on Lake Rinihue in a tiny steamboat, and sailed some miles over its exquisitely clear, green waters. Steep hills from two to three thousand feet high enclose it, and at its upper end, where it winds in towards the central range of the Andes, small glaciers descend from between high snowpeaks. The view, looking across the deep green of the forests, broken here and there by a rocky cliff, up to these glittering pinnacles, had a beauty not only of color and form, but of mystery also, — that indefinable sense of mystery which belongs to little-known countries. In regions like Scotland or the Alps or Norway one has historical associations and the sense of a long human past to enhance the loveliness of hills and groves and streams. Here one has the compensating charm of an untouched and almost unexplored nature. The traveller in southern Chile feels as if he were a discoverer, so little visited is this land, and such a promise of wild beauty waiting to be revealed lies in the recesses of these mountains. Along the shores of Rinihue, which is twelve miles long, there is, save for a house or two at the place where we embarked, no trace of human life. Other such lakes, many of them much larger, lie scattered over a space some four hundred miles long and fifty miles wide on both the Argentine and the Chilean side of the Cordillera, a land of forests virtually unexplored and uninhabited, except by a few wandering Indians, standing now as it has stood ever since the Andes were raised. The day will come, perhaps less than a century hence, when the townsfolk of a then populous Argentina, weary of the flat monotony of their boundless Pampas, will find in this wilderness of lake and river and mountain such a place, wherein to find rest and recreation in the summer heats, as the North Americans of the Eastern states do in the Appalachian hills; and the North Americans of the West, in the glorious ranges along the Pacific coast. Superior to the former region in its possession of snow mountains, equal to the latter in climate and picturesque beauty, and to the naturalist more interesting than either from its still active volcanoes and its remarkable flora, this lake land of the southern Andes is an addition, the value of which the South Americans have hardly yet realized, to the scenic wealth of our planet.

CHAPTER VII

ACROSS THE ANDES

For more than two thousand miles the republics of Argentina and Chile are divided from one another by the gigantic barrier of the Andes. So great is the continuous elevation of the range, so little commercial intercourse can there be across it, so few are the points at which it can be crossed even on foot by any travellers who are not expert mountaineers, that the communications between those dwelling on opposite sides of the mountains have been at all times very scanty. The contrast between the two sides is marked. For eight hundred miles south of the Equator, the eastern slopes of the Andean chain have abundance of rain, while the central plateau is dry and the western declivity is a waterless desert. But in the region which lies south of the Tropic of Capricorn, outside the region of trade-winds, the exact reverse holds. In this southern section of the Andes it is the eastern side that is dry and the western side that is wet, because westerly winds prevail and bring up from the Pacific rain clouds that scatter their moisture on the heights they first meet and have none left to bestow on the Argentine side of the Cordillera. This great dividing range, checking intercourse between the peoples on its two flanks, is the dominant fact in the political and economic life as well as in the physical geography of the southern part of the continent. It has given these two neighbour peoples, Chileans and Argentines, different habits, different characters, and a different history.

The infrequency of communication across the mountains was increased by the fact that most of the country on the eastern side, being sterile, was thinly settled, so that there were few people who had any occasion to cross the mountains, while the approach to the passes was difficult, for there was little food or shelter to be had along this track. In the middle of the sixteenth century, however, Mendoza, Captain General of Chile, founded on the Argentine side the town which still bears his name. Placed at the foot of the mountains on the banks of a stream descending from the glaciers of Aconcagua, it was a well-watered spot in a thirsty land, and population slowly gathered to it. As Argentina began to fill up with settlers in the latter half of the nineteenth century and as railways began to be pushed farther and farther inland from the Atlantic coast, the notion of making a railway across the Andes began to dawn on enterprising minds, especially after the Brenner and Cenis lines had been constructed across and through the main chain of the Alps. At last an English company built a railroad up to this town of Mendoza, and nothing remained except to pierce the belt of mountain country. That, however, was no simple matter. The belt is indeed of no great width. The Cordillera, which in the latitude of Antofagasta is the western edge of a high plateau, has here narrowed itself down to a single very lofty ridge, the summits of which are from 18,000 to 23,000 feet in height. There are transverse lower ridges running at right angles to the main chain, both westward towards the Pacific and eastward to the Argentine plain, but as these ridges average only thirty-five miles in length on the latter and twenty-five on the former side, the whole distance from the low country on the eastern side to the low country on the western, does not exceed seventy miles, which is less than the width (between Luzern and Arona) of the much less lofty chain of the Alps at the point where the Gothard railway crosses it.

The central ridge of the Cordillera is, however, so continuously lofty and its slopes so steep as to be passable for beasts of burden at very few points and then only during the summer months. Among these points that which has for a long time, probably from days before the Spanish conquest, been most in use, is the Uspallata Pass, so called from a place about fifteen miles west of Mendoza on the mule track which runs from that town towards the mountains. As population increased, there was at last substituted for the mule track a road passable by vehicles. Finally, in 1887, a railroad began to be constructed up the long and winding river valley which leads from Mendoza to the main chain, while on the Chilean side, another railway was built up the shorter valley which rises to the western foot of the same ridge.

Thereafter, the work of construction stopped for a good while, passengers continuing to cross the ridge on foot or mule back, or in vehicles which painfully climbed the steep track that led over the top. At last a tunnel under this ridge was bored, and the whole line opened for traffic in 1909. The tunnel is only two and a half miles long, much shorter than those which penetrate the Alps at the Simplon, the Gothard and the Cenis. But its height above sea-level (12,000 feet) is much greater and the scenery along the line more striking. If any other trunk line of railroad in the world traverses a region so extraordinary, it has not yet been described. Till one is run from Kashmir to Kashgar, over or under the Karakoram Pass, this Andean line seems likely to "hold the record."

The description of the Uspallata route may begin from Valparaiso. From that port to the junction for Santiago at the station of Llai Llai the country is hilly, rather dry, with rolling pastures and meadows along the streams, and thickets of small trees or scrub on the slopes, — a country much like southern California, save that there are no oaks and no coniferous trees. Further on, the hills grow higher; there are rocks with patches of brilliant flowers, and occasional glimpses of the great range are caught up the openings of valleys. At a pretty place called Santa Rosa de los Andes, the Andean railway proper (Ferro Carril Transandino) begins, and we change into a car of narrower gauge.

This Transandine railroad, one of the few which does not belong to the Chilean government, is narrow gauge, and its construction involved difficulties unusual even in the case of mountain lines, not only because the grades were very steep, but also because the valleys leading up to the central ridge were, especially that on the Chilean side, extremely narrow. To have bored corkscrew or zigzag tunnels, like those on the Gothard railway in Switzerland, would have involved an ex· penditure altogether disproportionate to the returns to be expected from the traffic. It was therefore found necessary to adopt the cog-wheel system; and on those parts of the line where the grade is too steep for the ordinary locomotive a rack or cog-wheel apparatus is fixed between the rails, and the locomotive, fitted with a corresponding apparatus, climbs by its help. This reduces the speed of the train in ascending those steep parts, most of which are on the Chilean side, and una-voidably reduces also the freight-carrying capacity of the line. There is, therefore, not much heavy goods traffic passing over it.[1] But to passengers who wish to save time and escape a sea voyage the gain is enor-mous, for while the transit from Valparaiso to Buenos Aires through the Straits of Magellan takes eleven days, the land journey by this Transandine railway can be accomplished in forty hours. The regular working of the trains had been interrupted in the winter before our visit by heavy falls of snow, but the construction of snowsheds, which was in progress, has probably by this time overcome such difficulties.

Travellers sleep at Santa Rosa in order to start early

---

[1] Many cattle are exported from Argentine to Chile, but these can here, as in the passes of southern Chile, be driven over the top of the ridge, though many now go by rail.

in the morning by the tri-weekly train which in twelve hours crosses the mountains to Mendoza. From the hotel at the station, we looked straight up a long, narrow valley to tremendous peaks of black rock thirty miles away to the east. How they stood out against the bright morning sky behind them, a few white clouds hovering above! One felt at a glance that this is one of the great ranges of the world, just as one feels the great musician in the first few chords of a symphony.

Up this valley runs the railway past little farm-houses, surrounded by stiff poplars, which thrive well here, though the tree is not a native, but brought from Europe. Fields, irrigated from the rushing stream beneath, are green with young corn; weeping willows droop over the watercourses, vines trail along the fronts of the cottages, and the pastures are bright with spring flowers. A cart road runs parallel to the line, and here one sees better than in the cities the true Chilean *roto* (peasant of mixed Spanish and Indian blood), in his rough coat and cotton shirt, baggy trousers and high boots fitted with large spurs, his low-crowned, narrow-brimmed felt or straw hat, and on his shoulders the thick homespun poncho characteristic of South America. His horse is usually near him, for they are all riders, a sturdy little animal with many saddle-cloths and a heavy, high-peaked saddle and heavy bit.

After eight or ten miles the valley narrows, and at its bottom there is only the torrent with sometimes a few yards of grass on one or other bank. The rock walls begin to rise more steeply, and the trees give place to shrubs.   At a spot called the Soldier's Leap, the train runs on a shelf in the rock through a gorge over which the converging crags almost touch one another and shut out the light, the torrent roaring sixty feet below. One considerable stream, the Rio Blanco, descends from the south, but otherwise there are no side glens. Vast black precipices rise on the northern bank six or seven thousand feet above the river.   Slender streamlets, perhaps the children of unseen snows behind, fall slowly from ledge to ledge, some of them lost in mid-air when a gust of the west wind sweeps them along.

At last, vegetation having now disappeared, a great black ridge rises in front across the end of the valley and seems to bar further progress.   On its steep face, however, one can presently discover a sort of track, winding up it in zigzags.   This is the old mule path by which travellers used to climb slowly to the pass, itself still far behind.   The spot at its foot, where there are a few houses, is Juncal, the last place where the wayfarer halted to rest before he started for the for-midable passage of the mountains.   Here two glens open-ing from opposite sides meet at the foot of the great ridge.   The glen to the north is short, descending abruptly from a semicircle of savage black peaks, the hollows between them filled with snow and ice.   That to the south is long, narrow, and nearly level; it is a deep cleft which runs into the heart of the mountains as far as the west side of the mighty Tupungato, whose glaciers feed its torrent.   Up this southern valley the railway, turning at right angles from its previous easterly direction, runs for some miles, then crosses and leaves the torrent, turns north and mounts along a narrow shelf cut out in the side of the great black ridge of Juncal, already mentioned. The slope rising above the line and falling below it to the valley is of terrific steepness. The grade is also steep and the locomotive toils and pants slowly upward by the aid of the cog-wheel, passing through tunnel after tunnel till at last it comes out, two thousand feet above Juncal, into a wide hollow surrounded by sharp peaks, those to the north streaked with beds of snow, those on the south of bare rock, because the snow has been melted off their sunward turned slopes. The bottom of this hollow is covered with enormous blocks that have fallen from the cliffs, and its northern end is filled by a small lake, part of whose surface was covered with ice. The fanciful name of Lago del Inca has been given to it. A scene more savage in its black desolation it would be hard to imagine. Compared to this frozen lake, the glacier lakes of the Swiss Alps, like the Märjelen See on the Aletsch glacier, are gentle and smiling. The strong sunlight and brilliant blue of the sky seemed to make the rocks blacker and bring out their absolute bareness with not so much as a moss or a lichen to relieve it. From the lake the railway, making another great sweep, climbs another slope and enters another still higher hollow, where it stops at the base of a steep ridge. Here a cluster of huts of corrugated iron, more than usually hideous in such a landscape, marks the mouth of the great tunnel, at a point 10,486 feet above the sea. In winter everything is covered deep with snow and now, in October, patches were still lying about and the cold, except in the sun, was severe. Big icicles were hanging from the eaves of the iron hut roofs.

Reserving for a later page some account of the top of the Pass and the colossal statue of Christ which has been set up there, I will describe the route, as travellers now take it, through the tunnel into Argentina and down the valley to the plains at Mendoza. The tunnel, cut through hard andesite rock, under a ridge fifteen hundred feet higher, is nearly three miles long, and the passage through it takes ten minutes. The air is cool and free from that sense of oppression which people complain of in the Gothard. The Duke of Wellington used to say that the business of a general in war consists largely in guessing what is on the other side of the hill. Whoever crosses a hill on foot or horseback sees the surrounding landscape change by degrees, and is more or less prepared for the view which the hilltop gives of what lies beyond. But when carried along in the darkness through the very core of a great mountain range expectation is more excited, and the sudden burst of a new landscape is more startling. So when, after the few minutes of darkness, we rushed out into the light of the Argentine side, there was a striking contrast. This eastern valley was wider and the peaks rose with a bolder, smoother sweep, their flanks covered with long slides of dark sand and gravel, their tops a line of bare precipices, not less lofty than those on the Chilean side but shewing less snow. The air was drier and the aspect of things not, indeed, less green, for there had been neither shrub nor plant visible since we passed Juncal, but more scorched and more aggressively sterile. There was far more colour, for on each side of the long valley that stretched before us to the eastward the declivities of the ridges that one behind another dipped towards it on both sides glowed with many tints of yellow, brown, and grey. A great flat-topped summit of a rich red, passing into purple, closed the valley in the distance. The mountains immediately above this upper hollow of the glen — it is called Las Cuevas — though nineteen or twenty thousand feet high, are imposing, not so much by their height, for the bottom of the hollow is itself ten thousand feet above sea-level, but rather by the grand lines with which they rise, the middle and lower slopes covered by sloping beds of grey ash and black sand, thousands of feet long, while at the head of the glen to the northwest glaciers hang from the crags that stand along the central range, the boundary of the two countries. In the presence of such majesty, the grim desolation of the scene is half forgotten.

From Las Cuevas the train runs rapidly down eastward, following the torrent through a confused mass of gigantic blocks that have fallen from the cliffs above, and after seven or eight miles, it passes the opening of a lateral glen down which there comes a far fuller torrent, bearing the water that has melted from the glaciers of Aconcagua. The huge mass of that mountain, loftiest of all the summits of the Western Hemisphere, is seen fifteen miles away, standing athwart the head of this lateral valley. It is a long ridge of snow, arching into two domes with a tremendous precipice of black rock facing south, on the upper edge of which is a cliff of névé. The falling fragments of thin ice feed a glacier below, just as a similar ice cliff above a similar precipice makes a little glacier thousands of feet below on the side of Mount Ararat. The top of Aconcagua is nearly twenty-three thousand feet high, and the valley at this point about eight thousand. Only in the Himalayas and the Andes can one see a peak close at hand soar into air fifteen thousand feet above the eye, and I doubt if there be any other peak even in the Andes which rises so near and so grandly above the spectator. It was first ascended in 1897 by an Englishman, Mr. Vines. The steepness of the snow slopes offered less difficulty than did the rarity of the air, the violence of the winds, the severity of the cold, besides the other hardships which are incident to camp life in this desolate region, where the climber, far from all supplies, waits day after day for weather steady enough to permit an attempt highly dangerous except under favouring climatic conditions.

A little below this point one reaches the spot called Puente del Inca (the Inca's bridge). Unusual natural

[1] An account of the ascent and of all this region will be found in Mr. E. A. Fitzgerald's *High Andes*, the author of which was prevented by illness from reaching the summit.

phenomena are called after the Incas in these countries, just as they are after the Devil in Europe. Hot springs of some medicinal value which gush from the ground have been turned to account in a small bathing establishment to which a few visitors resort in summer. There is a real natural curiosity in the sort of bridge which the torrent has formed by cutting a way for itself underneath a detrital mass, the upper part of which has been bound hard together by the mineral deposits from the hot springs, so that it makes a firm roadway above the river roaring below. The place is, however, unspeakably lonely and dreary, bare and shelterless, too sterile for aught but a few low, prickly shrubs to grow. Over it whistles that fierce west wind which comes up from the Pacific in the afternoon, and sweeps down this valley chilled by the snowy heights which it has crossed.

The journey down the valley from this point is a piece of scenery to which it would be hard to find a parallel on any other railroad. It is like traversing the interior of an extinct volcano, for the rocks are all volcanic, of different ages and different colours, black and grey lavas, yellow and pink and whitish and bluish beds of tufa and indurated ash, sometimes with long streaks of gravel or dark sand streaming down from the base of the precipices above. At one place there is seen just under such a precipice, a row of sharp black pinnacles, not unlike miniature aiguilles, apparently the remains of a lava bed that has disintegrated, leaving its harder parts to stand erect. These are called the Penitentes, from a fancied resemblance to sinners in black robes standing or kneeling to do penance.[1]   I could perceive no trace of any defined craters or, indeed, of any recent volcanic phenomena in the valley, and should conjecture that subterranean fires had died out here many ages ago.   Of the former presence of glaciers and the action of water on a great scale there are abundant signs in the remains of large moraines and in the masses of alluvium, through which the streams have cut deep trenches all the way down the valley.   Its mountain walls rise so high and steep that the snow mountains behind are hidden.   But at one point where a narrow glen comes down from the south, there is seen at the end of a long vista, thirty miles away, the great, blunt pyramid of Tupungato.[2]   Tupungato attains 22,000 feet, the upper six thousand of which are draped in white, and is, among the southern Andes, inferior only to Aconcagua and to Mercedario.

About thirty miles below the tunnel the valley opens into the little plain of Uspallata, bounded on the opposite or eastern side by a range of flat-topped hills, across which the old mule track and carriage road ran to Mendoza.   This range, running parallel to the main chain of the Cordillera and therefore at right

[1] This name is in the Andes usually applied ,to the sharp little peaks of ice that stand up, like the pyramidal points of seracs, on the surface of Andean glaciers, and it suits them better, because penitents wear white garments.   The similarity of form has however caused it to be applied to these black towers also.

[2] It was first ascended by Mr. Vines in 1897.   The measurements of Aconcagua vary from 23,200 to 22,425 feet.   Mercedario is given at 22,300 and Tupungato at 22,015.

angles to the valley down which we had come, turns the course of the torrent southward, forcing it to find its way out to the level country through a deep gorge or cañon. The railway follows the river. As we reached Uspallata, the declining sun was turning to a rosy pink the mists that hung upon the peaks to the northwest, now hiding and now revealing the snow fields that filled their highest hollows. The dry eastern hills glowed purple under its rays, and the purple was deepening into violet in the fading light when the train plunged into the depths of the cañon along the banks of the swirling stream. Here we were at once in different scenery. The rocks were of red and grey granite, and there were shrubs enough to give some greenness to the slopes. Stern and wild as the landscape was, it seemed cheerful and homelike compared with the black grimness of the volcanic region above. Night descended before we had emerged into the Argentine plain, and when we drove through the friendly lights of Mendoza to our hotel in the handsome Plaza, it was hard to believe that four hours before we had been in the awesome Valley of Desolation between Aconcagua and Tupungato.

To these two mountains Mendoza owes its existence. It stands in an oasis watered by the torrent which brings down the melting of their snows, the rest of this part of Argentina being an almost rainless tract, where coarse grass and sometimes low scrub-woods cover ground that is barely fit for pasturage and hopeless for tillage. At this spot, however, the perennial flow of the glacier-born river suffices to fill numerous channels by which water is carried through fields and vineyards over a wide area, giving verdure and fertility. It was the good fortune of this position that made Mendoza's lieutenant, Castillo, choose this spot so far back as 1560 for the first Spanish settlement made on this side of the mountains. For a long time it remained a tiny and isolated outpost, useful only as a resting place on the track from Chile to the Atlantic coast. But it was never forsaken, and though frequently shaken and as late as 1860 laid in ruins by earthquakes, it has of late years recovered itself and become a prosperous centre of commerce.

It stands on the great Pampa, just at the point where the last declivities of that low, flat-topped range to which I have referred sink into the vast and almost unbroken level, slightly declining · eastward, which extends six hundred miles from here to Buenos Aires. As the fear of earthquakes keeps the houses low, and the streets are wide, it covers a space of ground large in proportion to its population which is 45,000. The principal business thoroughfare is quite handsome with double rows of lofty Carolina poplars and a cool stream of reddish glacier water coursing along beneath. In the ample Plaza, planted with plane trees, there is a colossal statue of San Martin the Liberator of Argentina and Chile ; and quite recently a large park with an artificial lake has been laid out on the slope of the hill. All these adornments are due to the Mendoza River (the one which descends from Aconcagua) and two other smaller streams, whose combined waters have been skilfully used not only to beautify the city, but to irrigate a wide space round. Most of the land is planted with vines, but all sorts of fruit trees, particularly peaches, pears, and cherries, are grown and despatched by rail to the eastern cities. Vine culture is in the hands of the Italians, who have settled here in large numbers, and brought with them their skill in wine making. In an establishment which we saw, managed by an Italian gentleman from Lombardy, it was interesting to note how chemical science and mechanical invention have changed the forms of this oldest of human industries. Thirty-five years before in the port wine country of the Douro I had seen the ancient wine-press scarcely changed, if changed at all, from the days of Virgil, perhaps from the days of Isaiah, perhaps from the days of Noah, with the old simple methods of casking and keeping the wine still in use. Now it is all factory work, done like that of a foundry or a cotton mill by all sorts of modern scientific methods and appliances. The wine made here is of common quality, intended for the humbler part of the Argentine population, who have happily not exchanged their South European habits for the modern love of ardent spirits. Nearly all the country is supplied from Mendoza because eastern Argentina is ill fitted for viticulture. The vineyards, interspersed with meadows of the bright blue-green alfalfa, give some beauty to the oasis, though the vines are mostly trained on sticks, not made to climb the poplar or mulberry as they do in north Italy. The land both north and south outside the range of irrigation is a sterile wilderness, except along the banks of a few streams that descend from the Andes, and to the east also it remains barren for a long way, bearing nothing except the algaroba tree, which is of use for firewood, but for little else. Travelling still farther eastward, one reaches a region where a moister climate gives grass sufficient for ranching, and thereafter, the rainfall growing more copious as one approaches the Atlantic, comes the region of those prodigious wheat fields which are now making the wealth of this country.

Here in Argentina we were "on the other side of the hill," in a social as well as in a physical sense, and we soon found ourselves trying to note the differences between Chileans and Argentines, peoples of the same origin, dwelling side by side but divided by a lofty mountain chain. Two contrasts are evident. Chile is, always excepting Santiago and Valparaiso, a quiet tranquil country, developing itself in a leisurely way. But in Mendoza, though it is one of the smaller Argentine towns, there is a stir and bustle like that of England or Germany or North America. Land values are going up. Branch lines of railway are being run through the outskirts of the city among the vineyards. The main streets are crowded, and there is a general air of "expansion" and money making. Then in Chile the population is stable and comparatively homogeneous. The Germans who are found in some of the small southern towns have settled down and become completely domesticated. But here in Argentina the Italians who flock in daily are conspicuous as a growing element, which is contributing effectively to the wealth of the country, for most of the immigrants are hard-working and intelligent people from Lombardy and Piedmont. To describe with precision the differences between the Argentines proper, that is to say, those of Spanish stock, and the Chileans, is not easy for a passing foreign visitor, nor can he attempt to judge whether the Chilean is justified in claiming that he is more frank and open, and the Argentine that he is more perfectly a child of his time. One does, however, receive the impression that the Argentine, being usually better off, is more disposed to enjoy himself. In both nations Castilian courtesy has lost some of its elaborateness, but those who know both say that the change has tended to make the Chilean of the less educated class more abrupt even to the verge of brusqueness, and the Argentine more offhand and "casual." The prosperous Argentine gathers money quickly and spends it freely; the Chilean retains the frugality of old Spain, and while the former is more vivacious, the latter is more solid.

Placed on the edge of a monotonous desert, and far from all other cities, Mendoza may seem a depressing place to dwell in, yet it has some attractions for those to whom natural environment means something. At the end of those streets which open to the west glimpses are caught of the distant richly coloured mountains; and the man who goes to and fro amidst the crowd on his daily tasks is reminded of the beauty of a far-off lonely nature. Then there is the view of the Andes from the southwestern outskirts of the city. It is a view specially noble just at sunrise, when the level light reddens the long line of ghostly snows that stretches south for more than a hundred miles from where the cone of Tupungato, towering above its fellows, is the first to catch the rays. It is like the view of the Alps from Turin, and even grander, since not only the height, but also the immense length of the Andean range, trending away towards distant Patagonia till its furthest peaks sink below the horizon, lays upon the imagination the spell of vastness and mystery.

A third equally striking prospect is that over the Pampa from the high ground of the new park. There is something in looking over a boundless plain that inspires more awe than even the grandest mountain landscape. The latter is limited, the former thrills the mind with a sense of infinity, land and sky meeting at a point which one cannot fix. There is little colour on this plain and little variety of aspect except that given by the shadows of the coursing clouds. But its uniformity seems to make it the more solemn.

Over that plain lay our shortest way to Buenos Aires and Europe, along the line of railroad that runs for hundreds of miles without a curve or a rise or a bridge, always steadily eastward to the sea. But it is a dull and dusty journey through a monotonous landscape, at first mostly desert, then mostly pasture, at last mostly wheat fields, but always flat as a table, possibly the widest perfectly level plain in the whole world. And we had the stronger reason for not taking this route that it had been a main object of our journey to see the Straits of Magellan, that great sea highway from ocean to ocean, the finding and traversing of which was an achievement second only to the voyage of Columbus. So leaving Mendoza before dawn, we threaded the windings of the granite cañon, and then, passing the little plain of Uspallata, took our way up the long volcanic Valley of Desolation, that leads to the pass, finding it not less strange and terrible than it had seemed two days before. When we reached the Argentine end of the tunnel at Las Cuevas, we quitted the train in order to mount to and cross the top of the pass, the *Cumbre*, as it is called, which is fifteen hundred feet above, and over which, until the tunnel was pierced, all travellers walked or rode. The ridge is composed of friable volcanic rock, decomposed to a sort of coarse gravel, steep on both sides, but most so on the Argentine. The road, which, although rough, is still barely passable for light vehicles, is not likely long to remain so, as no one now crosses the ridge, unless indeed he wishes to see the statue on the top.

We took mules, for in this thin air it is well to save effort by riding when one can, and as there was no vegetation, there could be no gathering of alpine plants. But more than once we had occasion to feel that we should have been happier on our feet, for in heading the animals across short cuts between the windings of the track we got on slopes so steep that it was a marvel how the creatures could keep their feet. It was now past midday, so a furious west wind was careering over this gap between the far loftier heights on either side, and making it hard for the mules to resist it, and for us to keep in the saddle. Once upset, one might have rolled down for hundreds of feet, for there was nothing for beast or rider to catch at.

The Cumbre is a flattish ridge hardly a quarter of a mile across, with towers of rock rising on each side, the cold intense and no shelter anywhere from the biting blast. There is a small stone hut, but it was half full of snow. One thought of the hapless travellers of former days caught here in some blinding snowstorm far from human help. One recalled the daring march of that detachment of the Argentine army of San Martin, when, in 1817, they crossed the pass in that hero's expedition to deliver Chile from the yoke of Spain, the rest of his force having taken the equally difficult though less lofty route by the Los Patos Pass to the north of Aconcagua. The passages of the Alps by Hannibal and by Napoleon were over ridges only half as high and only half as far from the dwellings of men.

The view to the west into Chile looking down into the abysmal depths of the valley that leads to Santa Rosa, with formidable spires and towers of rock nineteen thousand feet high rising on either hand, grand and terrible as it is, is less extensive and less imposing than that to the east into Argentina. Both Tupungato to the south and Aconcagua to the north are hidden by nearer heights, the latter by the huge Tolorsa, whose cliff-crested slope descends in singularly beautiful lines to the hollow of Las Cuevas. But to the east are the two great ranges that enclose the valley, their forms less bold than those of the Chilean mountains to the west, where rain and snow wear down the softer rocks, and leave the crags standing up like great teeth, but their colours richer and more various.

On the level summit of the pass stands the Christ of the Andes, a bronze statue of more than twice life size standing on a stone pedestal rough hewn from the natural rock of the mountain. The figure, which is turned northwards so as to look over both countries and bless them with its uplifted right hand, is dwarfed by the vast scale of the surrounding pinnacles, and although there is dignity in the attitude and tenderness in the face, it hardly satisfies the conception one forms of what such a figure might be. Rarely does any modern representation of the Redeemer approach the dignity and simplicity which the painters and sculptors of the Middle Ages and early Renaissance knew how to give.[1] But when one reflects on the feeling that placed this statue here and the meaning it has for the two peoples, it is profoundly impressive. There had been a long and bitter controversy between Chile and Argentina over the line of their boundary along the Andes, a controversy which more than once had threatened war. At last they agreed to refer the dispute to the arbitrament of Queen Victoria

[1] The finest representation I have ever seen is a twelfth-century mosaic figure of Christ in the apse of the Norman cathedral at Cefalu in Sicily.

of Great Britain.   A commission was authorized by her
and her successor to examine the documents which bore
upon the question and to survey the frontier.   After
years of careful enquiry an award was delivered and a
boundary line drawn in which both nations acquiesced.
Grateful for their escape from what might have been a
long and ruinous strife, they cast this figure out of the
metal of cannon, and set up here this monument of peace
and good-will, unique in its place and in its purpose,
to be an everlasting witness between them.

We descended the opposite side of the pass on foot
in the teeth of the raging blast, taking short cuts across
the broken rocks, and avoiding the steep snowbeds.
At Caracoles, the stopping place at the Chilean end of
the tunnel, the manager of the railway, a bright and
pleasant young North American engineer, who had
accompanied us over the top, and to whose courtesy we
had been much beholden on the whole trip, proposed
to run us down the first and steepest part of the descent to the station of Rio Blanco, on an open trolley.
By now the sun was near his setting, but there would
presently be some moon, so we welcomed the suggestion of this less familiar kind of locomotion and started
in the waning light, sitting on a low bench back to back,
so as to steady one another, while our friend the manager took his seat on the edge of the little car and grasped
the brake handle.   We ran swiftly down the first steep
incline to the Frozen Lake, while the orange glow of the
sky was paling to a cold and steely grey, then out to the
edge of the ridge which rises above Juncal, then down

into the black depths of the Juncal Valley, along the narrow shelf cut out of the rock, rushing down the steep incline in and out of the tunnels. The tunnels were hardly blacker than the night without, for the moon was still hidden behind the peaks. At length she rose over the crags, just where the torrent comes down from behind Tupungato, and for the rest of our twenty-six miles we could by her help see a little way ahead, just enough to know if some block had fallen from above upon the rails. It was bitterly cold, but cold is more easily borne in this keen, dry air than in humid England, and sometimes we forgot it in noting how the trolley quickened or reduced its speed as the practised hand on the brake loosened it on a straight run or pressed it hard when we entered a dangerous curve. Twice before I had made similar descents, once down the Himalayan railway from Darjiling to Siliguri, and once through the dismal solitudes of the Bolan Pass in Beluchistan. But those were in broad daylight. To get the thrills of such a ride in their brimming fulness one must take it in the pale moonlight, passing into and out of the shadow of black crags as one spins along the ringing lines of steel.

As it is here that I bid farewell to the Andes, this is a fitting place for some observations on their scenery, as compared with that of the mountain systems more familiar to most of us, such as the Alps and the Caucasus, and the Himalayas, in the Old World; the Rocky Mountains and Sierra Nevada in the New. It is, however, only of the central and southern parts of the Andes, and for the most part of their western side, that I can speak, for I had no time to visit the valleys which descend into the forests of eastern Peru and Bolivia. But before I come to the scenery, let a few words be said upon the mountains from the climber's point of view, as offering a field for his energy and skill.

The Andes are not only a longer and loftier chain than any of those just named, except the Himalayas, but are altogether on a vaster scale, the plateaux higher and wider, the valleys longer and deeper. Thus they bear what one may call a different ratio to man, — that is to say, his power of walking and climbing enables him to accomplish less in a given time in these two greater than in the lesser ranges. He is less able to cope with their heights and their distances, especially as above a certain height the rarity of the air reduces his powers. In Great Britain an active man can ascend two of the highest mountains in a day without fatigue. In the Alps a first-class peak demands the afternoon of one day and the forenoon of another. A little more time is required in the Caucasus, a little less in the Pyrenees or the Tatra. But in the central Andes he may probably have to give several days to one ascent, so much more effort is required to reach the summit from his base of operations. A *coup de main* is seldom possible; one must allow plenty of time and make elaborate preparations.

When huge mountains with spreading bases stand apart from one another, they less frequently combine to form a landscape perfect in the variety of its features than do the mountains of lower ranges. Size is only one element in grandeur. A single peak, or even one of its precipices, may be sublime in the boldness of its lines and its enormous bulk, yet too isolated for that kind of beauty which lies either in the combination of fine lines or in the contrast of rich colours. A mountain that rises alone in a desolate region, strewn with tumbled rocks and ancient moraines, or, if it be a volcano, with fields of ashes and lava spreading miles from its base, may want the elements which make the charm of scenery in Europe or the temperate parts of North America. Andean peaks are often seen best a long way off, so that they fall into groups or show one behind the other, giving variety of position and contrast of form. Then, the unlovely heaps of gravel and stones or ash cease to deface the landscape, because distance, touching them with delicate colour, gives them a beauty not their own.

These atmospheric effects are of supreme value in the scenery of the arid parts of South America, in which one may include nearly all of the higher Peruvian, Bolivian, and North Argentine Andes. Such a dryness as belongs to the Pacific coast and to the central plateau from Titicaca southward into the desert of Atacama withdraws an element which gives half their charm to the best parts of Europe, for it forbids grass to clothe the hillsides and groves to break the monotony of plains. From the Equator till one reaches central Chile, there is scarcely any water in Andean landscapes, very few

T

lakes, except Titicaca, few rivers, and those rivers usually torrents, raging at the bottom of deep gorges, where they are heard, but scarcely seen. There is, except in the deeper valleys, no wood, seldom even such glossy shrubs or stunted and gnarled trees as one finds on the dry isles and coasts of the Ægean and the Levant, or on the equally dry hills of California and Arizona. Neither, except in a few upland valleys, is there any verdure of grassy slopes. Green, the softest and most tender of hues, is almost wholly absent from the great ranges and the plateau. On the eastern side of the Andes there is, indeed, vegetation enough and to spare, but once plunged into the forest all distant views are lost, for it is everywhere so thick that neither it nor the mountains above can be seen at all. Except when cresting a ridge, the traveller swelters under an unbroken roof of impenetrable foliage.

What redeems the scenery of the high Andes is the richness and delicacy of the colours which the brilliant desert light gives to distant objects. A black peak becomes deep purple; a slope of dry, grey earth takes a tender lilac; and evening as it falls transfigures the stones that strew the sides of a valley with a soft glow. The snow sparkles and glitters at noonday and flushes in sunset with a radiance unknown to our climates. This is what replaces for these regions the charm of the thick woods and marshy pools of New England, of the deep grassed river meadows of France, or the heathery hillsides of Scotland, and brightens the sternness of those vast prospects which the Cordillera affords. Yet it cannot make them inspire the sort of affection we feel for the mountains of temperate countries, with their constant changes from rain to sunlight, their fresh streams and bubbling springs, and flowers starring the high pastures. So the finest things in the Andes are either the views of a single giant peak, like that of Aconcagua, described a few pages back, or some distant prospect of a great mountain group or range, such as that of the snowy line of the Cordillera Real as it rises beyond Titicaca, or the volcanic peaks of Arequipa seen from the desert of the coast.

It follows from what has been said that the Andes offer a much less favourable field for the landscape painter than do the lower mountains of European countries, such as Scotland or Norway, or the Pyrenees or Apennines. The nearer and lesser beauties which the painter loves are just those which are here wanting. Sometimes one finds landscapes which some master of the grand style might place upon a large canvas. Several such there are in the Vilcañota Valley, especially below Sicuani, and still further down at Ollantaytambo. But the want of what is called "atmosphere" and the comparative scarcity of the objects which make good foregrounds are serious disadvantages. Grandeur and wildness, not beauty, are the note of these regions. Immense depths and heights, vast spaces, too bleak and bare for human life, lying between the habitable valleys, the sense of tremendous forces at work piling up huge volcanic cones, of unthinkable periods of time during which the hard rocks have been crumbling away and fathomless gorges have been excavated by rivers, — these are the things of which the Andes speak, and they speak to the imagination rather than to the sense of beauty. They are awesome, not loveable.

It is with European scenery, as that likely to be most familiar to my readers, that I have been trying to compare the scenery of the Cordilleras. But a word may be added about the Himalayas, since they, too, are on a great scale and the fitter to be compared to the Andes because near, though not actually within, the tropics.

They resemble the Andes in being too vast for beauty and for the sort of enjoyment to be derived from wandering among mountains of a moderate size, whose heights one can reach with no excessive fatigue. It is even more difficult in them than in the Cordilleras to explore the valleys and reach the base of the great summits. They offer some prospects wider and grander than any in South America, such as that from Phalut on the borders of Nepal and Sikkim, where forty peaks, each of which exceeds twenty thousand feet, stand up east, north, and west of the beholder.[1] The capital difference between the two chains, besides that difference in the forms which arises from geological character, the Himalayas being composed of ancient crystalline rocks, while many of the high Andes are of volcanic origin, lies in the fact that the south side of the Himalayas receives abundance of rain and is covered with dense forests. This

[1] The distant view of Badrináth and Trisul from the heights above Naini Tal in Kumaon is also quite as imposing as anything we saw in the Andes.

adds to the sublimity of the great Himalayan views a certain measure of beauty which the Andes lack. On the other hand those effects of colour on bare surfaces which belong to dryness and a powerful sun, are absent in the parts of the Himalayas which front toward India. When one passes behind the outer peaks into the great tableland of Tibet, physical conditions resembling those of the Andean deserts appear; and the same remark applies to the inner valleys of the north-western Himalaya, such as that of the upper Indus. The parallel may be carried further, for just as the Himalayan chain has a dry side, that turned to the lofty northern plateau of Tibet, so the Andean Cordillera has a wet side, its eastern, turned to the Amazonian forests. This side I have not seen, but gather from those who have that its rock and river scenery is superbly beautiful in the valleys, but that it is more difficult than in the Himalayas to obtain a distant view of the great range, because the points are few at which one can get above the forest.

Europe, although the smallest, is, in point of the accessibility, and of what may be called the serviceability to man, of its beauty, the most fortunate of the continents. Less grand and extensive than either the Himalayas or the Andes, the Alps have more of varied charm, and contain more of mingled magnificence and loveliness than any other mountain chain. It would lead me too far afield to discuss the respective merits of South American and of North American scenery. But those who have seen both will agree that there is nothing in the Andes which better combines beauty with majesty than the Yosemite and its sister cañons in the Sierra Nevada of California, and nothing so extraordinary as the Grand Cañon of the Colorado River in Arizona.

It may seem more natural to compare the Andean Plateau with what most nearly corresponds to it in North America, the plateau of Anahuac, in the centre of which lie the lakes and the city of Mexico. The northern parts of that country are for the most part bare mountains and barren desert, but on this plateau seven thousand feet above sea level there is rain enough to give fertile fields and woods and a profusion of flowers upon the hillsides. There is the brilliant sunlight of the tropics without their too rank vegetation. Ranges of craggy hills traverse it, and a few great snowy cones, such as Popocatepetl and Citlaltetepl (near the town of Orizava), rise in solitary grandeur from its surface to a height of seventeen thousand feet. The presence together of all these elements creates landscapes of surpassing beauty. Even in Italy and on the coasts of Asia Minor I have seen nothing equal to the views of the plain and lakes of Mexico from the castle of Chapultepec and the views of the broad valley of Cuernavaca either from that city or from the heights around it. These landscapes are not only lovely in their combination of hill and plain, of rock and forest, with snowclad summits closing the distance: they are also "in the grand style," ample and harmonious landscapes such as one has in the greatest pieces of Claude Lorrain or Turner. Whether there are any equal to these on the east side of the Andes I cannot say. Those on the west side have equal amplitude and equal grandeur, but not such finished beauty.

Can a lover of nature in general and of mountains in particular be advised to take the long journey to western South America for the sake of its scenery ? If he be a mountain climber who enjoys exploration and pants for yet untrodden peaks, he will find an almost un-touched sphere for his energies, summits of all degrees of difficulty from eighteen thousand to twenty-two thousand feet, with the advantage of having at certain times of the year uninterruptedly fine weather and a marvellously clear air. If, not aiming so high, he nevertheless loves natural beauty enough not to regard some discomforts, and if, having a sound heart and lungs, he does not fear great altitudes, he will be repaid by seeing something different in kind from anything which the mountains of Europe and North America and Africa have to shew, and the like of which can be seen only in the Himalaya and the even less approachable desert ranges of central Asia, such as the Thian-Shan and Kuen-Lun. The Andes have a character that is all their own, while in the temperate region of the South Chilean Cordillera one finds landscapes which, while not so unlike as are the Peruvian to those of western Europe and the Pacific coast of North America, have also a charm peculiar to themselves, which will endear them to the memory of whoever has traversed their flowery forests and sailed upon their snow-girt lakes.

NOTE TO CHAPTER VII

GENERAL SAN MARTIN'S PASSAGE OF THE ANDES

THE passage of the Andes by the army of San Martin has been pronounced by military historians of authority to have been one of the most remarkable operations ever accomplished in mountain warfare. The forces which he led were no doubt small compared to those which Suvarof and Macdonald commanded in their famous Swiss campaigns, and small also when compared to those which Hannibal and Napoleon carried across the Alps. But the valleys which the two detachments of San Martin's army had to traverse lay in an arid and practically uninhabited region, and the passes to be crossed were much higher. This added immensely to the hardships and difficulties of the march, yet few men were lost.

San Martin divided his army into two parts. The smaller, in charge of Colonel Las Heras, consisted of eight hundred men, including two field guns and a few cavalry. It proceeded by the Uspallata Pass, over the Cumbre, while the larger, under San Martin himself, moved by the much longer and colder though not quite so lofty route over the pass of Los Patos to the north of Aconcagua. The rendezvous was successfully effected at the exact point chosen by San Martin, where the two lines of march down the two valleys on the Chilean side of the Cordillera converge a little below the village of Santa Rosa de los Andes, now the terminus of the Trans-Andine railway. San Martin, screened by the Andes, had from his position at Mendoza so skilfully contrived to deceive and perplex the commander of the Spanish army in Chile as to induce him to scatter his greatly superior force over much too long a line, so as to guard the various passes, all very difficult, which lie to the south of the Uspallata. Thus when San Martin, having effected his own concentration near Santa Rosa, marched straight upon Santiago, he was able to overpower the Spanish army, still somewhat larger than his own, when it tried to bar his path at Chacabuco. The Spanish general fled to the coast, and though some time had yet to pass before San Martin won his decisive victory at Maipo, and before Lord Cochrane drove the Spaniards out of their last maritime strongholds at Corral, the crossing of the Andes was not only the most brilliant operation of the whole war, but was also that which most contributed to the liberation of Chile and Peru.

The best account I have been able to find of this campaign is in Mitre's elaborate *Historia de San Martin*, with the accompanying volumes of *Documentos*. The description there given of the crossing of the passes is, however, sadly wanting in topographical details.

José de San Martin, a strong and silent man, whose character and achievements have been little known or appreciated outside his own country, had learnt war under the Duke of Wellington in Spain. He comes nearer than any one else to being the George Washington of Spanish America.

CHAPTER VIII

In the annals of maritime discovery three great voyages stand out as the most daring in their inception, the most striking in their incidents, the most momentous in their results. They are those of Columbus in 1492, of Vasco da Gama to the coast of India in 1498, of Magellan in 1519–1522, and of these three, Magellan's was in some ways the most wonderful. It was by far the longest, and was performed under hardships and sufferings which were absent from the others. Vasco da Gama had a powerful armament, could obtain pilots, and knew where he was going. Columbus had a short and easy crossing, though it was into an unknown region. But Magellan ventured down into the stormiest seas of our globe, and after he had found a channel leading through savage solitudes to the Pacific, had eight thousand miles of ocean to traverse before he sighted those Asiatic isles among which he found his fate. As the interest of the Straits, apart from the grandeur of their scenery, lies largely in the circumstances of their discovery and the heroic character of the man who first proved experimentally (so to speak) that our earth is a globe, a few lines may be given to some account of his exploit before I describe the channel itself.

Columbus seems to have set forth not so much to discover new countries as to find a shorter way to India from the west than that known to exist *via* the Red Sea,[1] and which Bartholomew Diaz, by passing the Cape of Good Hope, had almost proved to exist round Africa. As James Russell Lowell happily said, "meaning to enter the back door of the Old World, Columbus knocked at the front door of a New World." To the end of his life, after four voyages, in two of which he coasted for hundreds of miles along the shores of what we now call Central and South America, he continued to believe that he had reached the Indies, though he had not been able to hit upon any one of the islands or districts supposed to exist there. When it began to be clear that there were masses of land extending a long way to the north and south of the part which Columbus had first struck, men tried to find a way through this land by which Asia, still supposed to be quite near, might be reached. Portuguese and Spanish navigators followed the coast of what we call South America a long way to the south, while others explored northwards. In 1513 Vasco Nuñez de Balboa, crossing the Isthmus of Darien, discovered the Pacific Ocean, which he called the South Sea; and it began to be conjectured that there might well be a great space of water to be crossed before India could be reached, though nothing shewed how wide it was or whether it was anywhere connected with

---

[1] Whether the discovery of India was his original aim, a point recently brought into question, there is no doubt that he thought after his first voyage that he had found some part of eastern Asia.

the Atlantic. Six years later, in 1519, Magellan was commissioned by Charles, king of Spain (not yet the Emperor Charles V) to try to find a passage from the Atlantic into the sea which washed eastern Asia and so to reach, if possible, the rich Spice islands (the Moluccas) already known to lie off the Asiatic coast. He sailed with three ships in August of that year, and began his search for a westward passage at the Rio de la Plata, which had already been reached (in 1516) by Spanish sailors. He wintered on the coast of Patagonia at a spot where Francis Drake also spent the winter fifty-eight years later, and on the 21st of October, being the day of the Eleven Thousand Virgins, sighted a low promontory which he called after those saints and which is still the Cape Virgenes of our charts. Just beyond and inside this promontory there opens to the west an inlet of the sea, which he sent two ships to explore. They seem, from the description given by Pigafetta, the Italian chronicler of the expedition, who was on board, to have gone through two channels, now called the First and Second Narrows, into the great piece of open water opposite the place we call Punta Arenas (though possibly they stopped at the entrance of the Second Narrows), and they returned thence with an account so favourable that Magellan entered the strait on All Saints Day (November 1). Had he not found it, his purpose was to sail on steadily southward till he reached latitude 75° south. Long before that he would have been stopped by the frozen shores of Graham Land, nor did any one get down to latitude 75° till 1823, He passed both Narrows, crossed the open piece of water, and then, halting at a point where the channel forks, he sent out two of his ships to examine the southeasterly one while he took the southwestern. Thereafter, stopping again, and making a pilot climb a hill to see if the channel came to an end, he sent on boats to explore further. They returned—so says Pigafetta[1] — in three days and reported that they had seen a cape and beyond it open sea. Thereupon Magellan cast loose from the shore to which he was moored and with two out of his three ships (for one of those sent to reconnoitre had deserted and gone back to Spain) sailed out to the west, and on November 28 entered the Pacific. When he perceived that there was a vast sea before him, he called the cape Deseado (the desired) and wept for joy. Thence, turning first north and then northwest, he got into the southeast trade-wind, and sped along before it, making from fifty to seventy leagues a day. Before this steady breeze he sailed for three months and twenty days over the boundless waste of waters, his crews reduced to the last extremity by famine and scurvy, till he reached the Ladrone Islands. "Had not God and His Blessed Mother given us good weather," says the Italian chronicler, " we should all have died of hunger in that exceeding vast sea. I do not believe that any such voyage will ever be made again." Perhaps it was because the subsequent sufferings made their time in the Straits seem agreeable by

[1] Unless Magellan had got farther to the west than the rest of the narrative would imply, three days seems a short time for the boats to proceed to the western opening and back again.

comparison that Pigafetta has nothing but good to say of the latter. "There were," he says, "safe ports every half league, and plenty of water and good wood. I do not believe there is a more beautiful country or a better strait than that in the world."

Sir Francis Drake, whose passage of the Straits in 1578, on his famous circumnavigation of the globe, seems to have been the next recorded one after Magellan's, got through in sixteen days, but encountered frightful weather when he emerged into the Pacific, which drove him a long way south, perhaps nearly as far as Cape Horn.[1] The passage from east to west which Magellan and Drake took is more impressive than that from west to east, because it begins between low shores in quiet and even tame scenery, which rises into grandeur as one approaches the Pacific. We, however, had to take the Strait the opposite way, and so I will describe it.

The last Chilean port at which the ocean-going steamers bound for the Atlantic call is Lota, near Talcahuano, of which I have already spoken (see page 227). From this it is a voyage of three days to the west end of the Strait. The steamer keeps so far out that in the cloudy weather which usually prevails it is only at intervals that one can see the lofty hills. This is one of the wettest and windiest parts of the Pacific, and it is in this region, between latitude 45° south and Cape Horn, that seas heavier than elsewhere in the world are apt to be encountered. We had the usual weather,

[1] Cape Horn was discovered in 1616 by Van Schouten and Le Maire sailing from the East.

cold and wet, with a southwest wind which sometimes rose to three-quarters of a gale. It is, however,
a good rule to keep the deck whenever you can do so
without the risk of being drenched or perhaps knocked
down and swept along by a wave coming on board;
and the want of anything else to occupy the eyes was
compensated by the delight of watching the flocks of
sea-birds which followed and circled round the ship
day after day. Chief among them was the albatross,
whose aspect is that of a gigantic gull. There were
usually two or three, and, as has often been observed,
they seemed scarcely to move their wings, but to float
along, rising and falling without effort and often moving faster than the ship, of which they usually kept
astern. Steady as was their flight, it would have
needed a good marksman to hit one with a cross-bow,
had such a weapon been by ill luck on board. Among
the other birds, — there were at least forty or fifty
playing round the ship, but it was impossible to count
them accurately, — the largest was the giant petrel
or "bone breaker," which somewhat resembles an
albatross, save that he is dark, and the handsomest
was the so-called Cape pigeon. He is bigger than a
pigeon and no more like one than is implied by the fact
that he is more like a pigeon than a gull. The grace
of his circling flight, and the black or dark brown
spots on the dazzling white of his wings, made it a
constant pleasure to watch him, but it was hard either
to follow the course of any particular bird or to be
sure that our count of the spots was correct. When

any remains of food were thrown overboard, the whole swarm darted at once upon it, fluttering and cluttering together on the surface of the sea, with much splashing and jostling, but never, so far as we could observe, fighting with one another. Even the great albatross did not seem to abuse his strength against the Cape pigeon. When they had seized what they could, all easily overtook the ship, though by that time perhaps two or three hundred yards away. The dulness of three tempestuous days under gloomy skies was redeemed by the joy of watching these beautiful creatures, happy in having their lot cast on a wild and lonely coast, where they are safe from the predatory instincts of man.

This long line of islands, stretching along the coast from Chiloe seven hundred miles to the opening of the Straits, is practically uninhabited, though a few wretched Indians wandering about in canoes support life by fishing. Between the isles and the mainland is a labyrinth of sounds and bays studded with other islands, great and small, all covered with wood so close and thick as to be almost impenetrable. The scenery, especially towards the south in the long inland sea called Smyth's Channel, has excited the admiration of those few travellers who have been fortunate enough to see it. This we had hoped to do, but found that the German steamers which used to take the route through these channels into the Straits had ceased to do so on account of the dangers of the navigation, there being so much fog and rain, such strong and uncertain currents, and so many sunken rocks that even with the help of the charts which the British Admiralty has published, it is hazardous to move except in broad daylight. Lighthouses there are none. One line of small steamers does run from Punta Arenas in the Straits through the channels up to the south Chilean ports, but to have waited for a boat of this line would have involved a month's delay, so we had to comfort ourselves by reflecting that had we been able to catch a vessel traversing this fairyland of wood and water and snowpeaks rising above land-locked fjords, still the chances of weather good enough to enable it to be seen and enjoyed would have been slender. For a description of it the reader may be referred to the book of Mr. Ball.[1] Were it not so far from the countries where rich men own yachts, it would be a superb yachting ground for those who could spare the time to explore its recesses, moving only by day, and with unceasing circumspection.

Among the headlands which we saw along this stern and lofty coast, two were especially striking from their height and form. One is called Tres Montes. Heavy clouds hid its top, but two thousand feet were visible of the steep face that rose above the sea. Further south the huge tabular mass of Cape St. George, grand and grey in its drapery of mists, looked out over billows, the spray of whose crests as they broke upon the rocks could be seen fifteen miles away. There is not in the world a coast more terrible than this. No hope for a ship driven in against it by the strong currents and the resistless western swell. Still further south,

[1] *Notes of a Naturalist in South America.*

U

on the fourth day of our voyage, after a night in which
the vessel, steady sea boat as she was, rolled so heavily
that it was hard to avoid being pitched out of one's berth,
we reached a group of high rocky islands, called the
Evangelists, — they seem from a distance to be four,
but are really five, — on which the Chilean government
has lately, in spite of the difficulty of landing in an
always troubled sea, erected a lighthouse. Its light,
190 feet high, is visible for thirty miles, and was
greatly needed, for vessels found it hard in the
thick weather that is frequent here to make the
entrance to the Straits. The group is conspicuous
by a hole through one of the highest cliffs, and a long
curved and contorted stratum of white quartz along
the face of another. Not even on the coast of Norway
can I remember anything grander than this wild
sea, flashing and seething round these lonely isles.
No other land was in sight, though the blackness of a
distant cloud shewed that there were hills behind
it. An hour and a half later there loomed up in
the south, through driving rain-clouds, a dark mass
which presently revealed itself as a tower of rock
springing out of the sea, with crag rising above
crag to a lofty peak behind. This rock tower — Cape
Pilar — marks the entrance to the Straits. Beyond
it an ironbound coast runs down four hundred miles
southeast to Cape Horn. It is a coast which ships
seldom see, for steamers, of course, prefer the Straits;
and the very few sailing vessels that still come round
this way to the Atlantic from San Francisco or Val-

paraiso or Australia give a wide berth to these savage and storm-swept shores. When we had gone some ten miles further, the steamer turned her course eastward, and entered the opening, about fifteen miles wide, between Cape Pilar on the south and Cape Formosa on the north. We were now on the track of Magellan, for Pilar is the cape which he saw and named the Desired Cape (Cabo Deseado) when the seaway opening to the west assured him that the ocean he was seeking had been found. Standing high on the bow of our ship and looking along it as it plunged in the great rollers, how small this ocean steamer seemed compared to the vast landscape around. Yet how much tinier were the two vessels with which Magellan ventured out into the billows of an unknown sea.

Before us the inlet narrowed to a point scarcely seen in the vaporous haze. To the south the bare peaks of Desolation Island, beginning from Cape Pilar, rose with terrific boldness, unscaleable shafts and towers of rock that recalled the shapes of the Coolin hills in Skye or the still loftier summits of the Lofoten Isles in Norway. To the north a mysterious fringe of islands and foam-girt reefs, grey and dim among their mists, hid the entrance to Smyth's Channel and the labyrinth of almost unexplored sounds and inlets along the Chilean coast beyond. Behind us the sun, now near his setting, threw from among the scattering clouds a flood of yellow light over the white-topped surges that were racing in our wake. One thought of Magellan's tears of joy when these long surges on which his little vessel rose told him that here at last was that ocean he had set forth to find and over which lay the path of glory that for him led only to the grave. Such a moment was worth a lifetime.

As our ship passed further and further in between the narrowing shores, the birds began to drop away from us, first the great albatross, which loves the open sea, and then the smaller kinds. So, too, the billows slowly subsided, though the wind was still strong and the water still deep and the sea wide open behind us, until when we had gone some fifteen miles beyond Cape Pilar the ocean swell was scarcely perceptible.

Among the isles on the north side of the Strait the most conspicuous is that to which, from its high-gabled central ridge, the name of Westminster Hall has been given. It seemed strange to find in this remote region nearly all the headlands, bays, and channels bearing English names, but the explanation is simple. As there were no native names at all, the Fuegians not having reached that grade of civilization in which distinctive proper names are given to places, and extremely few Spanish names, because the colonial government never surveyed the Straits and few colonial vessels entered them, the British naval officers who did their hydrographic work in and around the Fuegian archipelago were obliged to find names. Like Cook and Vancouver in the north Pacific they bestowed upon places the names of their ships, or of their brother seamen, or of persons connected with the British Admiralty at home. Hence Smyth's Channel and Cockburn Channel and

Croker Peninsula and Beagle Sound and Cape Fitzroy and Fury Island and Mount Darwin. The Dutch captains, sea-rovers or whalers, have contributed other names, such as Barnevelt Island and Staten Island and Nassau Bay and Cape Horn itself. Thus a chart has here the sort of historic interest which the plan of an old city has, where the names of streets and squares speak of the persons who were famous when each was built, like Queen Anne Street and Harley Street and Wellington Street in London, or the list of Napoleonic victories which one has in the street names of Paris.

The Admiralty surveys have also named the different parts of the long line of the Straits. First comes, beginning from the westward, Sea Reach, which, narrowing gradually till it is about four miles wide, has a length of about thirty miles; then Long Reach,thirty-five miles long, and averaging two to three miles wide; then the shorter, and in parts narrower, Crooked Reach, and English Reach, which brings one to Cape Froward, nearly halfway to the Atlantic. Darkness fell before we came to the end of Sea Reach, and we had our last view of the range of formidable pinnacles and precipices which, beginning from Cape Pilar, run along the shore of Desolation Island, the northernmost of the mountainous isles that lie between the Straits and Cape Horn. It is separated from the two isles next to it on the southeast by channels so narrow that the three were long supposed to form one island. The peaks, some of them apparently inaccessible, are of bare rock and run up to four thousand feet. On

the slopes near the shore there is a little short grass,
but no wood, so violent and unceasing are the winds.
The sea was absolutely solitary.   For three days we had
seen no ship.   Formerly a few Fuegians in their canoes
haunted these shores, but they now come no longer.
Scattered remnants of their small tribes, Yahgans and
Alakalufs, wander along the shores of the more southerly islands, supporting existence on shell-fish and
wild berries.   With the exception of the now all but
extinct Bushmen of South Africa and the Veddas of
Ceylon, they are the lowest kind of savage known to
exist, going almost or quite naked, rigorous as is the
climate, possessing no dwellings, and having learned
from civilized man nothing except a passion for tobacco.   There are missionaries at work among them
who have done what can be done to ameliorate their
lot, which would be even more wretched if they knew
it to be wretched.   They would appear, from the vast
remains of their ancient middens, to have inhabited these
inhospitable regions for untold ages, and their low state
contrasts remarkably with the superior intelligence
and the progress in some of the arts of life which mark
the Lapps and Esquimaux and other barbarous tribes
of regions far nearer to the North Pole than this is to the
South.   The contrast may possibly be due to the greater
scarcity of wild creatures both on land and sea in this
extremity of South America.[1]   Here are no bears, black

[1] It is hardly necessary to refer for information regarding the
Fuegians to the classic book of Charles Darwin, the *Voyage of the
Beagle*, in which the genius for observation and speculation of that
great man was first made known to the world.

or brown or polar, and no creature like the reindeer of Lapland, and no musk-ox; nor has the dog ever been harnessed.

Next morning we were up on the bridge beside our friendly captain at the first glimmer of dawn. The vessel, going at half speed during the night, had covered no great distance, but the character of the scenery had already changed. Here in Long Reach the Strait was only three miles wide. The spiry pinnacles of Desolation Island had been replaced by mountains nearly or quite as high, but of more rounded forms, their faces breaking down sometimes in cliffs, but more frequently in steep, bare slopes of rock to the deep waters, their glens filled with blue glaciers, which sometimes came within two hundred yards of the sea, their upper slopes covered with snow or névé, which seemed to form vast ice fields stretching far back inland. Clouds lay heavy on these snows, so only here and there could one discern the outlines of a peak, and conjecture its height. The tops seemed to average from twenty-five hundred to four thousand feet, and the level of the line of perpetual snow to be somewhat over three thousand feet, varying according to the exposure, the line being, of course, a little higher on the south side, whose slopes face the north. On the lower declivities towards the sea there was now some grass, and in sheltered places, such as the heads of inlets, a little thick, low scrub of trees, probably of the two Antarctic beeches,[1] which are here the commonest trees.

[1] *Fagus* (or *Nothofagus*) *betuloides*, or *Fagus antarctica*.

What most struck us was the similarity of the mountain lines and their general character to those of the extreme north of Norway, between Tromsö and the North Cape. Everything seemed to point to an epoch when the glaciers, formerly more extensive than now, rounded off the tops of the ridges, and smoothed the surfaces, just as one finds them rounded and smoothed along the Lyngen fjord on this side the North Cape. It is also natural to suppose that rain and wind, which seem to be less copious and less violent in this part of the Straits than at their western opening, have done less here than they do there to carve the peaks into sharp spires and jagged precipices.

The day, when it came, was dark, for a grey pall of cloud covered sea and mountains; but as this was the usual weather, and suited the sternness of the landscape, we regretted only the impossibility of seeing the tops of the highest hills that rose out of the undulating snow plateau which lies back from the shores. Very solemn was this long, slightly winding channel, deep and smooth, broken rarely by an island or a rock, but now and then shewing a seductive little bay with a patch of green. Sometimes in a glen running back to the foot of a glacier one caught the white flash of a waterfall. The remarkable purity of the ice and smallness of the moraines may be attributed to the fact that the glaciers seemed to be seldom overhung by cliffs whence stone would fall, and that the rocks were evidently extremely hard. They seemed to belong to the ancient crystalline group, granite and gneiss or mica schist, with masses of white quartz, shewing no trace anywhere of volcanic action. This region on both sides of the Straits may be a prolongation not of the great Andean Cordillera, but of the Coast Range of Chile, which (as already observed) mostly consists of those older rocks which I have just mentioned.

At Crooked Reach the view, looking back westward, was specially noble. On a green slope above a sheltered inlet upon the south side are a few houses, the melancholy remains of a Swiss colony, founded some twenty years ago, which failed to support itself in this inclement nature. Behind there was a long curtain-like line of snows. On the north two or three small isles fringed the steep rocky shore with a background of peaks dimly seen through drifting snow showers. In the middle the eye rested on the smooth, grey-blue surface of the great waterway, here only a mile wide, dark as the clouds above and darker still in spots where a gust from the hill fell upon it, silent as when Magellan's prow first clove it. For steam vessels the navigation is not dangerous, since, though there are in this narrow part no lights, there are few sunken rocks. A rock is always indicated by the masses of very long, yellowish brown seaweed which root on it and wave in the tide. But squalls or williwaws (as they are called) come down from the glens with terrific suddenness, and the water is so deep that it is often hard to anchor, or to keep the ship, if anchored, from dragging. Magellan moored his vessels to the shore every night. How did he manage to get through so quickly, against the prevailing west winds, by tacking in a channel so narrow, especially as in those days mariners could not sail so near the wind as we do? Perhaps he may have made much use of the tide, mooring when it was against him and pushing ahead when the ebb set out to the Pacific. The tide flow is, however, not so strong here as is that which enters on the Atlantic side, and it there rises to a much greater height.

About this point another change comes over the scenery. There begins to be more wood, and though it is still stunted, one notes patches of it up to eight hundred feet. On the north shore more recent sedimentary strata, apparently of sandstone and lime-stone, replace the gneiss, and a growth of herbaceous plants and ferns drapes the face of the cliffs. Then at the end of English Reach rises a bold headland, Cape Froward, twelve hundred feet high, projecting from the much loftier Mount Victoria behind. It marks the southernmost extremity of the South American Continent in latitude 52°. Here the coast-line, which had been running in a generally east southeasterly direction all the way from the Pacific, turns sharply to the north, and in a few miles a new scene is disclosed. The Strait widens out, an open expanse of water is seen to the northeast with a low shore scarcely visible behind it; and to the south, nearly opposite Cape Froward, a channel diverges to the southeast between high mountains on its west side and lower hills on the east. This is the north end of Cockburn Channel, which, after many windings among islands, opens out southwestward into the Pacific, and this seems to be the place where Magellan halted, sending out the two ships — one of which deserted him — to explore the southeastward channel. Looking up it one can see in clear weather, some forty miles away, the peak of Sarmiento, highest of all the mountains of this region, a double pyramid of rock peaks rising out of snow. It is of old crystalline rock and is described as by far the most striking object in all the Magellanic landscapes. Thick clouds hid it from our longing eyes. Its height is estimated at six thousand feet, and so far as I know it has never been ascended. That dauntless climber, Sir Martin Conway, who got nearer to its top than any one else has ever done, was turned back by a frightful tempest below the last rock peak.

East of Cape Froward, one is at once in a different region with a different climate. The air is drier and clearer. The shores are lower, the wood, still mostly of the Antarctic beech, is thicker, with many dead white trunks which take fire easily. The hills recede from the sea, and grow smoother in outline, finally disposing themselves in low flat-topped ridges, six or eight miles behind the shore-line. A wide expanse of water, and of land almost as level as the water, stretches out to the eastern horizon, so that at first one fancies that this apparently shoreless sea is part of the Atlantic, which is in fact still nearly a hundred miles away. Signs of civilization appear in a lighthouse at San Isidro, and near it at a small harbour on the mainland to which a few whalers resort, boiling down into oil the produce

of their catch. Presently the masts and funnels of
vessels lying off shore at anchor rise out of the sea, and
we heave to and disembark at the little town of Punta
Arenas on the Patagonian coast, which English-speaking
men call Sandy Point. This is the southernmost town
not only in Chile, but in the whole world, twenty
degrees further from the South Pole than Hammerfest,
an older and larger place, is from the North Pole.
It consists of about six very wide streets, only partially built up, running parallel to the shore, which
are crossed at right angles by as many other similar
streets, running up the hill, the houses low, many of
them built, and nearly all of them roofed, with corrugated iron. It has, therefore, no beauty at all except
what is given by its wide view of the open sea basin
of the Strait, here twenty miles wide, and beyond over
the plains of Tierra del Fuego, the great island which lies
opposite. In the far distance mountains can in clear
weather be seen in the south of that island, Mount
Sarmiento conspicuous among them.

Punta Arenas was for many years only a place of
call for whalers, since hardly any trading vessels passed
through the Straits before the days of steam, and thereafter for a while a Chilean penal settlement. It grew
by degrees and has profited by the discovery of lignite
coal in its neighbourhood, though the seam is small and
of poor quality ; and within the last twenty years it has
increased and thriven because sheep farming has been
started on an extensive scale on the mainland of Patagonia as well as in Tierra del Fuego and some of the

adjoining islands. All the sheep ranchmen within a range exceeding several days' journey come here for their supplies and all ship their wool from here, so it can now boast to be the leading commercial centre of the region, having no rival within a thousand miles. Whether it can develop much further may be doubtful, for traffic through the Straits will not greatly increase against the competition of the Trans-Andine railway for passengers and that of the Panama Canal for goods, and most of the land fit for sheep farming has been already taken up. Neither the whale fishery nor sealing is now prosecuted on a large scale.

The town is a cosmopolitan place, in which English, as well as Spanish and to a less extent German (for the steamers of a well-appointed German line call frequently), is spoken; people engaged in the sheep trade come and go from the Falkland Islands, and the ocean liners keep it in touch with the distant world of Valparaiso and Buenos Aires and Europe. It is the same distance to the south of the Equator as the Straits of Belleisle in Labrador is to the north, but the climate here is far more equable. It is never warm, but the winters are not severe, there is little snow, and frosts are moderated by the adjoining sea. The air is dry and healthy with a rainfall of only ten inches in the year. Though the landscape is bare, for trees can with difficulty be induced to grow, and though there is much wind and no shelter, still we found something attractive in this remote and singular spot, for one has a constantly stimulative sense of the vast expanse of sky and sea and the distant plain of Tierra del Fuego, with a touch of mystery in the still more distant ranges of that island which just shew their snowy peaks on the horizon. The light over sea and shore has an exquisite pearly clearness which reminds one of the similar light that floats over the lagoons between Venice and Aquileia. Can this peculiar quality in the atmosphere be due, here as there, to the presence of a large body of comparatively smooth and shallow water, mirroring back to heaven the light that it receives?

Tierra del Fuego, which one had been wont to think of as a land of dense forests and wild mountains, is, as seen from Punta Arenas, and all along the eastern part of the Straits from this point to the Atlantic, a featureless level. Its northern part is flat, like the Patagonian mainland, which is itself the southernmost part of the great Argentine plain. Some parts are arid, but most of it is well grassed, excellent for sheep. Only in the far south are there mountains, the eastern prolongation of the range that runs (interrupted by channels between the isles) southeast from Cape Pilar. Neither along the shores of the Strait nor in those southern mountains are there any signs of volcanic action, but I was told that such evidences do exist at the extreme eastern end of the island, and there are in the Patagonian mainland, a little way north of the Straits, a large crater and a lava stream eighteen miles in length, the last manifestations to the south of those volcanic forces which are visible along the whole line of the Andes northward to Panama. Both in Tierra del Fuego and on the mainland there are left a few Patagonian aborigines. Those who dwell in the island are of the Ona tribe, tall men who, like the Tehuelches that roam over the mainland, answer to the description of the Patagonian giants given by the early Spanish and English navigators. Pigafetta relates that when Magellan's men had, near Port St. Julian, where he wintered, guilefully entrapped and fettered one of these giants, he cried out on Setebos to aid him, "that is," says Pigafetta, "the big devil" (*il gran demonio*). Shakespeare would seem to have taken from this account, through Eden's *Decades of the New World*, the Setebos whom Caliban names as "his dam's god" in the *Tempest*.[1] The Onas who used to come down to Punta Arenas to sell guanaco skins and obtain ardent spirits, are now seldom seen. Strong liquor was too much for them, as it was for Caliban, and has reduced their numbers. It is curious that the far more abject Fuegians, who love tobacco, detest

[1] He is called Settaboth in the record of Sir Francis Drake's voyage (*The World Encompassed*, p. 487, Hakluyt Society Edition). (I take this reference from Robertson's edition of Pigafetta.) "Sycorax my dam," "the foul witch Sycorax," does not appear in Pigafetta, and comes from somewhere else : the name sounds Greek. As to Caliban and the Patagonians, see the notes to Dr. H. H. Furness's monumental edition of the *Tempest*, p. 379. Every one remembers Robert Browning's *Caliban upon Setebos, or Natural Theology in the Island*. The Settaboth mentioned in Drake's voyage is probably a mere repetition from Eden, for the Indians to whom Fletcher (in narrating that voyage) refers were encountered on the Chilean coast in lat. 38° S., a different set of people altogether. Fletcher's account is in many points hardly credible. See Barrow's *Life of Sir Francis Drake*, p. 121.

intoxicating liquors. But the chief calamity that befell this interesting tribe was the discovery that the more level parts of Tierra del Fuego are fit for sheep. The ranchmen drove off the Onas : the Onas retaliated by stealing the sheep and when they got a chance, shooting the ranchmen with arrows, for they have scarcely any firearms. The ranchmen then took to shooting the Onas at sight, so that now, out of three thousand who used to inhabit Tierra del Fuego, there are said to remain only three hundred, defending themselves in the recesses of the wooded mountains in the extreme south of the island. They are manly fellows of great strength and courage, and go about clothed only with a guanaco skin. Few guanacos are now left, for they also have had to make way for the sheep.[1]

After midnight the steamer left Punta Arenas for the Atlantic. Rising at daybreak I saw the eastern half of the Straits, than which nothing could be less like the western half. After traversing for some distance the wide basin between the mainland and Tierra del Fuego, on the west shore of which Punta Arenas stands, we reached the part of the Strait called the Second Narrows, where the passage, between low bluffs of hard earth on each side, is only a few miles wide, and then emerged from this into another large basin. Twenty miles further come the First Narrows, narrower than

---

[1] The guanaco is the only large wild quadruped of these regions. He belongs to the same genus (*Auchenia*) as the llama, alpaca, and vicuña, but is bigger than any of them. Pigafetta describes him as having " the head of a mule, the body of a camel, the feet of a stag, and the tail of a horse."

the Second, and then a wide bay, which in its turn opens into the Atlantic between two low capes, that on the north being Virgenes, and that on the south Espiritu Santo. Here it was that Magellan anchored while his two small ships went ahead to explore. The space between the capes, which is the eastern mouth of the Straits, is about ten miles wide. The coast here, as well as both shores of the Straits all the way from Punta Arenas, is perfectly flat, with a very slight rise of ground some miles back on the Patagonian side. Clear as was the air, no hills were visible in the distance, neither those in the south of Tierra del Fuego nor those westwards behind Cape Froward, where the Andes end. Over all this vast plain not a dwelling or sign of life could be discerned save the lighthouse on Cape Virgenes, where the boundary line between Chile and Argentina strikes the sea. The northeastern part of Tierra del Fuego belongs to the latter, the southwestern part to Chile. From below the cape, a low point runs out into the sea, to which British mariners have given the familiar name of Dungeness from its similarity to that curious shingle bank which the tides of the English Channel have piled up on the coast of Kent. It is, however, much shorter than our Dungeness and the pebbles of the shingle are smaller.

Before I close this account of the Straits, a few remarks may be added on their general physical character, which some of my readers may have pictured to themselves as very different from what one finds them to be. I had myself done this, fancying them to be a channel long and

x

narrow all the way from ocean to ocean, a channel between steep, dark hills, covered with dense forests, with
volcanoes, more or less extinct, rising behind. Nothing
could be further from the reality.

Magellan's Straits are unlike any other straits in
this respect, that the physical aspect of the two ends is
entirely different. The character of the shores on each
side is the same in each part of the channel, but both
shores of the eastern half, from the Atlantic to Cape
Froward, are unlike those of the western half from
Cape Froward to the Pacific. The former has low banks,
with smooth outlines, slopes of earth or sand dipping
into shallow water, and a climate extremely dry. The
latter half is enclosed between high, steep mountains
which are drenched by incessant rains. The eastern half
is a channel, narrow at two points only, leading through
the southernmost part of the vast Argentine plain, which
has apparently been raised from the sea bottom in comparatively recent times. The western half is a deep
narrow cut through the extremity of a great mountain
system that stretches north for thousands of miles,
forming the western edge of South America, and the
rocks on each side of it are ancient (palæozoic or
earlier). The western half is grand and solemn, with its
deep waters mirroring white crags and blue glaciers.
The low eastern half has no beauty save that which
belongs to vast open spaces of level land and smooth
water over which broods the silence of a clear and
lucent air. A more singular contrast, all within a few
hours' steaming, it would be hard to find. Unlike,

however, as these two halves of the Straits are, they are both impressive in the sense they give of remoteness and mystery, a passage between two oceans through a wilderness most of which is likely to be forever left to those overwhelming forces of nature, rain and wind and cold, which make it useless to man.

Magellan's discovery of the Straits and circumnavigation of the globe was an event of the highest geographical significance, for it finally proved not only that the earth was round, and that the western sea route to India, of which Columbus dreamed, really existed, but also that the earth was immensely larger than had been supposed. A few years after Magellan, Pizarro and his companions, sailing southward from Panama to northern Chile, proved that the "South Sea" discovered by Balboa stretched so far to the south that it must be continuous with that which Magellan had crossed to the Philippines. Thereafter, not much was done in the Southern Hemisphere until the discovery of New Zealand and Australia two centuries later. But no great importance, either commercial or political, belonged to a long and narrow strait which it was extremely difficult to navigate against the prevalent west winds, so when it was presently discovered that there was an open sea not much farther south, it was round Cape Horn and not through the Straits that most of the English and Dutch adventurers made their way to plunder the Spaniards on the Pacific coast; and when the trade restrictions Spain had imposed finally disappeared at the end of the eighteenth century, commerce also went round Cape

Horn, tedious and dangerous as was the passage to those who had to face the prevailing westerly gales. Even in the days when Charles Darwin sailed in the *Beagle* under Captain Fitzroy, hardly any merchant vessels traversed the Straits. It was the application of steam to ocean-going vessels that gave to this route the importance it has since possessed.[1] It is now threatened, as respects passenger traffic, with the competition of the Transandine railway; as respects goods traffic, with that of the Panama Canal, and it may possibly retain only so much of the latter as passes between Pacific ports south of Callao and Atlantic ports south of the Equator.

The morning was brilliant with blue wavelets sparkling under a light breeze as we passed out to the east and saw the low, flat bluff of Cape Virgenes sink below the horizon. But the wind rose steadily, and next morning the spray was dashing over the vessel when we caught sight, through drifting clouds, of the shores of the Falkland Isles. They were wild and dreary shores bordered by rocky islands and scattered reefs, no dwellings anywhere visible on land, nor any boats on sea. In the afternoon, having passed, without seeing it, the mouth of the channel which separates the East from the West Falkland, we anchored in the deep bay which forms the outer harbour of Port Stanley, the chief harbour and village of the islands. The wind was still so strong that our careful captain decided not to take his vessel through the very narrow passage which

---

[1] The steamers of the Pacific Steam Navigation Company began to run through the Straits about 1840.

leads to the inner harbour, so we got into the tiny launch which had come out with the mails, and after a tumble in the waves and a run through the narrows found ourselves in a landlocked inlet, on the shore of which stands the capital city of this remote and lonely part of the British Empire, a place of a few hundred inhabitants. Here was Government House, a substantial villa of grey stone. Indoors we found a cheerful little drawing-room with a cheerful blaze in the grate, a welcome sight to those who had not seen a fire during three weeks of almost constant cold. There was a tree beside the house, the only tree in the islands, and a conservatory full of gay flowers, looking all the prettier in such a spot. And from the top of its tall staff the meteor flag of England was streaming straight out in the gale. The village — it seems to be the only village in the colony — consists of one street built mostly of wood and corrugated iron, with a few better houses of stone whitewashed, and reminded us faintly of the little seaside hamlets of Shetland or the Hebrides, though here there was neither a fishlike smell nor any signs of the industry which dominates those islands. All was plain and humble, but decent, and not without a suggestion of internal comfort. The only colour was given by some splendid bushes of yellow gorse in full flower, an evidence that though it is never warm here, the thermometer never falls very low. The climate is extremely healthy, but the winds are so strong and incessant that everybody goes about stooping forward.

The isles were uninhabited when discovered, a fact

creditable to the aborigines of South America, for a more
unpromising spot for a settlement of savages could not
be imagined ; no wood and no food either on the land
or on the sea.   At present there are about two thousand
three hundred inhabitants, nearly all of British origin,
including a good many Scots brought hither as shepherds, for the colony is now one enormous sheep-farm,
probably the biggest in the world, and lives off the wool
and skins it sends home and the living sheep it exports
for breeding purposes to Punta Arenas.   Wild cattle,
descendants of a few brought long ago by the earlier
settlers, were once numerous, but have now almost disappeared; and the tall tussock grass, which was such a
feature in the days of Sir James Ross's Antarctic Expedition (1840), has vanished, except from some of the
smaller isles.   Poor is the prospect for an agriculturist,
for the climate permits nothing to ripen except potatoes
and turnips with a few gooseberries and currants.   As
in most oceanic islands, the native land fauna, especially
of mammals, is extremely scanty, and, what is stranger,
there are, so one is told, so few fish in the sea that it
is not worth while to face the storms to catch them.
Perhaps this is an exaggeration, meant to justify the
laziness as timidity of those who won't go out.   Certain it is that the sea is always rough, and there are no
fishing boats about.   Neither are there roads; the population is so thin that they would cost more than its
needs justify, and locomotion, even on horseback, is hin-
dered by the bogs and swamps that fill the hollows.

One naturally asks in the spirit which fills us all to-day,

whether anything can be done to "develop the place," *i.e.* to find some resources for the people and help them to make something more of the islands. Well, there are the seals which frequent the coast. They belong to a species different from that of the North Pacific, but with an equally valuable fur. Some are now taken by the few whaling vessels which still resort to these tempestuous seas, but nothing is done to prevent their destruction within territorial waters or to preserve a land herd, and it would no doubt be difficult to exercise effective control on such a wild and thinly peopled coast. Yet what one heard on the spot seemed to suggest that steps might be taken by international agreement for the protection and utilization of these and other large marine mammals both here and in the other islands in this part of the ocean. Some of the rarer species are threatened with extinction.[1] The arrangements recently made by a treaty between Great Britain, the United States, Russia, and Japan, for the benefit of the North Pacific sealing industry constitute a useful precedent.

There are ports enough to furnish all the west coast of South America with harbours of refuge, but no use for them, for few ships come this way, and, as has been said, nobody goes fishing. Yet far out of the world's highways as they lie, and slight as is their economic or political value, the Falkland Isles have had a long and chequered history. An English navigator, Davis, dis-

[1] The enormous herds of fur seals which existed a century ago in the islands of South Georgia, the South Orkneys, and the South Shetlands have vanished. 300,000 are said to have been killed within five years in the South Shetlands alone.

covered them in A.D. 1592, and they were afterwards explored by a French voyager from the port of St. Malo, whence the name of Iles Malouines, by which the French still call them. In 1764 Bougainville, one of those famous seamen who adorned the annals of France in that century, and whose name is now preserved from oblivion by the pretty, mauve-coloured flower which grows over all the bungalows and railway stations of India, planted a little colony here, with the view, fantastic as it seems to us now, of making this remote corner of the earth a central point from which to establish a transoceanic dominion of France in the Southern Hemisphere to replace that which had been lost at Quebec in 1759. The Spaniards, desiring no neighbours in that hemisphere, dispossessed these settlers. An English colony planted shortly afterwards, presently driven out by the Spaniards, and then re-established, was withdrawn in 1774. Finally, in 1832, the British government resumed possession of the islands, then practically uninhabited, for the sake of the whale fishery, and in 1843 a government was organized. In its present form, it is of the type usual in small British colonies, viz. a governor with an executive and a legislative council, the two bodies nominated, and consisting almost entirely of the same persons.

These political vicissitudes have left no abiding mark, except in a few remains at the station of Port Louis which the French made their capital, for there never was any population to speak of till sheep-farming began. The Pacific liners call once a month on their outward and inland voyages, and steamers go now and then to Punta Arenas, but there are no British possessions nearer than Cape Colony to the northeast and Pitcairn Island to the northwest, thousands of miles away.

We walked with the Acting Governor to the top of a hill behind Port Stanley to get some impressions of nature. There were as yet only two or three flowers in bloom, and what chiefly struck us was the resemblance of the thick, low mats and cushions of the plants to some species that grow on the upper parts of the Scottish Highland mountains. Among these, there was one producing a sweet berry, the dillydilly, from which excellent jam is made, the only edible wild product of the country. The prevailing strata are quartzose schists and sandstones, which rise in two mountains to heights exceeding two thousand three hundred feet, and as there is no trace of volcanic action anywhere, the islands are evidently not a link between the great Antarctic volcanoes and those of the Andean system, but perhaps a detached part of the older rocks through which those volcanoes have risen.

From the hilltop we looked over a wide stretch of rolling hills covered with short grass, which in the wet hollows was yellowish or brown. Ridges or peaklets of bare white or blue rock rose here and there into miniature mountains, and there were runs of loose stones on the slopes below the ridges, — altogether a wild landscape, with no woods, no fields, no signs of human life except in the village beneath, yet redeemed from dreariness by the emerald brilliance of the air and the variety of lights and shadows falling on the far-off slopes. The evening tints were mirrored in the landlocked inlet below, and beyond the outer bay the cold, grey, ever-troubled sea stretched away towards the South Pole. We felt as if quite near the South Pole, yet were no nearer to it than the North Pole is to Liverpool. One seemed to have reached the very end of the world. Though one might be reminded a little of the Hebrides, — all windswept islands have points of resemblance, — still the scenery was not really like any part of our Northern Hemisphere, but had a character of its own. I have seen many wild islands in many stormy seas, and some of them more bare and forbidding than this, but never any inhabited spot that seemed so entirely desolate and solitary and featureless. There was nothing for the eye to dwell upon, no lake, no river, no mountain, — only scattered and shapeless hills, — a land without form or expression, yet with a certain simple and primitive beauty in the colours of the yellow grass and grey-blue rocks, shining through clear air, with the sea-wind singing over them. No spot could better have met the wishes of the hermits who, in early Christian centuries, planted themselves on rocky islets and lonely mountain tops on the coasts of Ireland, for here there is nothing, even in Nature her-self, to distract a pious soul from meditation. Any one who to-day desires seclusion to think out a new philos-ophy might find this a fitting place of peace, if only he could learn to endure the perpetual drive of the wind.

The last flush of sunset was reddening on the inlet when we re-joined our steamer and sailed down past the lighthouse out into the ocean, a fresh flock of sea-birds appearing to bear us company. Three more stormy days and stormy nights northward to Montevideo!

CHAPTER IX

THE interest which Argentina arouses is entirely unlike that which appeals to the traveller's eye and mind in Peru or Bolivia or Chile. In each of these three countries there is scenery grand in scale and different in type from what any other part of the world has to shew. In Peru and Bolivia there are also the remains of a primitive civilization, scanty, no doubt, but all the more attractive because they stimulate rather than satisfy our curiosity. They speak of antiquity, and indeed all three countries have a flavour of antiquity, though Chile has scarcely any relics coming down from it. But in the River Plate regions there is (except along the Andes and in the far north) little natural beauty, and nothing that recalls the past. All is modern and new; all belongs to the prosperous present and betokens a still more prosperous future. Argentina is like western North America. The swift and steady increase in its agricultural production, with an increase correspondingly large in means of internal transportation, is what gives its importance to the country and shews that it will have a great part to play in the world. It is the United States of the Southern Hemisphere.

Not even the approach by sea to Alexandria or to the mouth of the Hooghly below Calcutta, is duller than

that to Buenos Aires.   Before land is seen, the vessel
enters a muddy, reddish brown sea, and presently
the winding channel, marked for a long way by buoys,
shews how shallow is the water on either side.   This
is the estuary, two hundred miles long and at this point
about thirty miles broad, of the Rio de la Plata,
formed by the union of the great river Uruguay with
the still greater Paraná, streams which between them
drain nearly one-fourth part of the South American
continent.   Approaching the Argentine shore, one sees
a few masts and many funnels rising above the tall
hulls of steamships, docked in lines alongside huge
wharves.   Beyond the open space of the wharf runs a
row of offices and warehouses, but nothing else is seen,
nor can one tell, except from the size of the docks and
the crowd of vessels, that a great city lies behind.   Nothing can be seen, because Buenos Aires stands only some
thirty feet above high-water mark in a perfectly flat
alluvial plain, with scarcely any rise in the ground for
hundreds of miles, and not a rock anywhere.   On entering the city one is surprised to find that with a boundless prairie all around, the streets should be so narrow
that in most of them wheeled traffic is allowed to move
only one way.   One great thoroughfare, the Avenida
de Mayo, traverses the centre of the city from the
large plaza in which the government buildings stand
to the still larger and very handsome plaza which is
adorned by the palace of the legislature.   Fortunately it
is wide, and being well planted with trees is altogether a
noble street, statelier than Piccadilly in London, or Unter

den Linden in Berlin, or Pennsylvania Avenue in Washington. In the newer parts of the city more width is now being given to streets as they are from time to time laid out, but the congestion of the nucleus is a serious obstacle to rapid locomotion, which is otherwise well provided for by numerous electric car lines. No North American city has a better car service. Though skyscrapers have scarcely yet made their appearance, the houses are much higher than in the west coast cities, because earthquakes are not feared; and many mansions in the residential quarters, built in the modern French style, have architectural merit. So, too, the numerous small plazas, usually planted with trees or shrubs and furnished with seats, partly atone for the want of space in the streets. It must be added that the statues which adorn these plazas do not tempt the passer-by to linger in æsthetic enjoyment. One is too acutely reminded of the bronze equestrian warriors so numerous in Washington. The cities of the western world, having a short history, seem to run to the commemoration of heroes whose names, little known to other nations, will soon be forgotten in their own, whereas the old countries, except Italy, seem forgetful of those whom the western stranger would like to have seen held up to reverence.

Buenos Aires deserves its name, for its air is clear as well as keen, there being no large manufacturing works to pollute it with coal smoke. The streets are well kept; everything is fresh and bright. The most striking buildings besides those of the new Legislative

Chambers, with their tall and handsome dome, are the Opera-house, the interior of which equals any in Europe, and the Jockey Club, whose scale and elaborate appointments surpass even the club-houses of New York.

Buenos Aires is something between Paris and New York. It has the business rush and the luxury of the one, the gaiety and pleasure-loving aspect of the other. Everybody seems to have money, and to like spending it, and to like letting everybody else know that it is being spent. Betting on horses is the favourite amusement, and the races the greatest occasion for social display. An immense concourse gathers at the racing enclosure and fills the grand-stand. The highest officials of state and city are there, as well as the world of wealth and fashion. The ladies are decked out with all the Parisian finery and jewels that money can buy; and although nature has given to many of them good features and to most of them fine eyes, custom seems to prescribe that nature shall not be left to herself. On fine afternoons, there is a wonderful turnout of carriages drawn by handsome horses, and still more of costly motor cars, in the principal avenues of the Park; they press so thick that vehicles are often jammed together for fifteen or twenty minutes, unable to move on. Nowhere in the world does one get a stronger impression of exuberant wealth and extravagance. The Park itself, called Palermo, lies on the edge of the city towards the river, and is approached by a well-designed and well-planted avenue. It suffers from the absolute flatness of the ground in which there is no point high enough to give a good view over the estuary, and also from the newness of the trees, for all this region was till lately a bare pampa. But what with its great extent and the money and skill that are being expended on it, this park will in thirty years be a glory to the city. The Botanical Garden, though all too small, is extremely well arranged and of the highest interest to a naturalist, who finds in it an excellent collection of South American trees and shrubs.

As the Opera-house and the races and the Park shew one side of the activities of this sanguine community, so the docks and port shew another. Twenty years ago sea-going vessels had to lie two or three miles off Buenos Aires, discharging their cargo by lighters and their passengers partly by small launches and partly by high-wheeled carts which carried people from the launches ashore through the shallow water. Now a long, deep channel has been dug, and is kept open by dredging, up which large steamers find their way to the very edge of the city. Docks many miles in length have been constructed to receive the shipping, and large stretches of land reclaimed, and huge warehouses erected and railway lines laid down alongside the wharves. Not Glasgow when she deepened her river to admit the largest ships, nor Manchester when she made her ship canal, hardly even Chicago when she planned a new park and lagoons in the lake that washes her front, shewed greater enterprise and bolder conceptions than did the men of Buenos Aires when on this exposed and shallow coast they made

alongside their city a great ocean harbour. They are
a type of our time, in their equal devotion to business
and pleasure, the two and only deities of this latest
phase of humanity.

If the best parts of Buenos Aires are as tasteful as
those of Paris, there is plenty of ugliness in the worst
suburbs. On its land side, the city dies out into a
waste of scattered shanties, or "shacks" (as they
are called in the United States), dirty and squalid,
with corrugated iron roofs, their wooden boards
gaping like rents in tattered clothes. These are inhabited by the newest and poorest of the immigrants
from southern Italy and southern Spain, a large and
not very desirable element among whom anarchism is
rife. This district which, if it can hardly be called city,
can still less be called country, stretches far out over the
Pampa. Thus, although the central parts are built
closely, these suburbs are built so sparsely that the town
as a whole covers an immense space of ground. Further
out and after passing for some miles between market
gardens and fields divided by wire fences, with never a
hedge, one reaches real country, an outer zone in which
some of the wealthy landowners have laid out their
estates and erected pleasant country houses. We were
invited to one such, and admired the art with which
the ground had been planted, various kinds of trees
having been selected with so much taste that even on
this unpromising level picturesqueness and beauty had
been attained. Everything that does not need much
moisture grows luxuriantly. We saw rosebushes forty

feet high, pouring down a cataract of blossoms. The
hospitable owner had spent, as rich *estancieros* often
do, large sums upon his live stock, purchasing in Great
Britain valuable pedigree bulls and cows, and by crossing the best European breeds with the Argentine stock
(originally Spanish) had succeeded in getting together
a herd comparable to the best in England. To have
first-rate animals is here a matter of pride, even more
than a matter of business. It is the only interest that
competes with horse-racing. Our friend had a number of Gauchos as stockmen, and they shewed us feats
of riding and lassoing which recalled the old days of the
open Pampas, before high stock-breeding was dreamt
of, when the Gaucho horsemen disputed the control of
these regions with the now vanished Indian.

Though Buenos Aires is often described as a cosmopolitan place, its population has far fewer elements than would
be found in any of the great cities of the United States.
There are English and German colonies, both composed
almost wholly of business and railway men, and each
keeping, for social purposes, pretty closely to itself.
There is a French colony, its upper section including
men of intellectual mark, while the humbler members
serve pleasure rather than business. From the United
States not many persons have come to settle as mer-
chants or ranch owners, but the great meat companies
are already at work. Of the so-called "Latin" element
in the inhabitants, half or a little more is Argentine
born, less than a quarter Spanish or Basque, more than
a quarter Italian, largely from Sicily and Calabria.

Y

Those Slavonic parts of central and eastern Europe which have recently flooded the United States with immigrants have sent very few to South America. Thus the mass of the population in Buenos Aires is entirely Spanish or Italian in speech, and the two languages are so similar that the Italians easily learn Spanish while also modifying it by their own words and idioms. A mixed, not to say corrupt, Spanish is the result. That there should be an endless diversity of types of face is not surprising, when one remembers how great are the diversities as well in Spain as in Italy among the natives of the various provinces in both those kingdoms.

The growth of a few great cities at a rate more rapid than that of the countries to which they belong is one of the most remarkable facts of recent years and fraught with many consequences. It is especially visible in the newest countries. In New South Wales the population of Sydney is nearly two-fifths that of the whole state, in Victoria that of Melbourne more than two-fifths. In California two great cities, San Francisco and Los Angeles, have one-third of the whole population.[1] The same tendency is apparently in South America. Of the whole population of Argentina, with its immense area of 1,135,000 square miles, one-fifth dwell in the city of Buenos Aires.[2] It is probable that this ratio may be maintained so that when,

[1] I reckon Oakland and Berkeley as, for this purpose, parts of San Francisco.

[2] The population of the Republic is about 7,000,000, and that of Buenos Aires 1,300,000.

thirty years hence, Argentina counts twenty millions of inhabitants, Buenos Aires will count four millions. There are other large cities, and one of them, Cordova, has an ancient university and a society of cultivated men. But business life and political life, as well as literary and intellectual life, are so concentrated in Buenos Aires as to make it to dwarf all the other cities and give to it an influence comparable to that of Paris in France. The history of the republic was for many years a history of the struggles between the capital — already pre-eminent in revolutionary days — and the provinces. So the people of Buenos Aires divide the Argentine nation into two classes, themselves, who are called the Porteños (men of the Port), and all the rest, the dwellers in the Campo or open country.[1] And though the wonderful development of the railway system has accelerated the settlement of the interior and brought the comforts of civilization to its towns, Buenos Aires has continued to maintain its supremacy by constantly drawing people from the interior. It is, moreover, the gateway through which all must pass to and from Europe. Thus the Porteño is the type and flower of Argentina, — the type of its character, the flower of its civilization. When we try to understand and appraise the Argentine nation, which for Argentina is the most interesting and indeed (apart from statistics of production) the only subject of study, it is on him

[1] The English, adopting this term, talk of the rural parts of Argentina as " the Camp," an expression which at first puzzles the visitor.

that the eye must be fixed. Nevertheless he is far from being the only factor. The nation is spread over a vast space. To conjecture its future we must think of the physical and economic conditions under which it will develop. These, therefore, I will try to sketch briefly, admitting that my own personal knowledge is confined to Buenos Aires and its neighbourhood, and to the region round Mendoza, mentioned in Chapter VII. I shall speak first of the natural features of the country, and then of the natives and of the colonists who came among them, before describing the Argentina of our own time.

The northwestern part of the republic, lying east of northern Chile and south of western Bolivia, is a table-land, sometimes rugged, sometimes undulating, the higher parts of it much like the adjoining plateau of Bolivia. But the rest of the country, nine-tenths of the whole, is an immense plain more than two thousand miles long from Magellan's Straits to the frontiers of eastern Bolivia and Paraguay. It is interrupted in a few points by low ranges, but, speaking generally, is a prairie like that which in North America lies between the hills of southern Oklahoma and the Canadian border, though more level, for it wants the undulating swells and ridges of Kansas and Iowa, and is less seamed by river beds. The climate varies with the latitude. It is severe in the Patagonian south, and almost tropical in the north. But in the region called the Pampas, that is to say, a sort of square, six hundred miles wide from the estuary of the Rio de la Plata to the outlying foothills of the Andes and about as long from north to south, it resembles that of west central Europe, for the heat is great only during the middle of summer and the winter cold is moderate.   Except in the far north, which has a wet summer season with a heavy precipitation, the rainfall is scanty and diminishes as one goes from east to west, so that much of the western belt, lying under the Andes, is too dry to be cultivated except by irrigation.   Fortunately, the streams that descend from the snows provide irrigation along their banks.   Many of them lose themselves in the arid ground on their course further eastward, but as this ground has a slight uniform fall towards the east, they supply a certain amount of subterranean moisture, so that in many districts where there are no superficial streams, water can be had by digging.

All this level Pampa, except that subtropical northern section I have referred to, is bare and open prairie, covered, as were the former prairies of North America, with grass and flowers, the grass sometimes six or seven feet high; but with no trees save here and there along the beds of the few and feeble streams.   The native fauna, especially in the families to which the larger mammals belong, was poorer than that of western North America and far scantier than that of the southern parts of Africa in the same latitude.   There were no buffaloes or elk, and few horned creatures corresponding to the elands and hartebeests and antelopes of South Africa. So remarkable a contrast is doubtless explicable by the different geological histories of the two continents.

When the Spaniards arrived, this vast region was occupied only by a few wandering Indian tribes, most of
them low in the scale of civilization.   They did not cultivate the soil, they had no milk-giving animals, and indeed
hardly any animals to feed upon except the guanaco
and the small South American ostrich.   As the chase
furnished but little food to these nomads, their numbers
did not increase.   Only in the hilly regions of the northwest were there settled tribes which had learnt some of
the arts of life from their Peruvian neighbours.   The rest
of the country was a vast open wilderness like the lands
beyond the Missouri, but the tribes were fewer and less
formidable than the Sioux or Pawnees or Comanches.

For three centuries after their arrival the Spaniards
did little to explore or settle the western or southern
parts of the country.   They founded small posts from
Buenos Aires northwards along the Paraná and Paraguay rivers, and through them kept up communication
with Potosi and Lima across the vast Andean plateau.
As the government forbade the Argentines to trade with
Europe direct, Spanish merchandise had to be brought
to them by a long and difficult land route *via* Panama
and the ports of Peru, and thence over the Andes.   The
inconveniences of this monstrous system, devised in the
interests of a group of Spanish traders, were mitigated
by the smuggling into Buenos Aires, which was carried
on by means of English and Dutch ships.   Life was not
secure, for the Indian tribes sometimes raided up to the
gates of the little towns, such as Cordova and Tucuman,
but as the savages had no firearms and no discipline,

it was generally easy to repulse them. Meanwhile some cattle and horses which had been turned loose in the Pampas after the middle of the sixteenth century began to multiply, till by the beginning of the eighteenth there were vast herds of both all over the plains, wherever grass grew, as far south as Patagonia.

When the development of the country had received an impetus by the creation in 1776 of a viceroyalty at Buenos Aires, and by the permission given to the Atlantic ports to trade with Europe, the cattle and horses became a source of wealth, men took to ranching, and colonization spread out into the wilderness. Then, in 1810, came the revolution which freed Argentina from Spain, and gave her people the opportunity of making their own prosperity. Unfortunately a period of civil wars followed, and it was not till the fall of the dictator Rosas in 1852 that the era of real progress began.

All this time the native Indians had been disappearing, partly by war, partly from the causes which usually break down aborigines in contact with white men. A campaign organized against them in 1879 practically blotted out the last of those who had roved over the central Pampas. The more civilized Indians of the northwestern plateau are quiet and industrious. A few nomads, now quite harmless, survive in Patagonia, and some fiercer tribes maintain a virtual independence in the forest and swamp country of the Gran Chaco in the far north. Otherwise the aborigines have vanished, leaving no trace, and having poured only a very slight infusion of native blood into the veins of

the modern Argentine.   Meanwhile the strife with the
Indians and the long civil wars which followed independence, as well as the occupation first of catching
wild cattle and horses and then of herding tame ones,
had produced a type of frontiersman and cattle-
man not unlike that of western North America between
1800 and 1880 and more distantly resembling the
Cossack of southern Russia a century and a half
ago.   This was the Gaucho, a word said to be drawn
from one of the native languages, in which it means
"stranger."   He was above all things a horseman,
never dismounting from his animal except to sleep
beside it.   His weapons against cattle and men were
the lasso and the *boletas*, balls of metal (or stone)
fastened together by a thong, and so hurled as to coil
round the legs of the creature at which they were
aimed.   Such missiles were used in war by some of
the Andean tribes.   His dress was the poncho, a square
piece of woollen cloth with a hole cut for the head to
go through, and a pair of drawers.   He could live on
next to nothing and knew no fatigue.   Round him
clings all the romance of the Pampas, for he was taken
as the embodiment of the primitive virtues of daring,
endurance, and loyalty.   Now he, too, is gone, as
North American frontiersmen like Daniel Boone went
eighty or ninety years ago, and as the cow-boy of
Texas and Wyoming is now fast going.

Such was the country and such those who dwelt in it:
boundless plains, bare and featureless, but fertile
wherever there was rain enough to water them, and not

too hot for the outdoor labour of a south European
race, a land fit for cattle and for crops, easy to traverse,
easy to till, because there were neither stones to be
removed nor trees to be felled. Yet in 1852 only an insignificant fraction of it was used for tillage, and such
wealth as there was consisted of the vast herds of cattle.
The population had scarcely reached a million and a
half. What is it now?

With the comparative peace that followed the fall of
Rosas there came the new factors which have enabled
the country to advance so quickly: the entrance of European capital, chiefly expended in providing means of
transportation, and the arrival of immigrants from Italy
and Spain. No country offers greater facilities for the
construction of railways. Quickly and cheaply built over
a surface everywhere smooth and level, they radiate
out from the capital, and have now penetrated every
part of the country except the marshy wilderness
of the Gran Chaco in the north and the arid
wilderness of remote Patagonia in the south. The
central part of the republic within three hundred
miles of Buenos Aires is as thickly scored with lines
of steel as is Westphalia or Ohio. Settlers, mostly
following the railroads, have now put under crops or
laid out in well-appointed stock farms all this central
region and a good deal more of land to the north of it.
The rest of the plain is occupied by cattle ranches or
sheep-farms, except where the want of water makes
stock raising impossible. Out of the 253,000,000
acres which are roughly estimated as being the area

available for agricultural or pastural purposes in Argentina — the total area of the country being 728,-000,000 acres — 47,000,000 were under cultivation in 1910, this, of course, including the slopes of the Andes in the northwest round Tucuman and Jujuy, where sugar and other semi-tropical products are grown.

An enormous area still remains available for tillage, though nothing but experiment can determine to what extent lands hitherto deemed too arid may be made productive by the new methods of dry farming, now prosecuted so successfully in western North America, and beginning to be tried in South Africa and Australia also. Of this central tract already brought under cultivation, by far the largest part is fertile. There are sandy bits here and there, but the bulk of it is a rich, deep loam, giving large returns in its natural state. Thus the waving plains of grass over which the wandering Indian roamed and the Gaucho careered lassoing the wild cattle are now being rapidly turned into a settled farming country.

The history of these regions and the process of their settlement resembles in many points that of the western United States and western Canada, but differs in one point of great significance. In North America the settlement of the new lands has from first to last been conducted by agricultural settlers drawn from the middle or working-class of the older parts of the country or of Europe, and the land has been allotted to them in small properties, seldom exceeding one hundred and sixty acres. Thus over all the

Mississippi Valley states and over the Canadian northwest there has grown up a population of small farmers, owning the land they till, and furnishing a solid basis for the establishment of democratic institutions among intelligent and educated men who have an interest in order and good administration. In Argentina, however, — and the same is generally true of Mexico, Chile, Peru, and Brazil, — the land, before or when it began to be regularly settled, passed in large blocks into comparatively few hands. There was no class like the men who settled New England in the seventeenth century and whose descendants settled the Great West in the nineteenth. The ideas of Spanish feudalism still lived among the Argentine colonists of a century ago. Leading men or rich men took as much land as they could get on the Pampas; and, seeing that there was little competition, each could get pretty much all he wanted. Thus the country became and is a country of great estates. They are measured by the square league, which contains about six thousand acres. Though a tendency to subdivision has set in and will doubtless continue, *estancias* of sixty thousand acres are not uncommon; and the average holding is said to be even now about six square miles.

This feature has, of course, had important effects on the character of the rural population. It consists, broadly speaking, of two classes, the rich *estancieros* or landholders, and the labourers. Though a good many Englishmen and other foreigners have bought farms and mean to stay on them, so that they or their

children will doubtless end by becoming Argentines,
still most of the large landholders are Argentine born.
Many have become or are becoming opulent, not only by
the sale of their crops and their live stock, but simply
by the rapid rise in the value of land. They live in
a liberal, easy, open-air way in straggling mansions of
the bungalow type, low and large, which they are now,
thanks to the railways, able to furnish with the modern appliances of comfort. The labouring class, who
gather like feudal dependents round the *estancia*, are of
two classes. Some are native, largely the offspring of
the old Gauchos, who have now settled down to work
as *peons* (labourers), unlearning their wild ways,
and beginning to send their children to school. The
rest are immigrants drawn from Italy and Spain by
the immense demand for labour. Most numerous are
the natives of northern Italy, hard-working men who
do not fear the heat and can live on very little. Many
of them come out for the harvesting weeks of December and January, and return home to reap their own
harvest or gather their own vines in the Italian summer
and autumn, thus making the best of both hemi-
spheres, much as the sleepless herdsman in the Odyssey
could earn wages by working day and night. As the
native peons are the men qualified to handle live stock,
so these Italians are the most valuable for all kinds of
agriculture. Some receive wages: some who stay for
a few years on the farm receive land to till and bring
into condition, and pay a part, perhaps one-quarter,
of the crop by way of rent. They seem to take to the

country, and though many return to Europe when they have accumulated what is to them a fortune, a large and increasing number remain.   Probably more and more of them will try to acquire small holdings, and as the price of land rises, many great landowners may, since the habit of extravagance is always growing, be tempted to sell off bits of their estates.   Thus a middle class of peasant proprietors may grow up between the big *estanciero* and the lowly peon.   But at the present moment small properties are rare.   The country is not, like western Canada, a place suitable for British or Scandinavian immigrants of small means, not merely on account of the climate, but because they could not easily get small farms and the means of working them. At present it is only persons with some capital who can be advised to come hither from England to farm.

Agricultural prosperity, more general here than almost anywhere else in the world, is tempered by two risks, either of which may destroy the profits of the year.   One is drought.   As the average rainfall is, in most parts of the country, only just sufficient to give moisture to the arable land, together with drink and grass to the animals, a deficient rainfall means scanty crops and the loss of cattle.   It is only along the skirts of the Andes that much can be done by irrigation, for the permanent rivers are few and the lagoons, which at one time were frequent, have been drying up.   Besides, they are often brackish.   The other danger is a plague of locusts.   These horrible creatures come in swarms so vast as to be practically irresistible.

Expedients may be used to destroy them while they are walking along the ground by digging trenches in their path, tumbling them in and burning them, but many survive these efforts, and when they get on the wing, nothing can be done to check their devastating flight. Did the swarms come every year, the land would not be worth tilling, but at present the yield of good years more than covers the losses both of droughts and of locust invasions. Men talk of erecting a gigantic fence of zinc to stop the march of the creatures southward from the Gran Chaco, for here, as in South Africa, they seem to come out of a wilderness. When the Gran Chaco itself begins to be reclaimed, the plague may perhaps be stayed.

As aridity is the weak point of the Pampas in their agricultural aspect, so monotony is the defect of their scenery. There is a certain beauty in a vast plain, but this one is so absolutely dead a level that you cannot see its vastness. There would be a charming variety of colour in it, the vivid green of the alfalfa and the light blue profusion of the flax blossoms contrasting with the yellowing wheat and the more sober greyish tints of the maize and the bleached pasture, but all these, as well as the shadows of the passing clouds, are not visible when one is standing on the ground and can see no further than a mile or two. The Pampa country has now been turned from a prairie of grass and flowers into huge fields divided by wire fences and intersected by straight roads, or rather cart tracks, marked by the line of brown dust that a drove of cattle or a ve-

hicle raises. The landscape was in Gaucho days the same
for hundreds of miles. It is so still, but now it wants
the wildness and the flowers, nor has it the deep river
channels and their overhanging bluffs which here and
there relieve the uniformity of the North American
prairie states. However, in many places orchards and
clumps of other trees are being grown round the man-
sion house. Such a clump, being the only sort of eminence that breaks the skyline, is called a *Monte*. The
swift-growing Australian gum, which has now domesticated itself in most of the warmer parts of the world,
waves its pliant tops in the breeze, more picturesque
in the distance than it is close at hand. If man's hand
takes something away from the wild charm of nature,
he also by degrees creates that other charm which belongs to rural life, so this land will come in time to be
less dull and more homelike. Pleasure grounds round
the *estancias* will mitigate the roughness of a first settlement, and there will be groves with dim recesses
in their thickets to stir the imagination of children.
There is always in the Pampas an amplitude of air
and a solemn splendour of the sunset glow to carry the
mind away beyond its near surroundings.

Nevertheless one is glad not to have been born in the
Pampas.

Perhaps those whose early years have been passed in
flat countries do not feel the need for hills in the landscape in the same way as do the natives of Scotland or
New England. Could any one of the latter class dwell
for twelve months in Argentina without longing to rush

off for refreshment to the mountains and lakes of the South Chilean Andes.

One word more on the economic aspects of Argentina before I come to the people. The wealth of the land is in tillage and live stock. Its three great agricultural products are wheat, maize, and linseed, in each of which it is now in the front rank of exporting countries. Sugar and cotton are grown in the north, and may increase largely there as that region gets settled, and wine is made at Mendoza for home consumption. Cereals will, however, remain the most important crops. Vast as has been the increase of live stock, the limits of the ranching area have not yet been reached.[1] The export of meat received a great stimulus from the introduction of systems of cold storage and transport, and now an enormous amount of European and North American as well as Argentine capital is embarked in this trade. There is, so far as known, hardly any coal in the country, and the sources of water-power are only along the Southern Andes, so that manufacturing industries have not been established on any large scale. The slopes of the Cordilleras furnish mines of gold, silver, copper, and lead, but the production of these minerals is small compared to that of Peru and Bolivia. The people have not taken to the sea either as mercantile mariners or as fishermen, and the demand for agricultural labour has been so large that there was no occasion for any one to seek his living in those employments.

[1] There were, in 1911, 30,000,000 cattle, 68,000,000 sheep, and 7,500,000 horses.

Thus we may say that among those great countries of the world which Europeans have peopled, Argentina is that which is now, and is likely to continue, the most purely agricultural in its industrial character.

The best evidence or illustration of the swift progress of the republic and of the confidence which European investors feel in its resources is to be found in the development of its railway system. The first railway line was opened in 1857 and was twelve miles long. In 1911 there were nearly 20,000 miles in operation, and the receipts in 1910 amounted to £20,000,000. Most of these railways, many of which are of a gauge broader than those of the United States or Great Britain, have been built and are worked by British companies, a few by the government.[1]

In this immense fertile and temperate country with hardly six people to a square mile, what limit can we set to the growth of wealth and population? Already the nation is larger than the Dutch or Portuguese or Swedish. Within thirty years it may equal Italy. Within fifty years it may approach France or England, even if the present rate of its increase be reduced. It may one day be the most numerous among all the peoples that speak a tongue of Latin origin, as the United States is already the most numerous of all that speak a Teutonic one. Many things may happen to change its present char-

[1] The total amount of British capital invested in Argentine railroads, tramways, banks, and land was, in 1910, £295,000,000. In writing about a country which attracts the world chiefly by its material development it is impossible to avoid figures, but I wish to give the reader no more than are absolutely needed.

acter, yet the unformed character of the youth before
whom such a future seems to lie is well worth studying.

First a few words about the race.   No other Spanish-
American state, except Uruguay, has a people of a stock
so predominantly European.   The aboriginal Indian
element is too small to be worth regarding.   It is now
practically confined to the Gran Chaco in the extreme
north, but elsewhere the influence of Indian blood is
undiscernible among the people to-day.[1]   The aborigines of the central Pampas have disappeared, — nearly
all were killed off, — and those of Patagonia have been
dying out.   We have, therefore, a nation practically of
pure South European blood, whose differences from the
parent stock are due, not to the infusion of native elements, but to local and historical causes.

Till thirty or forty years ago this population was almost entirely of Spanish stock.   Then the rapid development of the Pampas for tillage began to create a demand
for labour, which, while it increased immigration from
Spain, brought in a new and larger flow from Italy.
The Spaniards who came were largely from the northern
provinces and among them there were many Basques, a
race as honest and energetic as any in Europe.   So far
back as 1875 one used to see in the French Basque
country between Biarritz and the pass of Roncesvalles
plenty of neat and comfortable houses erected by men
who had bought back their savings from the River

[1] There is, however, a small population of mixed Indian and
colonial stock in the plateau of the Andean northwest adjoining
Bolivia.

Plate. The Italians have flocked in from all parts of their peninsula, but the natives of the north take to the land, and furnish a very large part of the agricultural labour, while the men from the southern provinces, usually called Napolitanos, stay in the towns and work as railway and wharf porters, or as boatmen, and at various odd jobs. In 1909, out of 1,750,000 persons of foreign birth in the republic,[1] there were twice as many Italians as Spaniards, besides one hundred thousand from France, the latter including many French Basques, who are no more French than Spanish. Between 1904 and 1909 the influx of immigrants had risen from 125,-000 annually to 255,000. The Spaniards, of course, blend naturally and quickly with the natives, who speak the same tongue. The Italians have not yet blent, for there has hardly yet been time for them to do so, but there is so much similarity, not indeed in character but in language and ways of life, that they will evidently become absorbed into the general population. Children born in the country grow up to be Argentines in sentiment, and are, perhaps, even more vehemently patriotic than the youth of native stock.

Here, as in the United States, the birth-rate is higher among immigrants than among natives. In the case of Italians it is twice, in that of Spaniards one and a half times, as great.

What effect upon the type and tendencies of the future nation this Italian infusion will have it is hard to predict, because no one knows how far national charac-

[1] 844,000 were from Italy, 424,000 from Spain.

ter is affected by blood admixture.   We have no data
for estimating the comparative importance of heredity
and of environment upon a population which is the
product of two elements, the foreign one injected into
a larger native element whose prepotent influences
modify the offspring of new-comers.[1]

In considering the probable result of the commingling,
and as a fact explaining the readiness with which Italian
immigrants allow themselves to be Argentinized, one
must remember that these come from the humblest and
least educated strata of Italian society.   They are, like
all Italians, naturally intelligent, but they have not
reached that grade of knowledge which attaches men
to the literature and the historical traditions of their
own country.   Thus, the scantiness of their education
prevents them from making either to the intellectual
life or to the art of their adopted country those contributions which one might expect from a people which
has always held a place in the front rank of European
letters, art, and science.   It may be expected, however,
that in the course of a generation or two inborn Italian
capacity will assert itself in the descendants of the immigrants.

The other foreigners, French, English (business men
and landowning farmers), and German (chiefly business
men in the cities) are hardly numerous enough to affect
the Argentine type, and the two latter have hitherto re-

[1] Some remarks upon this obscure question will be found in
Chapter XCII of the author's *American Commonwealth* (edition of
1910).   The problem is rather simpler here than in the United
States because the recently injected elements are here less various.

mained as distinct elements, being mostly Protestants and marrying persons of their own race. They occupy themselves entirely with business and have not entered Argentine public life; yet as many of them mean to remain in the country, and their children born in it become thereby Argentine citizens, it is likely that they, also, will presently be absorbed, and their Argentine descendants may figure in politics here, as families of Irish and British origin do in Chile.

The social structure of the nation is the result of the economic conditions already described. In the rural districts there are two classes only,—landowners, often with vast domains, and labourers, the native labourers settled, the Italians to some extent migratory. In the cities there exists, between the wealthy and the workingmen, a considerable body of professional men, shopkeepers, and clerks, who are rather less of a defined middle class than they would be in European countries. Society is something like that of North American cities, for the lines between classes are not sharply drawn, and the spirit of social equality has gone further than in France, and, of course, far further than in Germany or Spain. One cannot speak of an aristocracy, even in the qualified sense in which the word could be used in Peru or Chile, for though a few old colonial families have the Spanish pride of lineage, it is, as a rule, wealth and wealth only that gives station and social eminence. Manners, which everywhere in South America have lost something of the courtliness of Castile, are here rather more "modern" than in Mexico or Lima, because the growth of wealth has brought up new men and has made money the criterion of eminence, or at least of prominence. Here, as in England and the United States, one sees that though the constitution is democratic, society has some of the characteristics of a plutocracy.

The little that I have to say about the political life of the country must be reserved for another and more general chapter, so I will here note only two facts peculiar to Argentina. It is, of all the Spanish-American republics, that in which the church has least to do with politics. Though Roman Catholicism is declared by the constitution to be supported by the state, and the president and vice-president must profess it, that freedom of religious worship which is guaranteed by law is fully carried out in practice, and all denominations may, without let or hindrance, erect churches and preach and teach. The legislature has shewn itself so broad-minded as to grant subventions to a system of Protestant schools founded originally as a missionary enterprise by a Protestant Episcopal clergyman, and many of the Roman Catholic families of Buenos Aires send their children to schools provided by the American Methodist Episcopal Church. In liberality of spirit, Argentina is rather more advanced than either Peru or Chile, not to speak of bigoted Ecuador. Still more noteworthy is it that there seems to be little or no effort on the part of the church to influence public affairs. No political party is allied with the clergy, no clerical influence is felt in elections. The happy detachment of the two spheres which travellers observe and admire in North America deserves even more credit when found in a country where intolerance long reigned ·supreme.

The other phenomenon which no one will connect with religious freedom, inasmuch as it has appeared in nearly every country of Europe and of North America, whatever be the religious conditions that prevail, is the emergence here and nowhere else in South America of a vehement anarchist propaganda. Among the immigrants from Italy and from eastern Spain there have been enough persons engaged in this movement to cause great alarm to the government. Not long ago the chief of the police was killed by an explosive thrown by a Russian anarchist, and in the summer of 1910 a bomb was exploded in the great Opera-house during a performance, wounding a number of persons. These occurrences led to the proclamation of a state of siege which was maintained for many weeks. The police is said to be efficient,[1] and the Executive did not hesitate to use powers which it would be less easy to obtain or use in the United States or in England. Our age has seen too many strange incidents to be surprised that these acts of violence should be perpetrated in a country where, though no doubt there is an ostentatious display of wealth, work is more abundant and wages are higher than in any other part of the world. Such acts are aimed not at oppression, nor at bad industrial conditions, but at government itself.

[1] I was told that many of the street police are Indians from the north of the country.

Here, as generally in South America, though less in Chile than elsewhere, politics is mainly in the hands of the lawyers. A great deal of the best intellect of the country, probably more in proportion than in any European country or in the United States, goes into this profession; and the contributions to the world's store of thought and learning made by Argentine writers have been perhaps more considerable in this branch of enquiry than in any other. In the sphere of historical or philosophical or imaginative literature, not much has yet been done, nor is the class prepared to read such books a large one. Fiction is supplied by France. The press is a factor in public affairs whose power is comparable to that exercised by the leading newspapers in Australia. It is conducted on large and bold lines, especially conspicuous in two journals of the capital[1] which have now a long record of vigour and success behind them. The concentration of political and commercial activities in Buenos Aires gives to them the same advantage that belongs to the leading organs of Sydney and Melbourne.

The world is to-day ruled by physical science and by business, which, in the vast proportions industry and commerce have now attained, is itself the child of

---

[1] They have a mass of readers near at hand and a revenue from advertisements comparable to those which are found in the United States and Australia, but are not found in Spanish America outside Buenos Aires.

Mr. F. Seebey states that, in 1903, 212 periodicals were published in Buenos Aires in various languages or dialects, including Basque, Catalan, and Genoese.

physical science. Argentina is thoroughly modern in the predominance of business over all other interests. Only one other comes near it. The Bostonian man of letters who complained that London was no place to live in because people talked of nothing but sport and politics, would have been even less happy in Buenos Aires, because there, when men do not talk of sport, they talk of business. Politics is left to the politicians; it is the *estancia*, its cattle and its crops, and the race-course, with its betting, that are always in the mind and on the tongue, and are moulding the character, of the wealthier class. Business is no doubt still so largely in the hands of foreigners that one cannot say that the average Argentine has developed a talent for it comparable to that of those whom he calls the North Americans, seeing that much of his wealth has come to him by the rise in the values of his land and the immense demand for its products. He is seldom a hard worker, for it has been his ill fortune to be able to get by sitting still what others have had to work for, but he does not yield to New York in what is called a "go-ahead spirit." He is completely up to date. He has both that jubilant patriotism and that exuberant confidence in his country which marked the North American of 1830–1860. His pride in his city has had the excellent result of making him eager to put it, and keep it, in the forefront of progress, with buildings as fine, parks as large, a water supply as ample, provisions for public health as perfect, as money can buy or science can devise. The wealth and the expansion of Buenos Aires inspire him, as the wealth and expansion of Chicago have inspired her citizens, and give him, if not all of their forceful energy, yet a great deal of their civic idealism.

It is the only kind of idealism that one finds in the city or the country. Every visitor is struck by the dominance of material interests and a material view of things. Compared with the raking in of money and the spending it in betting or in ostentatious luxury, a passion for the development of the country's resources and the adornment of its capital stand out as aims that widen the vision and elevate the soul. A recent acute and friendly observer has said that patriotism among the Argentines amounts to a mania. Such excess of sentiment is not only natural in a young and growing nation, and innocent too (so long as it is not aggressive), but is helpful in giving men something beyond their own material enjoyments and vanities to think of and to work for. It makes them wish to stand well in the world's eyes, and do in the best way what they see others doing. If there is an excess, time will correct it.

Loitering in the great Avenida de Mayo and watching the hurrying crowd and the whirl of motor cars, and the gay shop-windows, and the open-air cafés on the sidewalks, and the Parisian glitter of the women's dresses, one feels much nearer to Europe than anywhere else in South America. Bolivia suggests the seventeenth century and Peru the eighteenth, and even in energetic Chile there is an air of the elder time, and a soothing sense of detachment. But here all is twentieth century, with suggestions of the twenty-first.

Yet, modern as they are, and reminding one sometimes of the gaiety of Paris and sometimes of the stir and hurry of Kansas City, the Argentines are essentially unlike either Europeans or North Americans. To say in what the difference consists is all the harder because one doubts whether there yet exists a definite Argentine type. They have ceased to be Spaniards without becoming something new of their own. They seem to be a nation in the making, not yet made. Elements more than half of which are Spanish and Basque, and one-third of which are Italian, are all being shaken up together and beginning to mix and fuse under conditions not before seen in South American life. That which will emerge, if more Spanish than Italian in blood, will be entirely South American in sentiment and largely French in its ways of thinking, for from France come the intellectual influences that chiefly play upon it. It will spring from new conditions and new forces, acting on people who have left all their traditions and many of their habits behind them, and have retained but little of that religion which was the strongest of all powers in their former home. Men now living may see this nation, what with its growing numbers and its wealth, take rank beside France, Italy, and Spain. It may be, in the New World, the head and champion of what are called the Latin races. Will the artistic and literary genius of Italy, France, and Spain flower again in their transplanted descendants, now that they seem to have at last emerged from those long civil wars and revolutions which followed their separation from Spain? The very magnitude of the interests which any fresh civil wars would endanger furnishes a security against their recurrence, and the temper of the people seems entirely disposed to internal peace. No race or colour questions have arisen, and religious questions have ceased to vex them. They have an agricultural area still undeveloped which for fifty years to come will be large enough both to attract immigrants and to provide for the needs of their own citizens. Seldom has Nature lavished gifts upon a people with a more bountiful hand.

CHAPTER X

WHOEVER wishes to have something by which to distinguish Uruguay from its many sister republics, the size and character of each of which are unfamiliar to many of us in Europe, may learn to remember that it is the smallest of the South American states, and that it has neither mountains, nor deserts, nor antiquities, nor aboriginal Indians. Nevertheless, it is by no means a country to be described by negatives, but has, as we shall presently see, a marked character of its own.

Having belonged to the viceroyalty of Buenos Aires, and being peopled by men of the same pure Spanish stock as those who dwelt in Argentina, it would probably have continued to be a part of that country but for the fact that, as it lay close to Brazil, it was from time to time occupied and held by the Portuguese of that country, sometimes by conquest, sometimes by formal cession from the crown of Spain. Thus its people, who had, when part of the Spanish dominions, a governor of their own under the Viceroy, began to acquire a sort of national consciousness as a community distinct from their fellow-countrymen on the opposite shore of the Rio de la Plata and the Uruguay river. They got the name of the *Banda Oriental* (East Side), as opposed to the rest of Argentina on the west side of the Uruguay. When the colonists began, from 1810 onwards, to assert their independence of the crown of Spain, the Orientales, as the Uruguayans were then usually called, had to fight their own battle and fought it valiantly. The Portuguese of Brazil, now allying themselves with Spain in defence of monarchy, invaded the country, and it was their expulsion in 1814, as the outcome of a long struggle under the famous patriot leader Artigas, that finally set Uruguay free. After the Argentines had tried more than once to force her into their federation, and the Portuguese had again invaded and occupied the devastated land, Uruguay was ultimately recognized as a sovereign State in 1828 by both Argentina and Brazil, the latter now independent of Portugal. By this time incessant wars and sufferings had formed a distinctive type of character and lit up a flame of national feeling which has burnt strongly ever since.

With an area of only 72,000 square miles, as against 1,135,000 in Argentina and 3,208,000 in Brazil, Uruguay seems like a garden plot between two vast estates. But she is a veritable garden. There is hardly an acre of useless ground within her borders. Except a few bare hilltops and a few sandy stretches on the coast, all is available, either for cattle and sheep, or for tillage, or for forest growth. No country is more favoured by nature. The surface is gently undulating along the sea and rises inland into swelling downs intersected here and there by ranges of hills. The abundant grass is deemed the

best for cattle in all South America, so for many years
ranching was practically the only industry. Latterly,
however, a great deal of land has been brought under
cultivation. Wheat and maize are the principal
crops, and there are now many vineyards. As the climate, while generally resembling that of central Argentina, is tempered by the neighbourhood of the Atlantic,
the winters are less cold and the summers cooler in
Montevideo than they are on the other side of the
Plate estuary. Further north, where Uruguay adjoins Brazil, the midsummer heats are severe and
the vegetation becomes subtropical. It is a cheerful
country, with scenery constructed, so to speak, on a small
scale, as befits a small republic. Broad uplands of
waving grass, with here and there tree clumps, and in
the centre and north of the country bosky glens winding through rocky hills, make the landscape always
pleasing and sometimes romantic. There are no great
forests, no deserts, no volcanoes, nothing half so grand
as the peaks of the Argentine Andes, but nothing
half so monotonous as the flats of the Argentine
Pampa.

Montevideo the capital has the same air of freshness
and cheerfulness which belong to Uruguayan landscape
and the Uruguayan climate. It has grown to be a
great and prosperous city in respect of its port, which
makes it the chief seat of the republic's commerce.
The estuary of the River Plate is much deeper on this
northern side than on the southern, so large ships
have always been able to approach nearer to this shore

than they could do to the Argentine. By deepening the
entrance and running out breakwaters, a good harbour
has now been created, accessible to vessels of exceptionally deep draught which could not (in 1910) come
up to the docks in Buenos Aires. The city is also more
fortunate in its site, for the ground, a dead flat on the
Argentine side, here rises from the shore in a slope steep
enough to afford fine views over the sea and to enable
the church towers and other tall buildings to present
an effective sky-line.

Montevideo, with its 300,000 inhabitants against the
1,300,000 of Buenos Aires, has streets by no means so
thronged as are those of the Argentine capital. Neither
are the houses quite so high, nor is there the same
sense of a vast country behind, pouring its products out
by this water-gate that leads to Europe. But here,
just as in Buenos Aires, everything is modern. Only
one public building, the old Town Hall in the chief plaza,
dates from colonial times and has, or seems by its quaint-
ness to have, a sort of artistic quality which is absent
from the work, all French rather than Spanish in character, of the last sixty years. The plazas are handsome,
well laid out and planted, and the street architecture
creditable, with fewer contrasts of meanness and magnificence than one usually sees in the growing cities of North
America. There is an absence not only of external
squalor, but of any marks of poverty, for the people seem
brisk and thriving, with plenty of money coming in. For
many miles round the environs are studded with tasteful villas, and the well-kept roads that traverse them

are lined by splendid rows of Australian blue gums.
Three points of interest deserve to be specially mentioned. One is the Cerro, an isolated conical hill on
the southwestern side of the bay, opposite the main city,
and an object so conspicuous and picturesque on this
generally tame coast that it has found a place in the arms
of the republic. The castle that surmounts it has
no merit as a building, but the view is superb
along the coast and out to sea where the pale grey
waters of the Paraná and Uruguay meet the ocean blue.
The second ornament of the suburbs is the Botanical
Garden. Its display of spring flowers, both native and
European, and the wonderful variety of trees from
semitropical and temperate regions, give a vivid sense
of the powers of this admirable climate, not oppressive
in the blaze of its sunlight, yet warm enough for roses
twice as luxuriant as the best that Europe can show.
Lastly, there is a fine collection of wild animals in a
garden belonging to a private gentleman of large means,
who is unique in the personal relations which his kindly
disposition has enabled him to establish with the creatures, even with the beasts of prey. There were
splendid jaguars and pumas, and there were South
American ant-eaters with tongues longer than themselves. But what most delighted the holiday crowd,
who are permitted to ramble through the gardens, was
to see a brace of lion cubs strolling about in a friendly
way among men, women, and children, while the owner
led us close up to the bars of the cage in which his pet
lion, a superb giant, sat peacefully blinking and made us

2 A

stroke it and rub its back. The lion took the attention
benignly and beamed on his master, but the attitude
of the lioness in the further corner of the cage did not
encourage any such familiarities.

Like Argentina, Uruguay is destined to be a pastoral
and agricultural, not a mining or manufacturing country. There are some minerals, including gold, manga-
nese, iron, and coal, but none of these is worked on a
large scale, and it has not yet been proved that either
coal or iron is present in quantities sufficient to form the
basis of any important industry. Cattle are at present
the chief source of wealth, the export of meat having
been greatly increased by the recently invented methods
of freezing and chilling. Meat, hides, wool, wheat,
and maize are likely to continue to be the mainstay
of the country's prosperity ; and as only about one-
eighth of the surface is at present under tillage, there
is room for great expansion.   No better evidence of
progress can be furnished than the extension of railways. The first was begun in 1866. There were, in
1910, 1472 miles in operation, and construction continues to go briskly forward. The chief centres of population are either on the coast or on the banks of the
great navigable river Uruguay, whence cattle, meat, and
wool are shipped.

So far, therefore, Uruguay has all the material conditions required for prosperity and happiness, an abundance of good land, a temperate and genial climate,
water highways for traffic provided by Nature in her
rivers, artificial iron highways on land, supplied by

enterprising British capitalists. What is to be said of her inhabitants?

They were, till recent years, almost entirely of Spanish stock. The warlike native Indians, one of whose tribes, the Charruas, were fierce fighters, having been killed off, and the weaker tribes having quietly melted away, very little aboriginal blood has mingled itself with the Iberian stock. Some negroes are to be found along the Brazilian frontier, but they do not seem to have perceptibly affected the European element. Of late years a stream of immigrants has flowed in from Italy, yet in no such volume as toward Argentina. There is also a steady, though smaller, inflow from Spain; among whom there are, fortunately, many industrious Basques. Rather more than a fifth of the population are of foreign birth, a proportion small compared to that of the foreign-born population of Rhode Island or Massachusetts. These new-comers will soon be assimilated and are not likely to modify the national type.

That type strikes the foreign observer as already distinct and well marked. The Uruguayan is, of course, first and foremost a Colonial Spaniard, but a Spaniard moulded by the conditions of his life during the last ninety years. He has been a man of the country and the open air, strong, active, and lawless, always in the saddle riding after his cattle, handy with his lasso and his gun. Fifty years ago he was a Gaucho, much like his Argentine cousin beyond the river. Now he, too, like that cousin, is settling down, but he has retained something of the breezy recklessness and audacity, the frankness and free-handedness, of the older days. A touch of this Gaucho quality, in a milder form, is felt through all classes of Uruguayan society. Democratic equality in manners is combined with a high sense of personal dignity, an immense hopefulness, an impulsive readiness to try all experiments, a national consciousness none the less intense because it already rejoices over the triumphs it is going to achieve. Whether there is more of "ideality" than in Argentina I will not venture to say, but there is less wealth and less ostentation. Englishmen and North Americans settled in Montevideo like the Uruguayans, and say they are good fellows. There is evidently something attractive about them when the sons of such settlers grow up fond of the country, willing and proud to be its citizens. You will hear an English-speaking youth of either race say, if asked whether he is an Englishman or an American, "I am an Uruguayan."

While we were in Montevideo a revolution broke out in the country. There was sharp fighting about forty miles away from the city and the railways were bringing in the wounded. It caused no great excitement, having been expected for some weeks, and the newspapers told their readers very little of what was happening. They did not know much, for the military authorities had stopped every channel of communication. That, however, would of itself have been a very poor reason for not furnishing details. There were other and more imperative grounds for reticence.

We were unfortunately unable to see anything and could learn little of the revolution, but its origin and especially the perfect *sang-froid* of the Montevideans, both natives and Englishmen, struck us as curious. A short explanation of the conditions attending such outbreaks may throw light on the phenomena of other republics as well as Uruguay.

Ever since the colonists declared their independence of Spain, fighting has been almost incessant in this smiling land. They fought first against the Spanish troops, and then against the Portuguese rulers of Brazil; they fought several times against Argentina and Paraguay, and almost incessantly against one another. As soon as independence had been secured and the Portuguese finally expelled, the two leading generals (Rivera and Oribe) who had led the patriots to victory quarrelled, and before long were striving in arms for the chief place in the republic. Their adherents grew into two factions, which soon divided the nation, or so much of it as took an active interest in politics. At the first battle General Oribe, who headed one of the parties, rode a white horse, and his lancers carried white pennons on their spearheads; so they were called the Blancos. The followers of the rival general, Rivera, had red pennons, and he rode a bay horse. They were, therefore, the Colorados. From that day on Uruguayans have been divided into Whites and Reds. Seventy-five years had passed and the grandsons of the men who had fought under Oribe and Rivera in 1835 were still fighting in 1910.

For what have they been fighting? At first there were no principles involved; it was a personal feud between two soldiers, who not long before had stood shoulder to shoulder against the Brazilian invader. But just as political parties sometimes drop the tenets with which they started and yet live on as organizations, so sometimes factions which started without tenets pick them up as they go along and make them watchwords. A party is apt to capture any current issue, or be captured by it, and to become, thereafter, committed to or entangled with it. Thus the Whites became in course of time the country party as opposed to the Reds of the towns, and especially of Montevideo, and thus, as the city is the home of new views and desires for change, the Reds have become the anticlerical and the Whites the church party. It would seem that the colours have nothing to do with the now almost forgotten term (common in France in 1848–1851) of the "Red Republic," but another sort of connection with Europe may be found in the story that the Garibaldian red shirt, which figured on so many battle-fields in Sicily and Italy, was due to Giuseppe Garibaldi's having fought on the Colorado side, in 1842–1846, against Rosas and the Argentine invaders, the emblem being retained when that last of the heroes raised his standard in the Italian revolution of 1848.[1]

[1] The account of the origin of the red shirt given by Mr. G. M. Trevelyan in his interesting book, *Garibaldi and the Defence of Rome*, is not quite the same as that which I heard in Uruguay, but not incompatible therewith.

When an insurrection is planned in Uruguay, word is sent round that its supporters are to rendezvous, armed and mounted, at certain spots on a certain day, and when the government gets to know of the plan, its first step is to seize all the horses in the disaffected districts and drive them to a place where they are kept under a strong guard. The horse is the life of a revolutionary movement, a tradition from the grand old Gaucho days; and without horses, the insurgents are powerless.

The Blancos have been out of power in Uruguay since 1864, but they hold well together and compose an opposition which acts by constitutional methods in the legislature (when any of its partisans can find an entrance) and by military methods outside the constitution, in the open country, whenever peaceful methods are deemed useless. The parties have become largely hereditary; a child is born a little Blanco or a little Colorado, and rarely deserts his colour. Feeling runs so high that in Blanco districts it is dangerous for a man to wear a red necktie, just as in driving through certain Irish towns a harmless botanist from Britain may, when his car approaches a particular quarter, be warned by the driver to throw away or cover over the ferns which he has gathered in a mountain glen, because the sight of the obnoxious colour will expose him to be stoned by those who regard its display as an affront.

These revolutions, however, have in the course of years been tending to become rather less frequent, and certainly less sanguinary, just as in parts of South America there are volcanoes once terrible by their tremendous eruptions which now content themselves with throwing out a few showers of ashes or discharging a stream of lava from a little crater near the base. This rising ended with a surrender, accompanied by an amnesty which included the absence of any decree of confiscation of property, so no blood was shed except in the field.

When I asked what were the grievances alleged to justify the revolt of November, 1910, the answer was that an election of the legislature was impending, that the new legislature would, when elected, proceed forthwith to the choice of a President of the republic for the next four years, that the Blancos fully expected that the elections would be so handled by the government in power as to secure a majority certain to choose a particular candidate whom the Blancos feared and disliked, and that therefore the only course open to the latter was to avert by an appeal to arms the wrong which would be done to the nation by tampering with the rights of the electors. How much truth there may have been in these allegations the passing traveller could not know, nor was it for him to judge whether, if true, they would warrant an appeal to force.

The conditions in some Latin-American republics are peculiar, and can be paralleled only in one or two other parts of the modern world. In the years between 1848 and 1859 when despotic governments held sway in most parts of Europe, the ingenuous youth of Britain used to assume, as Thomas Jefferson had done fifty years before, that every insurrection was presumably justifiable and entitled to the sympathy of all lovers of freedom. Of recent years, since constitutional governments have been established in nearly all countries, the presumption is deemed to be the other way, and revolts are *prima facie* disapproved. In some American republics, however, — and here I am speaking not of Uruguay, but of more backward communities, — there is no presumption at all either way. A government in Nicaragua or Honduras, for instance, has usually obtained power either by force of arms or by a mock election carried through under military pressure. To eject it by similar means is, therefore, in the eye of a constitutional lawyer, not a breach of law and order, because the government which it is sought to eject has no legal title, being itself the child of wrongdoing. On the other hand the insurgents are probably no better friends of law and order than is the government. If they succeed by arms, they will not hold an honest election, but will rule by force, just as did their predecessors. There is, accordingly, no ground for the award of sympathy or moral approval to either faction, while for foreign powers the problem of when to recognize a government that has come in by the sword, and will presently, like the Priest of the Grove at Nemi, perish by the sword, is no easy one, and must usually be solved by waiting till such a government has made itself so clearly master of the situation as to possess a *de facto* title likely to hold good for some time to come, and perhaps ultimately pass into a title *de iure*.[1]

[1] Such legal or quasi-legal questions have arisen several times in Central America.

Reverting to Uruguay, the most curious and histori-
cally instructive feature of her case is that these re-
current civil wars and attempts at revolution do not
seem to have retarded her prosperity. She saw more
incessant fighting from 1810 till 1876 than any other
part of the world has seen for the last hundred years.
Even since then risings and conflicts have been frequent, and though there has been no foreign war since
1870, when that with Paraguay ended, the presence
on either side of two great powers, not always friendly
to her or to each other, has often caused anxiety.
Nevertheless, the country has continued to grow in
wealth and population. Capital has flowed in freely to
build railways, and the good opinion which European
investors entertain is shewn by the fact that the Uruguayan five per cent bonds average just about par in
the London stock market. Foreign trade has increased
fivefold since 1862. Without forsaking their love of
fighting, the people have turned to work, and the land
or cattle owner depends less on foreign labour than he
does in Argentina. Thus it would seem that as there
have been countries ruined by war — as Central Asia
Minor was by the long strife between the Seljukian
Turks and the East Roman Emperors, and as Germany suffered from the Thirty Years' War injuries
it cost her nearly two centuries to repair, so there
are countries which have thriven in the midst of
war. In the sixth and fifth centuries B.C. the Greek
cities of Sicily were seldom at peace. They fought
with the Carthaginians, they fought with one another,

they fought for or against a Tyrant within their own walls; and all this fighting was done by citizen soldiers. Yet they throve and erected those majestic temples whose ruins we admire at Girgenti and Selinunte, while the iron peace of Rome in those later days, when the island had been made a province, brought to the country folk misery interrupted only by servile insurrections.

The occasional recurrence of such incidents as that of November, 1910, had not for some years prior to my visit prevented the government of Uruguay from emulating that of Argentina in efforts to keep abreast of Europe in all sorts of administrative schemes for the advancement of education, and for the development of the country. In two respects it has entered on a policy different from that of other South American states. It is the only one in which schemes or ideas tending towards state socialism have been countenanced by the Executive, and it is also the only one in which there is a distinctly antireligious party. In Peru the church has still some political influence. In Chile she has less, in Argentina practically none, but in neither is she the object of hostility. Here, however, a section of the dominant party is professedly antagonistic to the church, and this would seem to be due not to any provocation given recently by the clergy, whose Blanco friends have been long out of power, but rather to a spirit which seeks to strike at and eliminate religion itself.

Such a movement does not seem, any more than do socialistic ideas, to be a natural growth of the Uruguayan soil. Just as the anarchistic propaganda in

Argentina has been recently brought thither from Europe by immigrants, so this less fierce expression of the revolutionary spirit bears marks of having been transplanted from those parts of southern Europe where the more violent advocates of change regard not only the Roman Church, but religion itself, as hostile to progress and to the reconstruction of society on a new basis. The rural population of Uruguay are not the sort of people among whom such ideas would spontaneously arise, for they belong, so far as their beliefs and views of life are concerned, rather to the eighteenth than to the twentieth century. Elsewhere in South America, enmity to the church has been due to the power she has exercised in the secular world, or to the memory of her old habits of repression. One does not hear, however, that she has for a long time past been politically obnoxious here; nor can there have been any memories of serious persecution to provoke hatred, for the 'era of persecution was passing away when these regions began to be thickly settled.

With her temperate climate and her fertile soil, Uruguay is an attractive country. In no part of South America, except perhaps southern Chile, would a European feel more disposed to settle down for life. The people are of pure European stock and have many of the qualities — frankness and energy, courage, and a high sense of honour — which make for political progress. The country is no doubt comparatively small, and it is the fashion nowadays to worship bigness and disparage small nations. Yet the independent city communities, or the small nations — such as were England and Holland in the seventeenth century — have produced not only most of the best literature and art, but most of the great men and great achievements which history records. National life is apt to be more intense and more interesting where it is concentrated in an area not so wide as to forbid the people to know one another and their leaders. Thus one cannot but hope that the Uruguayans, with some favouring conditions, and without the disadvantage of excessive wealth suddenly acquired, will seriously endeavour to smooth the road, now rough and dangerous, over which the chariot of their republican government has to travel. It is not the Constitution that is at fault, but the way in which the Constitution is worked. The backward state of education and consequent incompetence of the ordinary citizen is usually assigned as the source of political troubles. There is certainly an inadequate provision both here and generally in South America of elementary and secondary schools. But the experience of many countries has shewn that the education of the masses is not enough to secure a reform in political methods. There is surely force in the view I heard expressed, that if the whole population, or even the whole of the educated class in the population, were to exert themselves to take more active part in politics, they could set things right by checking the abuses or grievances out of which revolutions grow and by moderating the party spirit which rushes to arms when grievances remain unredressed.

CHAPTER XI

THAT more than half of South America was settled by and still belongs to the men of Portugal is due to what may be called an historical accident. In the year following the discovery of the West Indies by Columbus, Pope Alexander the Sixth issued his famous Bull (A.D. 1493) which assigned to the Crown of Castile and Leon " all the islands and lands to be discovered in the seas to the west and the south of a meridian line to be drawn from the Arctic to the Antarctic Pole, one hundred leagues to the west of Cape Verde and the Azores." Though there is in the Bull no mention of Portugal, it was intended to reserve the rights of Portugal in whatever she had discovered or might discover on the other, *i.e.* the eastern, side of the line of delimitation. The Portuguese, however, were not satisfied, and next year a treaty between Spain and Portugal moved the line three hundred and seventy leagues farther west. This had the effect, as discovery progressed, of giving to Portugal the eastern, to Spain the western, part of the Continent which was first touched by Columbus in his third voyage (1498). Now it so happened that one of the first navigators who actually saw that eastern part was a Portuguese, named Cabral. Driven out of his course while sailing for India, in A.D.

1500, he touched the South American coast, in latitude 8° south, and took possession of it in the name of his sovereign. A few months earlier the Spanish sailor, Pinzon, had struck the same coast and had taken possession of it for Spain, but as Spain had plenty of discovered land already, and did not care to depart from her treaty of 1494, the territory was left to Portugal. Both nations had recognized the Pope as the authority entitled to dispose of all new-found lands, and possibly they may have supposed in 1500 that these new lands were part of the same Indies which Portugal had reached by the eastern route in 1498, six years after Columbus had, as was then supposed, reached them by the western.[1] Thus Brazil became and has ever since remained a Portuguese country, except during the eclipse of Portugal, when, after the death of King Sebastian, it fell for a time under the Crown of Spain.

The area of Brazil is about 3,300,000 square miles, larger than that of the United States, and more than double that of India. Most of its territory is inhabited only by aboriginal Indians, many of them wild savages, and a good deal is still practically unexplored. As I saw, and can attempt to describe, only a very small part, it may be proper, lest any reader should fancy that particular part to be typical of the whole, to sketch very briefly the general features of the country.

[1] This question is involved with that relating to the voyages, real or alleged, of Americus Vespuccius in 1497, and is too intricate to be discussed here.

It is geologically one of the oldest parts of the South American Continent. The mountains which form its central nucleus stood where they stand now long before the great volcanoes of the Andes, such as Aconcagua and Chimborazo, had been raised. This mountain centre of the country falls abruptly on the east to the Atlantic, more gently on the west towards the level ground in the middle of the Continent, and is composed of ancient crystalline rocks, which have probably been reduced from a much greater height by the action of rain, sun, and wind, continued through countless ages. It may be roughly described as an undulating plateau, 800 miles long by 300 broad, traversed by various ranges which are seldom of great height. Their loftiest summit is Italiaya, about fifty miles to the southwest of Rio de Janeiro and nearly 10,000 feet high. Few exceed 7000 feet, while the average elevation of the highlands as a whole is from 2000 to 3000. The scenery of their richly wooded eastern side, where they break down steeply towards the Atlantic, is as beautiful as can be found anywhere in the tropics. They are continued northward and southward in lower hills, and on the west subside gently, sometimes in long slopes, sometimes in a succession of broad terraces, into a vast plain, only slightly raised above sea-level, from which streams flow southward into the Paraná, northward into the Amazon. In this plain, still imperfectly explored, Brazil touches Paraguay and Bolivia. The inland regions, both highlands and plains, are less humid and, therefore, less densely wooded than is the line of mountains which faces the Atlantic, the climate steadily growing drier as one goes inland from the rain-giving ocean. Large parts of them are believed to be fit only for ranching, but settlement has in the western districts not gone far enough to determine their capacity for agriculture, though it is known that some are unprofitable because marshy and others because sandy. On the other hand the country south of latitude 20° is for the most part fertile and well watered, and more developed than any other part of Brazil except the coast strip.

There remains another and still larger region which lies in the northwest part of the republic; I mean the vast plain of the Amazon and its tributaries. It is the so-called Selvas, or woodland country, covered everywhere by a dense forest and for part of the year so flooded by the tropical rains which raise its rivers above their banks that much of it can be traversed only in boats. Except for a few white settlements here and there, its sole inhabitants are the uncivilized Indian tribes, of whom there may be several hundred thousands in all, a number very small when compared to the space over which they are scattered. To these Selvas and their possible future I shall return.[1] Meanwhile the reader will have gathered that: (1) The whole eastern part of Brazil from latitude 5° south to latitude 30° south is mountainous or undulating, with here and there wide valleys. All of this country is valuable either for cultivation, for pasture, or for tim-

[1] See Chapter XVI, *post.*

2 B

ber, and it contains rich mines.   (2) The western part and the whole plain of the Amazon and its tributaries is practically quite flat, and most of it is a forest wilderness.   (3) Though there are some arid districts along the coast north and south of the mouth of the Amazon, there are nowhere in Brazil such deserts as those which cover so large a space in Peru, Bolivia, Chile, and Argentina.   (4) The only parts that are as yet comparatively well-peopled are the coast strip and the fertile valleys debouching on that strip, some inland districts in the state of Minas Geraes, and in the southern states of São Paulo, Santa Catharina, and Rio Grande do Sul. Even in these the population is still far below the capacities of the country.

I have made these few remarks in order to give the reader some notion of the general features of this immense country.   The only parts I saw were on the east coast; and these I shall try to describe before returning to a discussion of the people and prospects of Brazil as a whole.

The south Atlantic all the way from Buenos Aires to the Amazon has the credit of giving passages as smooth and pleasant as any in the world.   Very different was our experience between Montevideo and Santos, for there was some rain, more wind, and quite a heavy sea, with weather so thick that little could be seen of the coast along which we sailed.   We were, of course, told that it was "quite exceptional weather," but old travellers know that nothing is commoner than exceptional weather.

When at last our steamer, rounding a lofty cape, turned her prow shoreward to enter the harbour of Santos, how unlike was the landscape to any which we had seen since passing the Equator at the northern extremity of Peru. All down the west coast there had been a stern and mostly barren coast, with cold grey clouds over a cold grey sea. But here at last were the tropics. Here was the region of abundant and luxuriant vegetation, a soft, moist air and a sea of vivid blue, with the strange thin-bodied, long-winged frigate birds hovering above it. As we came near enough to see the waves foaming on the rocks, an amphitheatre of mountains was disclosed, surrounding the broad, flat valley through which a river descends to form the port of Santos. To the north there ran along the coast a line of lofty promontories against which the surges rose. The mountains behind, all densely wooded, were shrouded with heavy mists, but the sun bathed in light the banks of the river, covered with low trees and flowering shrubs, and the gaily painted houses of the suburb which stretches out from the town of Santos, embowered in palm groves, to the white sands of the ocean beach.

Moving slowly up the winding channel into smooth water, we found many British and German ships lying at the wharves, for the harbour has now been so deepened as to admit large steamers, and its improvements, accompanied by draining operations, have made the place reasonably healthy. Twenty years ago it was a nest of yellow fever. I was told that once, during an inroad of that plague, forty-three British ships were lying idle in the river with their crews all dead or dying.   Now the disease has practically disappeared, and the port is one of the busiest in South America, since it is the exporting centre for the produce of the vast coffee country which lies inland.   All day long, and during the night, too, at some seasons, an endless string of stalwart porters may be seen carrying sacks of coffee from the railroad cars on the wharf to the ships lying alongside.   In 1910 coffee to the value of nearly £19,000,000 ($93,107,000) was exported from Santos, more than half of what went out of Brazil to all quarters of the globe.

Such a trade gives plenty of traffic to the railway which connects the coffee-planting interior and the thriving city of São Paulo with the sea.   It is quite a remarkable railway.   First built in 1867, its most difficult portion, which climbs a very steep slope, was laid out afresh along a better line between 1895 and 1901, and is a really skilful and interesting piece of engineering performed for a British company by British engineers and contractors.   As was observed a few pages back, there lies behind this part of the Brazilian coast a plateau, here averaging from 2500 to 3000 feet in height, which breaks down abruptly to the sea.   The edge of the plateau, which, from below, appears like a mountain range, is called the Serra do Mar (Sea Range). To reach the plateau from the flats at sea-level it was necessary to ascend some 2500 feet, and this had to be done in a distance of about six miles, which means an average gradient of about eight per cent from the bottom to the top of the slope. The line has accordingly been constructed in a series of five inclines, on which the trains are worked by wire-rope haulage, each incline having its own power-house and haulage plant, and safety being secured not only by the "locomotive brake" which is attached as a last car to each ascending and descending train, but also by the simultaneous descent and ascent of trains each way, and other devices too numerous to describe. These, taken together, are sufficient to ensure perfect safety. The extraordinary completeness and finish of every part not only of the roadbed and rails, but also of the stations and other buildings, and of the iron bridges and the thirteen tunnels, together with the neatly set tile drains which have been laid down the slopes to carry off in channels the rainwater which might otherwise dislodge loose earth from above and weaken the embankments below, — all these things witness to the unusual success and prosperity of the line as a business undertaking. It has been the best-paying one, next to that at Panama, in South America. Since the dividend assignable to the shareholders is restricted, the directors spend their surplus in securing not only efficiency and security, but even elegance. The saying, current among Europeans in Brazil, is that the only thing that remains to be done upon the São Paulo and Santos line is to gild the tops of the telegraph poles.

The scenery, which we saw to advantage from seats placed in front of the leading car, is extremely beautiful as the train winds along steep slopes from which one

looks down into richly wooded glens, with tiny waterfalls descending through ravines amid a profusion of tall
ferns.   It is a very wet bit of country, and before reaching the top, we were enveloped in clouds and heavy rain,
and so lost what are perhaps the finest views, those looking back from the higher levels down the main valley
and out to the now distant ocean.   On the top one
seemed suddenly to lose sight of the mountains, for we
came out upon level ground without any descent to
the other side of the hill.   The weather cleared, and
across a sparsely wooded undulating plain, in some
parts open moorland, in other parts under tillage,
we could descry distant peaks that rose sharp and clear
in the less humid air.   Whoever has travelled from
north to south in Spain will remember a similarly
abrupt transition when the railway, after climbing the
mountains south of Santander, dripping with the rain-
storms that constantly drive in from the Bay of Biscay,
emerges on the bare dry plateau of Old Castile.

The train, speeding along the perfectly smooth roadbed which this gilt-edged railroad boasts, brought us
after fifty miles to the city of São Paulo, the briskest
and most progressive place in all Brazil, though with
less than half the population of Rio de Janeiro.   It is one
of the oldest towns in the country, founded in 1553 by a
Jesuit missionary.   The early settlers, many of whom
intermarried with the native Indians, became the parents of a singularly bold and energetic race, who, in their
search for gold and silver, explored the land and raided
the Indians and whites, too, if there were any, all the way

down from here to the Uruguay and Paraná rivers.   In
those days the Portuguese government at Bahia, far off
and weak, seldom interfered with its subjects.   The free
spirit of these "Paulistas" has passed to their descendants. Living in healthy uplands, they have shewn more
industrial and political activity than the people of any
other state in the federation.   Since 1875 the planting
of enormous tracts of land with coffee has rapidly raised
the wealth of the region, and this city, being its heart
and centre, has risen in sixty years from a small country
town to be a place of four hundred thousand inhabitants.

It stands upon several hills, from the highest of
which there are charming views to the picturesque
ranges to the north and along the valley of its river,
the Tiete.   Rising only thirty miles from the sea,
this stream flows away northwestward to join the
Paraná and enter the ocean above Buenos Aires, the
slope of all this region, so soon as one has crossed the
Serra do Mar, being from east to west.   The city has
grown so fast as to shew few traces of its antiquity, except
in the centre, where the narrow and crooked streets
of the business quarter have a picturesque variety rarely
found in the rectangular towns of the New World. The
alert faces, and the air of stir and movement, as well as
handsome public buildings rising on all hands, with a
large, well-planted public garden in the middle of the city,
give the impression of energy and progress. This plateau
air is keen and bright, and, though the summer sun was
strong, for we were in mid November, the nights were
cool, and the winter, which sometimes brings slight frosts,

restores men to physical vigour.   We drove out a few
miles to see the Independence Building, a tall pile, which
from its hilltop looks over a wide stretch of rolling country.   It was erected to commemorate the revolt of Brazil
from Portugal in 1822, and contains what is one of the
largest fresco paintings in the world, shewing Dom Pedro
of Braganza, then Regent of Brazil, surrounded by his
generals, proclaiming the independence of the nation, a spirited if somewhat theatrical composition.
There is a collection of objects of natural history, as
well as of native weapons and ornaments, but both here
and elsewhere in Brazil, and, indeed, generally in South
America, one is struck by the small amount of interest
shewn in all branches of knowledge, except such as have
a direct practical bearing and pecuniary value.   Considering the enormous field of research which this
Continent presents, and what advances have been
made in scientific natural history during the last sixty
years, far too little is being done to gather or to arrange
and classify specimens illustrative either of the world of
nature or of prehistoric and savage man.   The collections
are for the most part inferior to what European museums were seventy years ago.   Let it be said, on the other
hand, that the state of São Paulo has set an admirable
example to the rest of Brazil in the liberal provision it
is making for elementary schools.

Many immigrants from Italy have in the last decade
entered the state and the city, and now by their labour
contribute largely to the prosperity of both.   Negroes
are comparatively few ; it is these Italians that do the

most and the best of the work. The larger business, both commercial and industrial, for there are now a good many factories, is chiefly in the hands of foreigners, Italians, Germans, and English, with a few French, a state of things which accelerates material progress and leaves the native or Portuguese Brazilians more free to devote themselves to politics, a sphere of action into which, as already observed, the modern Paulistas have carried the energy of their ancestors. The state is not only the most prosperous, but politically the most influential, in the republic. One way or another, what with Paulistas and foreigners, city and state are vigorous communities, and to see them disabuses the traveller of the common belief that the South Americans are slack and inert.

The railway — a government line — from São Paulo to Rio runs at first through that high, rolling country which lies behind the escarpment facing to the coast. Its variety of surface, and its patches of woodland, the trees handsome though seldom tall, make it very pretty, and there are glimpses of the mountain range to the west, one of whose summits is the loftiest in all Brazil. The line, as it approaches the coast, begins to descend, running along the edge of deep gorges, where the bright green herbage and luxuriant growths of shrubs and ferns contrast with the deep red of the soil produced by the decomposition of granitic rocks. After the arid severity of the Andean valleys of Argentina and Bolivia, and the sternness of chilly Patagonia, there was something cheering in this exuberance of vegetation, this sense that Nature is doing her best to give man a chance to live easily and happily. The train sweeps down a long ravine, and passes many a waterfall, till at last the ravine becomes a wide valley and opens into the outskirts of Rio de Janeiro.

How is one to describe Rio? I had read a score of descriptions, yet none of them had prepared me for the reality. Why should a twenty-first description be any more successful? Its bay has been compared to the bays of Naples, of Palermo, of Sydney, of San Francisco, of Hongkong, and of Bombay, as well as to the Bosphorus. It is not in the least like any of these, except in being beautiful, nor, I should fancy, is it like any other place in the world. Suppose the bottom of the Yosemite Valley, or that of the valley of Auronzo in the Venetian Alps, filled with water, and the effect would be something like the bay of Rio. Yet the superb vegetation would be wanting, and the views to far-away mountains, and the sense of the presence of the blue ocean outside the capes that guard the entrance.

The name (River of January) suggests a river, but this was a mistake of the Portuguese discoverers, for nothing but trifling streams enter this great inlet. It is a landlocked gulf, twenty miles long and from five to ten miles wide, approached from the ocean through a channel less than a mile wide between rocky promontories upon which forts have been erected. On the north side, inside the entrance, is the town of Nictheroy, whose name commemorates a long-extinct tribe of Indians. Bold rocky isles lie in front of it and high hills rise behind.

The city of Rio lies upon the south side of the gulf, the great bulk of it inside, though two or three suburbs have now grown up which stretch across a neck of land to the ocean. It runs along the shore for five or six miles, occupying all the space between the water and the mountains behind, and cut up into several sections by steep ridges which come down from the mountains and jut out into the water. The coast-line is extremely irregular, for between these jutting promontories it recedes into inlets, so that when one looks at Rio, either from offshore in front or from the mountain tops behind, it seems like a succession of towns planted around inlets and divided from one another by wooded heights. All these sections are connected by a line of avenues running nearly parallel to the coast, so that the city sometimes narrows to a couple of hundred yards, sometimes widens out where there is a level space between the water and the hills, sometimes climbs the hill slopes, and mingles its white houses with the groves that cover their sides. Behind all stands up the mountain wall, in most places clothed with luxuriant forests, but in others rising in precipices of grey granite or single shafts of rock. Thus Rio stands hemmed in between mountains and bays. There is hardly a spot where, looking up or down a street, one does not see the vista closed either by the waving green of forest or the sparkling blue of sea.

Other cities there are where mountains rising around form a noble background and refresh the heart of such town dwellers as have learnt to love them. "I will lift mine eyes unto the hills whence cometh my aid." Such cities are Athens and Smyrna, Genoa and Palermo, San Francisco and Santiago de Chile. But in Rio the mountains seem to be almost a part of the city, for it clings and laps round their spurs just as the sea below laps round the capes that project into the bay. Nor does one see elsewhere such weird forms rising directly from the yards and gardens of the houses. One can hardly take one's eyes off the two strangest among these, which are also the most prominent in every prospect. The Pan de Azucar (Sugar Loaf) is a cone of bare granite, so steep as to be scaleable at one point only by the boldest climbers, which stands on the ridge between the bay and the ocean. The other peak is the still loftier Corcovado, a vertical shaft of rock something like the Aiguille de Dru,[1] which springs right out of the houses to a height of over two thousand three hundred feet. Such strange mountain forms give to the landscape of the city a sort of bizarre air. They are things to dream of, not to tell. They remind one of those bits of fantastic rock scenery which Leonardo da Vinci loved to put in as backgrounds, though the rocks of Rio are far higher, and are also harder. A painter might think the landscapes altogether too startling for treatment, and few painters could handle so vast a canvas as would be needed to give the impression which a general view makes. Yet the grotesqueness of the shapes is lost in the splendour of the whole, — a flood of sunshine, a strand of dazzling

[1] Opposite the Montanvert at Chamouni.

white, a sea of turquoise blue, a feathery forest ready to fall from its cliff upon the city in a cascade of living green.

It is hard for man to make any city worthy of such surroundings as Nature has given to Rio. Except for two or three old-fashioned streets in the business quarter near the port and arsenal, it is all modern, and such picturesqueness as there is belongs to the varying lines of shore and hill, and to the interspersed gardens. A handsome modern thoroughfare, the Avenida Central, has been run through what used to be a crowded mass of mean houses, and it has the gay effectiveness of a Parisian boulevard. Villas surrounded by trees crown the hills that rise here and there; and one street is lined by two magnificent rows of Royal palms, their stems straight and smooth as marble pillars, crested by plumes of foliage. At the east end of the city the semicircular bay of Botafogo is surrounded by a superb palm-planted esplanade, whose parapet commands the finest general view over the entrance to the bay and the heights behind Nictheroy, and as far as the Organ Mountains which rise in a row of lofty pinnacles thirty miles away.

In such a city, the curious traveller does not need to hunt for sixteenth-century churches or quaint old colonial houses. Enough for him that the settings of the buildings are so striking. The strong light and the deep shadows, and the varied colours of the walls and roofs of the houses, the scarlet flowers climbing over the walls, and the great glossy dark green leaves of

the trees that fill the gardens, with incomparable backgrounds of rock and sea, — all these are enough to make
the streets delightful.

Not less delightful are the environs. The Botanic
Garden about a mile away has long been famous for
its wonderful avenue of royal palms, each one hundred
feet high, all grown from the seed of one planted a
hundred years ago, in the days when the king of Portugal held his court here. But it has other things to shew,
equally beautiful and more interesting to the botanist.
Not even the garden of Calcutta contains a more remarkable collection of tropical trees, and its vistas of
foliage and bowery hollows overarched by tall bamboos are enchanting. As respects situation, there is,
of course, no comparison ; for at Calcutta, as at our own
Kew, all is flat, while here the precipices of the Corcovado on the one side, and the still grander crags of
the Tijuca and Gavea on the other, shoot up thousands
of feet into the blue.

A longer excursion to the south of the city carries one
in the course of a five hours' drive through a succession
of mountain landscapes unsurpassed even in Brazil.
A road winds up the hillside through leafy glens, where
climbing plants and tree-ferns fill the space between the
trunks of the great trees. Now and then it comes
out on the top of a ridge, and one looks down into
the abysmal depths of forest, bathed in vaporous sunlight. Through a labyrinth of valleys one reaches a
clearing in the forest, above which is seen the beautiful
peak of Tijuca, and beyond it, still higher, the amazing

Gavea, a square-sided, flat-topped tower of granite. In their boldness of line these peaks remind one of those that stand up round the Mer de Glace at Chamouni. There moraines and masses of fallen stones are heaped upon the bases of these Aiguilles, and nothing breaks the savage bareness of their sides except snow beds in the couloirs. Here the peaks rise out of a billowy sea of verdure. The steepness of their faces seems to defy the climber; yet on their faces there are crevices just big enough for shrubs to root in, by the help of which a daring man might pull himself aloft. Nature, having first hewn out these peaks into appalling precipices, then set herself to deck them with climbing plants and to find foothold for trees on narrow ledges and to cover the surface with the bright hues of mosses and lichens, and fill chinks and crannies with ferns and pendulous flowers that wave and sway in the passing breeze. Some way further, from the top of a gap between the peaks, the open ocean is suddenly seen a thousand feet below, its intense blue framed between green hills, with long billows rushing up over the white sands of the bay, and lines of spray sparkling round the rocky isles that rise beyond, like the summits of submerged mountains.

Though the bay of Rio was discovered as far back as 1531 by the Portuguese sailor who took its mouth for a river, and was settled not long after, first by Frenchmen in 1558 and then by Portuguese in 1567, the settlement grew slowly, and it was not till 1762 that the seat of government was transferred here from Bahia, seven

hundred miles further to the north. Now the population, estimated at a million, is in South America ex-
ceeded by that of Buenos Aires only, and in recent
years much has been done to improve both the city
and its port and wharves. Still greater service has
been rendered by sanitary measures which have not
only cleared away slums, but have practically ex-
tinguished yellow fever, and reduced the mortality
from other tropical diseases. Rio is now a pleasant
place of residence in winter, and the sea-breeze
makes the climate agreeable in all but the hottest
months, during which Europeans find it debilitating.
Fifty years ago the then Emperor Dom Pedro the
Second built himself a summer residence among the
mountains which rise beyond the further end of the
bay, and this presently became the "hot weather station," as people say in India, for the richer class of
citizens and for the representatives of foreign countries.
Now that Rio itself is more healthy, the need for an
annual migration is less imperative, but the natural
charm as well as the much cooler air of Petropolis —
so the place is called — have maintained it as a summer
resort. It is an excellent centre both for the naturalist
and for the lover of scenic beauty.

The railway from Rio, after traversing the low
and marshy ground along the margin of the bay
for more than twenty miles, reaches the foot of the
Organ Mountains, which form a part of the Coast
Range already referred to.[1] These Organ Mountains

[1] See page 368.

(Serra dos Orgãos) rising in a row of granite towers to a height of 7300 feet, the ravines between their peaks filled with luxuriant forest, make a noble ending to the view from Rio along the length of the bay. A botanist could spend no more delightful week than in rambling among them at a season when the rains are not too heavy. The railway climbs the Serra at its lowest point, about 2600 feet above sea-level, descending a little on the other or northeastern side to Petropolis. The grade is so steep as to require trains to be hauled up by a wire rope. Nothing can surpass the beauty of the views which the ascent gives over the bay with its islands and all the way southeastward to the mountains that surround Rio.

Petropolis is a pretty little spot, nestling under steep hills, its streets well planted and shady, its rows of shops which address themselves to the summer visitor reminding one of a Pyrenean or Rhenish bathing place. But the charm of its surroundings is beyond that of any place in Europe, for in no temperate clime are such landscapes with such woods and such colours to be found. Here, better even than in the neighbourhood of Rio, one can explore the glens and penetrate the forests on foot, wherever a path can be found to follow, for to force one's way along without a path, by cutting openings through the tangle of shrubs and climbers with a *machete*, is a task beyond the powers of the solitary walker. It is not so easy as in Europe to get to know the mountains, for the pedestrian cannot go where he will. The thickness of the wood stops him. He cannot fix upon

2 c

some attractive summit and say he will climb there for a view, because access on foot, and, still more, access on horseback, is possible only where there exists a regular "trail" or well-marked path. Yet it is a genial country, fit to be loved, and not on too vast a scale, like the Himalayas or the Andes. When one rambles along the valleys, new beauties appear as the mountains group and regroup themselves with rock peaks springing unexpectedly out of the forest, and new waterfalls disclose themselves along the course of the brooks, for in this land of showers every hollow has its stream. The heights are sufficient to give dignity,[1] and the forms are endlessly varied, with here and there open pastures or slopes of rocky ground rising to a rocky peak, while the heat is tempered by the elevation and by the seldom failing breeze.

We learnt still more of the character of the country in an excursion over the Leopoldina railway, down into the valley of the Parahyba River, and back up one of its tributary glens, to the top of the Coast Range whence we descended to the coast at Nictheroy opposite Rio. In general one does not get the best impression of any scenery, and perhaps least of forest scenery, from a railroad. Here, however, a railroad must be turned to account, because roads are few and driving difficult. Our train moved slowly and the rains had laid the dust.

This Leopoldina railway (the property of a British company, to the kindness of whose managers we were

---

[1] The tops range from 4500 to 7000 feet.

greatly beholden) descends a narrow valley, hemmed in by steep mountains whose projecting spurs and buttresses turn hither and thither the course of the foaming river. Right and left waterfalls leap over the cliffs to swell its waters. The slopes are mostly too steep for tillage, but here and there a cluster of houses clings to the slopes, and round them there are fruit trees and maize fields or little gardens. At last the ravine widens and we emerge into the broad valley, bordered by lower hills, of the Parahyba, one of the chief rivers of the Atlantic side of Brazil. Running down it, through a rich country, we stopped at a wayside station to take horse and ride up to a *Fazenda* (estate) whose hospitable owner had invited us to see his coffee plantations and live stock. The house, set on a hill with a pretty garden below it and charming views all round, and inhabited by a large family of his children and grandchildren, gave a pleasant impression of Brazilian rural life. Here was simplicity with abundance, the beauty of groves and flowers, a bountiful Nature, labourers, nearly all negroes, who seemed contented and attached to their kindly master. A band of coloured people turned out to greet us and played the national air of Britain. The plantation and stock farms are managed by the owner and his son, who take pleasure in having everything done in the best way. We saw the process, quite an elaborate one, and carried on by machinery, of washing and drying the coffee-beans, sorting them out by size and quality, separating the husks and membranous coverings from the beans before they are fit to be packed and shipped. Coffee is an exhausting crop. Fresh land must be taken in from time to time and the old land allowed to rest; and we were to see next day many tracts where it used to be cultivated, which have now been abandoned to forest because the soil had ceased to repay tillage. A large piece of ground was ready to be planted with young coffeeplants, and we were asked to inaugurate it by planting the first trees, which was done to the accompaniment of rockets let off by the negroes in the full afternoon sunlight. The love of fireworks, carried by the peoples of southern Europe to the New World, reaches its acme among their coloured dependants.

Leaving with regret this idyllic home, we sped all too quickly down the vale of the Parahyba. Everyone knows that there is nothing more beautiful than the views one gets in following a river. But here we felt as if we had not known before how beautiful a valley can be till this Brazilian one was seen in its warm light, with the heavy shadows of tropic clouds falling upon woods and pastures, the broad stream now sparkling over the shallows, now reflecting the clouds from its placid bosom. The nearer ridges that fell softly on either side were crowned with villages clustering round white church spires; other ridges rose one behind another to the west, their outlines fading in the haze of distance. Not often in the tropics does one get the openness and the mingling of cornfields and meadows with forest which make the charm of south European scenery. Here the landscape had that

Italian quality one finds in Claude and in the backgrounds of Titian but bathed in the intenser light of a Brazilian sun. In Brazil, as in Mexico, scenery that is both splendid and romantic stands awaiting the painter who is worthy to place it on canvas.

At last, turning away from the Parahyba, which the main line of railway follows to the sea, we mounted by a branch up a lateral valley, passed through great stretches of rough pasture land into the higher region of thick woods, and halted for the night in the midst of a thunderstorm which pealed and growled and flashed all night long, as often happens in these latitudes where one bank of clouds comes up after another to renew the discharges. Next morning the line, after keeping along the heights for some miles, descended through a forest more wonderful in its exuberance than any we had yet seen. From the summit we looked over a wilderness of deep valleys, the waving green of their tree-tops seamed with the white flash of waterfalls, with many ranges and peaks rising in the far distance, few of whose tops any European foot had pressed, for it is only the bottoms of the valleys that are inhabited. The views were all the more beautiful because the precipices on the hillsides beneath which we passed were dripping with rivulets from last night's rain, and cascades leapt over a succession of rock ledges and hurried in foaming channels down the bottoms of the glens.

In the hollow of the valley lies a quiet little town called Novo Friburgo, because first inhabited by a Swiss colony brought here many years ago to grow coffee. These

Brazilian villages are loosely built, the houses scattered along wide streets, among spreading trees, and this one had retained something of the trimness of the industrious people who first settled it. Many of the coffee plantations of forty or even thirty years ago have been abandoned, and their sites are now practically undistinguishable from the rest of the forest. How long it will take for the land to recover its pristine vigour is not yet known, and there is still so much virgin land waiting to be planted that the question is of more importance to the individual owner than to the nation at large.

From this smiling vale the line climbs another high ridge and then descends once more through a long valley to the level land that lies behind the bay of Rio, coming out at last in the town of Nictheroy opposite the city.

This long run through the mountains on the top of the ridges and down along the terraces cut out in their sides, whence one can look over great spaces of woodland, completed the impressions of the forest which our excursions round Rio and Petropolis had given. Regarded as a piece of Nature's work, these Brazilian forests are more striking than those of the eastern Himalayas or of the Nilghiri Hills in India, more striking even than that beautiful little forest at Hilo in Hawaii, which no one who has visited that extraordinary island can ever forget. It is not that these Brazilian trees are very lofty. I was told that further north there are places where the great trunks reach two hundred feet, but here none seemed to exceed, and not very many to reach,

one hundred. Thus, as respects either height or girth
or general stateliness of aspect, these trees of the
Serra do Mar are not to be compared either to the so-
called "Big Trees" of California[1] or to the red woods
of the Pacific Coast Range,[2] nor do they equal the
forests of the Cascade Range above Puget Sound,
where many of the Douglas firs and the so-called
"cedars" approach, and some are said to exceed,
three hundred feet. But they have a marvellous
variety and richness of colour both in flowers and
leaves. Very few — in this part I could see none — are
coniferous, but very many are evergreen, changing their
leaves not all at the same time, like the deciduous trees
of temperate countries, but each tree at its own time, so
that there are always some with fresh leaves coming as
the others are beginning to go. The variety of tints
is endless, from the dark glossy green of many a forest
tree to the light green of the bamboos. Some leaves
have white undersurfaces, which when turned up by the
wind are bright enough to give the effect of flowers ; and
one tree, frequent in these mountains, has a group of
what seem white bracts round the corymb at the end of
its flower-shoots. Still more varied and still more brilliant are the flowers. These are seen best from above
because it is the highest boughs touched by the sun that
burst forth into the most abundant blossoms. Though
we were too early in the hot season to see the blossom-
bearing trees at their best, the wealth of colour was de-

[1] *Sequoia gigantea* of the Mariposa and Calaveras groves.
[2] *Sequoia sempervirens.*

lightful even in November. Yellow and white were
perhaps the most frequent, but there were also bright
pinks and purples and violets. Palms rising here and
there often high above the rest gave a variety of tint
and form, while the space between the trunks was filled
by tree-ferns rising to twenty feet and by a bewil-
dering profusion of climbing and hanging and parasitic
plants, many of them girdling the boughs with flowers.
There were far more than anybody could give me
names for, and as I had no means of ascertaining the
scientific names, it would not serve the reader to give
the popular Portuguese ones, especially as I found that
the same name was sometimes applied to quite different
plants because their colour was similar.

It is in a region like this that one begins to
realize the amazing energy of nature. In the Andes
we had seen the power of what are called the inanimate
forces acting from beneath to shake the earth and
break through its solid crust. There heat, acting
upon water, has produced volcanic explosions and
piled up gigantic cones like Misti and Tupungato,
and has destroyed by earthquakes cities like Valparaiso or Mendoza. Here heat and water are again
the force and the matter on which the force works;
but here it is through life that they act. Every inch of
ground is covered with some living and growing thing.
While the tall stems push upward to overtop their
fellows and let their highest shoots put forth flowers
under the sunlight, climbing plants slender as a vine-
shoot or stout as a liana embrace the trunk and mount

along the branches and hang in swinging festoons from tree to tree. The fallen trunks are covered thick with ferns and mosses. Orchids and many another parasite root themselves in the living stem, and make it gay, to its ultimate undoing, with blossoms not its own. Even the bare faces of gneiss rock, too steep for any soil to rest upon, support a plant with a thick whorl of succulent leaves that is somehow able to find sustenance from air and moisture only, its roots anchored into some slight roughness of the rock. When a patch of wood has been cut down to the very ground, five years suffice to cover the soil again with a growth of trees and shrubs so rank that the spot can scarcely be distinguished from the uncut forest all round. But this swift activity of life is hardly more wonderful than is the variety of forms. Each of the great forests of Europe and North America consists of a few species of trees. In the New Forest in England, most beautiful of all, in one place chiefly beeches are found, in another chiefly oaks, mixed, perhaps, with some birches and white thorns. The woods of Maine and New Hampshire are composed of maples and birches, white pines and hemlocks and spruces, with now and then some less frequent tree. In the majestic forests of the Pacific coast there are seldom more than three or four of the larger species present in any quantity and this is generally true also of the Eucalyptus forests of Australia. But on this Brazilian coast the diversity is endless. Those who have traversed the Amazonian forests have made the same remark. There as here you may find within a radius of eighty yards, forty kinds of trees growing side by side, species belonging to different families with myriad shapes and hues of leaf and flower. Not content with the abundance of its production, this creative energy of nature insists on expressing itself also in an endless variety of forms. Do any principles which naturalists have yet discovered quite explain such a marvellous diversity where the conditions are the same ?

After the doctrine of the Struggle for Life had been once propounded by two great naturalists who had seen, one of them South America, and the other, the tropical islands of the Further East, men soon learnt to recognize and observe the working of the principle in every part of the earth until in the arid desert or the freezing north a land was reached where life itself was extinct. But it is in Brazil that the principle is seen in the fulness of its potency. Here, where life is so profuse, so multiform, so incessantly surging around like the waves of a restless sea, this law of nature's action seems to speak from every rustling leaf, and the forest proclaims it with a thousand voices.

Rambling round Rio, and noting the physical characteristics of the ground it occupies, the rocky hills and the promontories and the islands, the traveller is reminded of the historic cities of Greece and Italy and naturally asks himself : Supposing Rio to have been one of those cities, where would the Acropolis have been, and where would the citizens have met in their assembly before they rushed to attack a tyrant, and to what sea-girt fortress would a ruler have sent his captives by water as the East Roman emperors seized their enemies and sent them into exile from the Bosphorus ? Then, remembering that few streets or hills in Rio have any associations with the past, he wonders whether such associations will come into being in the future, and whether insurrections and civic conflicts may ever render some of these spots famous. In old cities like Florence and Paris and Edinburgh historic memories make a great part of the interest of the place. How much of English history connects itself with the Tower of London and with Westminster Hall! It so happened that during our stay in Rio there befell an incident which shewed that the smooth surface of things may, even in our own days, be troubled by explosive passions, an incident which revealed a new kind of danger to which in times of domestic strife modern engines of warfare may subject a maritime town.

On the day when we were to embark for Bahia and Europe, we started early in the morning from Petropolis to come down by train to Rio, and heard at the station rumours of a revolution, confused rumours, for no one could say from whom the revolution, if there was one, proceeded or against whom it was directed. When we reached Rio, things cleared up a little. It was not a political revolution nor a military pronunciamento, but a marine mutiny. The crews, almost entirely negroes, of the two great Dreadnought battleships which the Brazilian government had recently ordered and purchased from an English firm of shipbuilders, and which had shortly before arrived in the harbour, had revolted during the night. The captain of one of the vessels, the *Minas Geraes*, had been murdered by his crew as he stepped on board upon his return from dining on a French ship. The story ran that he had been first pierced by bayonets and then hewed in pieces with hatchets. Of the other officers some few had been killed, the rest put on shore. The only white men left on board were some English engineers forcibly detained in order to work the engines. The crews of a cruiser and two smaller war vessels had joined in the revolt. All the ships were in the hands of the crews, who, however, were believed to be obeying non-commissioned officers of their own colour, and who were led by a negro named João Candido,[1] a big man of energy and resolution, who had shewn his grasp of the situation by ordering all the liquor on the *Minas Geraes* to be thrown overboard. The grievances alleged by the seamen were overwork, insufficient wages, and the frequency of corporal punishments. Rumours were busy connecting the names of prominent politicians with the outbreak, but so far as could be made out then or subsequently there was no foundation for these suspicions. The mutiny seems to have been the spontaneous act of the crews, who, it was remarked, had just arrived from Lisbon, lately the scene of a revolution, and might have there caught the infection of rebellion. In demanding the redress of their grievances, which was, of course, to be accompanied by an amnesty for themselves, they had threatened to lay the city in ashes,

[1] John White.

enforcing the threat by firing some shots into it (not, however, from the heavy guns). One shot killed two children, and several other persons were wounded.

The aspect of the city was rather less affected than might have been expected. Some troops were moving about, here cavalry, there infantry. Few carriages or motor cars and few women were to be seen. Business was slack, and groups of men stood talking at street corners, evidently imparting to one another those tales and suspicions and guesses at unseen causes with which the air was thick. All water traffic from the opposite side of the bay had been stopped by the mutineers, who had also compelled the submission of one of the forts at the entrance. Strolling along to the great Botafogo Esplanade under the palms, I found a battery of field artillery, their guns pointed at the two battleships, the *Minas* and the *São Paulo*, against which they would, of course, have been as useless as paper pellets. There the majestic yellow grey monsters lay, fresh from Messrs. Armstrong's yard at Newcastle, flying the ensign of Brazil, but also flying at the fore the red flag of rebellion. So the day wore on, terror abating, but the sense of helplessness increasing. We were lunching at the Ministry of Foreign Affairs — it was a small party, for considerations of safety had kept away the ladies who had been invited — when suddenly the heavy boom of the guns was heard, and continued at intervals all through the repast. When again in the streets, I found that the two Dreadnoughts were shelling some torpedo-boats, manned by crews still loyal, which had approached them. The practice was bad, and none of the boats was hit, but they prudently scurried off up the bay into shallow water where the ironclads could not follow.

So the hours passed and everybody was still asking, "What is to be done?" "The mutineers," so men said, "can't be starved out, because they have threatened to destroy the city if food is refused them, and the city is at their mercy. By this threat they have forced us to give them water. We cannot blow up the ships with torpedoes, first because they have stretched torpedo nets round the hulls, and secondly because it would be a serious thing to destroy property for which we have paid no small part of our annual revenue. Doesn't it look as if we should have to submit to the mutineers? What else can we do?" Later on the firing recommenced and I mounted to the third story of the British Consulate to see what was happening. The ships were shelling the naval barracks on the Isla das Cobras in the harbour, and the island was replying, and we were near enough to see the red flash from the iron lips just before the roar was heard. Lying out in the bay was the British liner by which we were to sail for Liverpool. The lighters that were carrying coal to her had been commandeered by the mutineers, but she had just enough in her bunkers to get to Bahia. The immediate difficulty was for the passengers to reach her across the line of fire. At last, however, a boat was sent out from shore bearing a flag of truce, and the *São Paulo* consented to cease firing and let the passengers get on board the British vessel. They were accordingly embarked in a launch which, flying the Consulate flag, crossed unharmed the danger zone. It was the only chance, but a sense of relief was visible in every face when we stepped on board, for if a negro gunner had been smitten by the desire to let fly once more at the Isla das Cobras, his ill-aimed shot might very well have sent the launch to the bottom. As we steamed slowly out to the ocean the magnificent *São Paulo* ran close alongside us, and we could see her decks crowded with negroes and the red flag still flying. "A study in black and red," someone observed. Outside the entrance were lying the *Minas Geraes* and the *Bahia*, partly to be out of harm's way from torpedoes, partly to guard the mouth of the bay. In the sober light of a grey sunset, the clouds hanging heavy on the Corcovado, but the lofty watch-tower of the Pan d'Azucar still visible through the gathering shades, we turned north-ward, and bade farewell to Rio. Two hours later, looking back through a moonless night, we could still see the flash, from beneath the horizon, of the search-lights which the *Minas Geraes* was casting on the sea all round her to guard against the stealthy approach of a loyal torpedo-boat.

A few days later, at Pernambuco, we heard that peace had been restored. The Chambers had voted an amnesty with eloquent speeches about the beauty of for-giveness, and had promised to redress the grievances of the mutineers. Another mutiny broke out afterwards, which, after many lives had been lost, was severely suppressed, but these later events happened when we were far away, nearing the coast of Europe, and of them I have nothing to tell.

The coast for some way north from Rio continues high, but the steamers keep too far out to permit its beauties to be seen. Before one approaches Bahia, the mountains have receded, and at that city, though picturesque heights are still visible, they lie further back, and scarcely figure in the landscape. Still further north, towards Pernambuco, and most of the way northwestward to Pará, the coast is much lower. The bay of Bahia is singularly beautiful in its vast sweep, as well as in the verdure that fringes its inlets, and the glimpses of distant sunlit hills. Nor is the city, long the capital of Brazil, wanting in interest; for, though none of the buildings have much architectural merit, there is a quaint, old-fashioned look about the streets and squares, with many a house that has stood unchanged since the eighteenth century. The upper city runs along the edge of a steep bluff, sixty or eighty feet above the lower town, which is a single line of street, even more dirty than it is picturesque, occupying the narrow strip between the harbour and the cliff. Here, far more than in Parisianized Rio, one finds the familiar features of a Portuguese town reproduced, irregular and narrow streets, houses, often high, roofed with red tiles, and coloured with all sorts of washes, pink, green, blue, and yellow. Sometimes the whole front or side of a house is covered with blue or yellowish brown tiles, a characteristic of Portuguese cities — it is frequent in Oporto and Braga — which has come down from

Moorish times. But a still greater contrast between this and southern Brazil is found in the population. In São Paulo there are few negroes, in Rio not very many, but here in Bahia all the town seems black. One might be in Africa or the West Indies. It is the same in Pernambuco and indeed all the way to the mouth of the Amazon.

Finding this to be a region filled with coloured people as São Paulo was with white people, and knowing that a thousand miles further west one would come into a region entirely Indian, one began to realize what a vast country Brazil is, big enough to be carved up into sixteen countries each as large as France. Were there natural boundaries, *i.e.* such physical features as mountain ranges or deserts, to divide this immense region into sections, the settled parts of Brazil might before now have split apart into different political communities. As it is, however, there are no such natural dividing lines, and if the Republic should ever break in pieces it will be differences in the character of the population or some conflict of material interests that will bring this about.

How has it happened that so huge a country has fallen to the lot of a people so much too small for it, since one can hardly reckon the true Brazilian white nation at more than seven millions ?

What did happen was that the French, English, and Dutch, having their hands full in Europe, did not pursue their attempts to occupy the country with sufficient persistence and with adequate forces, and so lost their

2 D

hold on the parts they had seized. Thus it became possible for a handful of Portuguese on the Atlantic coast to send out small colonizing parties into their un-occupied Hinterland, and as there were no civilized in-habitants to resist them, to go on acquiring a title to it without opposition until they met the outposts of the Spanish government who had advanced from the Pacific across the Andes just as the Portuguese had advanced from the Atlantic. Neither Portuguese nor Spaniards had been numerous enough to colonize this interior region of the continent, so it remains (save for a few trading posts on the rivers) an empty wilderness.

Nevertheless, though Brazil is physically all one coun-try, it contains regions differing in climate, in economic resources, and in population. I will try in a few sen-tences to indicate the character of each.

The most northerly part along the frontiers of Guiana and also along a good deal of the coast between the mouth of the Amazon and Cape St. Roque is the least valuable, for large tracts are stony and protracted droughts are not uncommon. The extreme north has been hardly at all settled.

The east central part, consisting of the mountain ridges and table-lands referred to on page 368, together with slopes which descend on all sides from these highlands, is a region of great natural resources where all tropical crops and fruits can be produced. Most of it is healthy, much of it not too hot for white men to work and thrive, and the magnificent forests, no less than the mines, will make the mountains for many years to come no less a source of wealth than are the more level tracts. Its weak point is the want of white labour and the inefficiency of black labour.

This tropical region passes imperceptibly into the temperate country which occupies the states of São Paulo, Paraná, Santa Catharina, and Rio Grande, a section of the country no less fertile than the last and better fitted for European constitutions. Here all sub-tropical products can be raised; here also are forests; and here, where the land has not yet been brought under tillage, there is abundant and excellent pasture for all sorts of live stock. As the east central region is the land of cotton and sugar, so this southern region is the land of coffee and cattle, — coffee in its northerly parts, cattle and the cereals in its southern.

There remain the vast spaces of the west and north-west, still so imperfectly explored that it is hard to estimate their economic value. To the Amazonian forests, the Selvas, I shall return in another chapter.[1] They are the land of another great Brazilian staple — rubber. Most parts of the region where Brazil adjoins Bolivia, a vast level or slightly undulating country, partly grassy, partly covered with wood or scrub, is believed to be available either for cultivation or for ranching. At present access is difficult, and markets are far away, but when the districts of Brazil, Uruguay, and Argentina that lie between this region and the coast have been more fully settled, its turn will come.

Taking Brazil as a whole, no great country in the

[1] Chapter XVI.

world owned by a European race possesses so
large a proportion of land available for the support
of human life and productive industry.   In the United
States there are deserts, and of the gigantic Russian
Empire much is desert, and much is frozen waste.   But
on the Portuguese of Brazil nature has bestowed nothing for which man cannot find a use.   Such a possession
as this was far more than enough to compensate the
little kingdom for the loss of the empire which it began
in the sixteenth century to build up in India, before the
evil days came after the death of King Sebastian.

The material prosperity of a country, however, depends less on its natural resources than on the quality
of the labour applied to its development and on the
intelligence that directs the labour.   In these respects
Brazil has been less fortunate.   When the Portuguese
first settled the coast lands, they forced the Indian aborigines to work for them, and in many places destroyed
by their severities the bulk of the native population.
Negroes began to be imported about A.D. 1600, but not in
great numbers until the discovery of diamond and other
mines in the inland country created a sudden demand
for labour.   After that, there came a large importation
of slaves, for agricultural as well as for mining purposes,
from all the Portuguese dominions of Africa, and from the
Congo regions ; and this went on, though latterly much
reduced, down to our own time.   Between 1825 and 1850
it is said that 1,250,000 slaves were landed, and cargoes
came in even later.   Thus the working population of
the tropical region, including the coast towns, became

largely, and in the north, predominantly negro. Slavery was abolished by successive stages, the last of which was reached in 1888. For a time the plantation culture was disorganized, but most of the freedmen ultimately returned to work. It is by their labour that sugar and cotton are raised to-day, though they take life very easily, and often content themselves with just so much exertion on just so many days a week as is needed to provide them with food and the other scanty necessaries of their life. Here, as elsewhere, the race is lighthearted and thoughtless, caring little for the future, loving amusement in its most childish forms. It is kindly and submissive, but dangerously excitable, and quickly demoralized by drink. The planters find it hard to count on their work people, who stay away if they feel more than usually lazy, and will, if displeased, transfer themselves to another planter, who, in the general scarcity of labour, is glad to have them. Many children are born to them, but many die, especially in infancy, so that, taking the country as a whole, they do not seem to increase faster than the other sections of the population.

Such are the cotton and sugar regions: now let us turn to those southerly states of the republic, whose staples are coffee and cattle and cereals. In them, and especially in São Paulo and Rio Grande, the conditions are altogether different. The number of negroes was never large there, and it does not grow. Owing to the elevation of the ground and to the less powerful sun, the heat is not excessive in either state, and European im-

migrants can work and thrive and be happy. So
Europeans have flocked hither. Between 1843 and
1859 about twenty thousand came from Germany to
Rio Grande do Sul, and there are now, it is said, about
two hundred thousand, forming a compact community
which preserves its national habits and manages its
own affairs with little interference by the central government.   It is, in fact, disposed to resent any such interference and to "run things" in its own solid German
way.   Even larger is the number of Italians who in
more recent years have entered these southern states.
The labour on the great coffee estates of São Paulo is
almost entirely Italian ; and in Rio Grande they have
become well-to-do peasant proprietors, living in less
comfort than their German neighbours, but working
just as steadily.   This better quality of population has
largely gone to making the southern states the most
progressive part of Brazil.   Should the Italians and the
native Brazilians of the south, who have far less negro
blood than those of the middle states, continue to
spread themselves out as settlers over the still thinly
peopled southwestern districts, they will probably
give prosperity to that region also.   Cattle ranching
is in the south carried on by Gauchos much like those
of Uruguay or Argentina.   They are said to have
communicated their love of horses to the Germans and
Italians, so that on holidays even the women of those
races appear on horseback in a way that would startle
their peasant cousins left at home in Swabia or Lombardy.

The foreign element in Brazil is more important by its energy and industry than by its numbers, for it probably little exceeds a million all told, and the total population of the republic may approach nineteen or twenty millions. In 1910 about 88,000 immigrants entered, most of them Italians, and the rest Portuguese, Spaniards, and Syrians, these last mostly travelling peddlers, or small dealers who establish themselves in the towns. The afflux of Syrians that has found its way to South America and the West Indies during the last few years is a new and curious feature in the currents of ethnic movement that mark our time.

But what of the Brazilian people itself? The influences that tend to make it vary from its original type are counterworked by the steady immigration from Portugal, and from Spain also, for though any sort of Spaniard (except a Gallego) differs materially from a Portuguese, the two races differ much less from one another than either does from any other European stock. The Brazilian is primarily a Portuguese in the outlines of his mind and character. He has, however, been modified by intermixture with two other races. The first of these is the native Indian. The settlers both in São Paulo and along the northeastern coast, while they killed most of the Indian men either in fight or by working them to death as slaves, intermarried freely with Indian women. The offspring were called Mamelucos, an Eastern term which it is odd to find here, and which is now beginning to pass out of use. In the south this mixed race as well as the pure Indian race has been

now absorbed into the rest of the population.[1] You
would as soon expect to see a Pawnee in Philadelphia
as an Indian in Santos.   In the north the half-breed
is generally called a *Caboclo*, a name originally given
to the tame native Indian, as opposed to the wild
Indio bravo; and in that region, a large part of the
agricultural population is of this mixed stock.

The second modifying influence is that of the imported
Africans.   When the first slave ships disgorged their
cargoes on the Atlantic coast, the aborigines of those
districts had already been either killed off or merged
in the Portuguese population, so that the mingling of
Indian and negro blood which is supposed to produce
an especially undesirable class of citizens was comparatively small.   The intermarriage of blacks and whites
has, however, gone on apace, and the negroes constitute a large, the mulattoes and quadroons a still larger,
percentage of the population.   Some observers hold
that the coloured people, taken all together, equal or
outnumber the whites.   The intermixture continues,
for here, as in Portuguese East Africa, no sentiment
of race repulsion opposes it.[2]   Any figures that might
be given would be quite conjectural; for the line be-

---

[1] How many Indians there are nobody knows, but the common
(probably exaggerated) estimate puts them at nearly 2,000,000, half
of these pagans in the Amazonian forests, while the mixed race is
calculated at 1,700,000.

[2] Sir H. H. Johnson (*The Negro in the New World*) conjectures
the pure blacks at about 2,720,000 and the mulattoes and quadroons
at about 5,600,000. The rest of the population, that which may be
described as white because it bears no conspicuous marks of any in-

tween the mixed black and white and the white cannot be drawn with any approach to accuracy. Even
in the United States, where conditions permit more
careful discrimination, no one can tell what is the percentage of mulattoes to the total coloured population,
nor how many quadroons and octoroons there are to
be found among those classed as whites, for many people
who have some negro blood succeed in concealing its
presence, while others are classed as coloured who in
Europe would pass as white. Much more difficult is it
to tell in Brazil who is to be deemed a person of colour.

How far the differences between the Brazilian and
the Portuguese of to-day are due to racial admixture,
and how far to the conditions of colonial life and a new
physical environment, is a matter on which one might
speculate for ever and come no nearer to a conclusion.
The descendants of Englishmen who were living in
Massachusetts and Virginia in 1840 before immigration
from Continental Europe had begun to affect the
English stock shewed already marked differences from
the Englishmen of old England, and it is impossible to
tell how far the changes that have passed on the people
of the United States since then are due to the influx of
new immigrants from Europe, how far to other causes.
The Brazilian is still more of a Portuguese than he is of
any other type. His ideas and tastes, his ways of life,

fusion of color, may approach 8,000,000. The Indians and half-breeds
(Indian and white) would make up the rest of the non-European
population. Of the pure blacks, from 20,000 to 30,000, living on the
northeast coast, are either Mussulmans or heathen fetichists.

his alternations of listlessness and activity, his kindly
good nature, his susceptibility to emotions and to a
rhetoric that can rouse emotion, belong to the country
whence he came.

Brazil was the latest country in the American continent to become a republic. This befell in 1888.
In 1807, when the armies of Napoleon Bonaparte
entered Portugal, the then reigning king, John, of the
house of Braganza, crossed the Atlantic and reigned at
Rio till the expulsion of the French enabled him to
resume his European throne. In 1822 the people had
become discontented under Portuguese misgovernment.
Republican ideas, stimulated by the destruction of Spanish power that was proceeding on the Pacific coasts,
were in the air, and the Regent, Dom Pedro, son of King
John, proclaimed the independence of Brazil which was,
after some fighting, conceded by the mother country
in 1825. His action probably saved monarchical
institutions, and when he abdicated in 1831, disgusted
with the difficulties that surrounded him, and with
the unpopularity to which his own faults had exposed him, he was succeeded by his son, who ruled
as the Emperor Pedro the Second. This amiable
and enlightened prince, a lover of natural science as
well as of art and letters, devoted himself chiefly to
European travel and to the economic and educa-
tional improvement of his country, interfering very
little with politics. A military conspiracy and the
resentment of the planters at the sudden abolition of
slavery brought about the revolution of 1888, in which

a republic was proclaimed and the Emperor shipped off to Europe. In 1891 a congress met and enacted a federal constitution modelled on that of the United States. The immense size of the country and its want of homogeneity suggested a federal system, the basis for which already existed in the legislative assemblies of the provinces. Since then Brazil has had its full share of armed risings and civil wars.

At first the states were allowed the full exercise of the large functions which the Constitution allotted to them, including the raising of revenue by duties on exports and the maintenance of a police force which in some states was undistinguishable from an army. Presently attempts were made to draw the reins tighter, and these attempts have continued till now. The national government has at its disposal the important field of financial and tariff legislation, the control of army and navy, and the opportunities of helping needy or slothful states by grants of money or by the execution of public works. Through the use of these powers it has latterly endeavoured to exert over the states a greater control than some of them seem willing to accept. Nor is this the only difficulty. While some of the states, and especially the southern, have an intelligent and energetic population, others remain far behind, their citizens too ignorant and lazy, or too unstable and emotional, to be fit for self-government. Universal suffrage in districts where the majority of the voters are illiterate persons of colour suggests, if it does not justify, extra-legal methods of handling elections.

One illegality breeds another, and there is perpetuated
a distrust of authority and a resort to violence.   As one
of the most recent and brilliant of European travellers [1]
observes, in a passage which conveys his admiration for
the attractive qualities he finds in the Brazilians, "The
Constitution enjoys a chiefly theoretic authority. . . .
There is a lack of balance between the states which have
already a highly perfected civilization and the districts
which in theory are on a footing of equality, but whose
black or Indian population can only permit of a nominal democracy stained by those irresponsible outbursts
which characterize primitive humanity."   That the authority of a constitution should be "theoretic rather than
practical" must be expected where "a democracy is nominal"; for if institutions the working of which requires
intelligence and public spirit are forced on Indians and
negroes, their failure is inevitable.

In the Brazilian politics of to-day there are many
factions, but no organized parties nor any definite principles or policies advocated by any group or groups of
men.   Federal issues are crossed and warped by state
issues, state issues confused by federal issues, and both
sets of issues turn rather on persons than on general
doctrines or specific practical proposals.   One source
of dissension is, however, absent, — that struggle of the
church and clericalism against the principles of religious equality which has distracted the Spanish-American republics.   In Brazil the separation of church
and state is complete, and though the diplomatic

[1] M. Georges Clémenceau in his *South America of To-day.*

corps enjoys the presence of a papal Nuncio as one of its members, this adherence to tradition has no present political significance. Here, moreover, as in Argentina and Uruguay, the church and religion seem to have little influence upon the thought or the conduct of laymen. The absence or the fluidity of parties makes the executive stronger than the legislature both in national and state politics. There are many men of talent, especially oratorical talent, and many men of force, but not enough who shew constructive power and the grasp of mind needed to handle the enormous economic problems which a country so vast, so rich, and so various presents.

Among the economic issues of to-day may be reckoned that of protection, as against free trade. Brazilian policy is at present highly protectionist, and does not hesitate, when some powerful interest asks for more protection, to double or more than double whatever protective duty it finds existing. The chief social questions are those relating to the extension of education and the enactment of better labour laws for the benefit of children and the security of workpeople. The chief constitutional question is the relations of the national and the state governments. European critics complain that upon none of these does any legislative group seem to put forward any definite and consistent policy. Yet such critics must be reminded that the country has been a republic only since 1891, and free from the taint of slavery only since 1888, and that her peace has been since those years frequently disturbed. It is too soon to be despondent.

Brazilian society seems to a passing observer to be in a state of transition, and may not for some time to come succeed in reconciling the contrasts between the old and the new, and between theory and practice, which it now displays. The old system was aristocratic not only because a number of respected families surrounding the imperial court enjoyed a preeminence of rank, but also because a newer class of rich men, chiefly landowners, had grown up. The aristocracy of rank is now almost gone, but the aristocracy of wealth remains and is in control of public affairs. In most parts of the country, it stands far above the labouring population, with little of a middle class between. Democratic principles have been proclaimed in the broadest terms, but thinking men see, and even unthinking men cannot but dimly feel, that no government, however good its intentions, can apply such principles in a country where seven-eighths of the people are ignorant, and half of them belong to backward races, unfit to exercise political rights. The conditions here noted may be thought to resemble those of the southern states in the North American Union. But there are two conspicuous differences. In Brazil no social "colour line" is sharply drawn, and the fusion of whites and blacks by intermarriage goes steadily on. In Brazil the pure white element, though it preponderates in the temperate districts of the south, is less than half of the whole nation, whereas in the United States it is eight-ninths. Yet in the southern United States nearly all the coloured population has been disfranchised and all declarations of democratic principles are understood to be subject to the now fundamental dogma that white supremacy must be absolutely assured.

Though the financial stability of Brazil is said to be hardly equal to that which Argentina was enjoying in 1910, and though the growth of national and individual wealth has been less rapid, there is a sense of abundance, and the upper classes live in an easy open-handed way. Slaveholding produces extravagant habits, especially among plantation owners, for what is the use of looking after the details of expenditure when one has thriftless labourers, whose carelessness infects all who are set over them? Like their Portuguese ancestors, the Brazilians are genial and hospitable, and they have the example and the excuse of a bounteous Nature around them. They seem less addicted to horse-racing and betting than are the Argentines and Chileans, but the gambling instinct finds plenty of opportunities in the fluctuations of exchange, as well as in the rapid changes of the produce markets.

The Brazilian is primarily a man of the country, not of the city. Rio, large as it is, is a less potent factor than Buenos Aires is in Argentina, or Santiago in Chile. The landowner loves his rural life, as did the Virginian planter in North America before the Civil War, and lives on the *fazenda* in a sort of semi-feudal patriarchal way, often with grown-up sons and daughters around him. Estates (except in the extreme south) are extensive; near neighbours are few; families are often large; the plantation is a sort of little principality, and its owner with his fellow-proprietors is allowed, despite all democratic theory, to direct the politics of the district just as in England, eighty years ago, the county families used to control local affairs and guide the choice of representatives in Parliament.

I have observed that the Brazilian, though modified in some parts of the country by Indian or negro blood, is primarily a Portuguese. Now the Portuguese, a people attractive to those who live among them, have also had a striking history. They are a spirited people, an adventurous people, a poetical people. For more than a century, when they were exploring the oceans and founding a dominion in India, they played a great part in the world, and though they have never quite recovered the position, wonderful for so small a country, which they then held, and have produced no later poet equal to Camoens, men of practical force and men of intellectual brilliance have not been wanting. Neither are they wanting in Brazil. A love of polite letters is common among the upper classes, and the power of writing good verse is not rare. The language has retained those qualities which it shewed in the Lusiads, and the possession of that great poem has helped to maintain the taste and talent of the nation. There are admirable speakers, subtle and ingenious lawyers, astute politicians, administrators whose gifts are approved by such feats as the extinction of yellow fever in Rio and Santos. The late Baron do Rio Branco was a statesman who would have been remarkable in any country. Yet it is strange to find that, both here and in other parts of South America, men of undoubted talent are often beguiled by phrases, and seem to prefer words to facts. Between the national vanities and self-glorifying habits of different nations, there is not much to choose, but in countries like England and the United States, the rhetoric of after-dinner speeches is known clearly and consciously by the more capable among the speakers, and almost as distinctly by the bulk of the audience, to be mere rhetoric. They are aware of their national faults and weaknesses and do not really suppose themselves more gifted or more virtuous than other peoples.

In Latin America, where eloquence comes by nature and seems to become a part of thought itself, the case is different. Exuberant imagination takes its hopes or predictions for realities, and finds in the gilded clouds of fancy a foundation on which to build practical policies. Proud of what they call their Democratic Idealism, they assume as already existing in their fellow-countrymen the virtues which the citizens of a free country ought to possess. To keep these unrealized ideals floating before one's eyes may be better than to have no ideals at all, but for the purposes of actual politics, the result is the same either way, for that which is secured for the principles embodied in the laws is what M. Clémenceau happily calls "an authority chiefly theoretic." Let us, nevertheless, remember that although the habit of mistaking words for facts and aspirations for achievements aggravates the difficulties of working constitutional government in South American

2 E

countries, these difficulties would in any case exist. They inhere in the conditions of the countries. It is vain to expect a constitution closely modelled on that of the United States to work smoothly in Brazil, just as it is impossible to expect the British Cabinet and Parliamentary system to work smoothly in those small nations which have recently been copying it, without an incessant and often ludicrous contrast between doctrine and practice. A nation is the child of its own past, as Cervantes says that a man is the child of his own works.

The Brazilians, who never forget that they were for a time, during the French invasion of Portugal, their own mother country, and head of the whole Portuguese people, cherish their national literary traditions with more warmth than do the Spaniards of the New World, and produce quite as much, in the way of poetry and *belles lettres*, as do the writers of Portugal. They have a quick susceptibility to ideas, like that of Frenchmen or Russians, but have not so far made any great contributions to science, either in the fields of physical enquiry or in those of economics, philology, or history. One can hardly be surprised that learning and the abstract side of natural science are undervalued in a country which has no university, nothing more than faculties for teaching the practical subjects of law, medicine, engineering, and agriculture. This deficiency of a taste for and interest in branches of knowledge not directly practical is the more noticeable, because the Brazilians do not strike one as a new people.

Less here than in Argentina or Uruguay, has one the
feeling that the nation is still in the first freshness of
youth, eagerly setting itself to explore and furnish its
home and to develop resources the possession of which
it has just begun to realize. Business and sport are
not such absorbing topics of conversation here as they
are in Argentina; there is neither such a display of
wealth nor such a passion for spending it. Yet one
doubts whether this freedom from the preoccupations of
industry and commerce, the latter mainly left to foreigners, enures to the benefit of public life. Most of those
who follow politics seem absorbed in personal intrigues.
Comparatively few shew themselves sensible of the tremendous problems which the nation has to face, with
its scattered centres of population to draw together,
its means of communication to extend, its public credit
to sustain, its revenues to be scrupulously husbanded
and applied to useful purposes, above all, its mass of
negro and Indian population to be educated and civilized. Nowhere in the world is there a more urgent
need for a wise constructive statesmanship.

It is hard to convey the impression with which one
sees the shores of Brazil sink below the horizon after
coasting along them for three thousand miles from
the Uruguayan border to Pernambuco, and coming to
know something of the boundless wealth which Nature
has lavished upon man in this vast land. Not even the
great North American republic has a territory at once
so large and so productive. What will be its future?
Is the people worthy of such an inheritance?

The first thought that rises in the mind of those who are possessed, as in this age we all more or less are, by the passion for the development of natural resources, is a feeling of regret that a West European race, powerful by its numbers and its skill, say the North American or German or English, has not, to use the familiar phrase, "got the thing in hand." The white part of the Brazilian nation — and it is only that part that need be considered — seems altogether too small for the tasks which the possession of this country imposes. "How men from the Mississippi would make things hum along the Amazon and the Paraná!" says the traveller from the United States. In thirty years, Brazil would have fifty millions of inhabitants. Steamers would ply upon the rivers, railways would thread the recesses of the forests, and this already vast dominion would almost inevitably be enlarged at the expense of weaker neighbours till it reached the foot of the Andes. Second or third thoughts suggest a doubt whether such a consummation is really in the interests of the world. May not territories be developed too quickly? Might it not have been better for the United States if their growth had been slower, if their public lands had not been so hastily disposed of, if in their eagerness to obtain the labour they needed they had not drawn in a multitude of ignorant immigrants from central and southern Europe? With so long a life in prospect as men of science grant to our planet, why should we seek to open all the mines and cut down all the forests and leave nothing in the exploitation of natural resources to succeeding generations ?   In the long run doubtles. the lands, like the tools, will go to those who can use them. But it may be well to wait and see what new conditions another century brings about for the world; and the Latin-American peoples may within that time grow into something different from what they now appear to the critical eyes of Europe and North America.

CHAPTER XII

THE RELATIONS OF RACES IN SOUTH AMERICA

ALTHOUGH races, unlike in character and differing in the scale of upward progress, must have come into contact from the earliest times, it is only in recent years that the phenomena attending that contact have been carefully observed and studied. From the end of the fifteenth century European nations have been conquering the backward races. In some countries they enslaved, in others they extirpated, these races. They have now portioned out the whole world of savagery, barbarism, and semicivilization among themselves, so that, as the result of discoveries, wars, and treaties, six great and three smaller powers [1] have now appropriated all the extra-European world, except three or four ancient Asiatic kingdoms. In our own day the questions connected with race contact have obtained both a new moral interest, because the old methods of killing off the so-called lower branches of mankind by the sword or by slavery have fallen into discredit, and also a new scientific interest, because we have become curious to know what are the effects of a mixture of markedly dissimilar racial stocks. Such mixture raises some of the most obscure problems in the doctrine of heredity. Does the

[1] Britain, France, Germany, Italy, Russia, the United States, Belgium, Holland, and Portugal.

blending of one race with another tend to weaken or to improve the breed, and how far are any marked qualities of one parent stock transmissible by blood to a mixed progeny which is placed in and powerfully affected by a different environment? Spanish America offers a large and varied field for the study of these and other similar questions, and a field which has been, so far, little examined. My own knowledge does not go far enough to enable me to do more than state a few broad facts and suggest to those who have better opportunities for enquiry some of the problems which the subject presents.

When the Spanish and Portuguese conquerors began to occupy the New World they found it peopled everywhere by native tribes whose physical characteristics and, to some extent, their languages also, indicated that although they had inhabited America during countless ages, they probably all had the same, and that an east Asiatic, origin. No part of the two continents from Behring's Straits to Cape Horn (except a few hopelessly utterly barren deserts) was uninhabited, but some regions were far more populous than others. These regions were the high plateaus of Anahuac (Mexico) with the adjoining lower regions of Yucatan and Guatemala, the plateau of Bogotá, and the plateau of Peru. It was in these that the greatest progress had been made toward civilization and a settled agricultural life; while the lower woodlands and the more or less arid prairies, such as those of the Missouri and of southern Argentina, were more thinly inhabited. There may well have been in Anahuac in Yucatan as many people as in all the rest of North America, and in the Peruvian realm of the Incas as many people as in all the rest of South America.

Now the existence of this aboriginal population has been and still is a factor of the first magnitude in all parts of the continent (except Argentina and Uruguay, where it hardly exists), and in this fact lies one of the most striking contrasts between the northern and southern halves of the Western Hemisphere. The importance of the native Indian element in South America — and the same thing holds true of Mexico and Central America — resides partly in the fact that it furnishes the bulk of the labouring people and a large part of the army, partly in the influence which it has exerted, and still exerts, on the whites, commingling its blood with theirs and affecting their habits and life in many ways.

When the Spaniards came to the New World, they came mainly for the sake of gold. Neither the extension of trade, the hope of which prompted the Dutch, nor the possession of lands to be settled and cultivated, thereby extending the dominion of their crowns, which moved most of the English and French, nor yet the desire of freedom to worship God in their own way, which sent out the Pilgrims and Puritans of New England, — none of these things were uppermost in the minds of the companions of Columbus and Ponce de Leon, of Vasco Nuñez and Cortes and Pizarro. No doubt they also desired to propagate the faith, but their spiritual aims were never suffered to interfere with their secular enterprises. Few settlers came from Spain to till the land. The first object was to seize all that could be found of the precious metals, much to the astonishment of the natives, who thought that gold must be to them a sort of fetich. The next was to discover mines of those metals and make the Indians work them. The third was to divide up the more fertile districts into large estates, allotting to each adventurer his share of labourer-natives along with his share of the lands. No settlers came out to clear the ground from wood and build homes upon it, as did the colonists of New England, and those also who sought to create a New France on the St. Lawrence. No Spaniard thought of tilling the soil himself. Why should he, when he could make others till it for him? Where it was already under cultivation by the native peasants, they were turned into serfs attached to the *encomienda*. Where there was forest, the conquerors seldom troubled themselves to fell it, and that which they found as wilderness remained wilderness in the hands of the savage tribes. Where it was open prairie, there was as little reason for disturbing the nomads who wandered over it. Accordingly, the invaders became a ruling caste, living on the labour of their Indian serfs, and for a long time they confined themselves to the lands on which the latter were already established. So it befell that the aborigines, who in the northern parts of North America were either destroyed or driven out to the west, continued to be in Spanish America one-half or more of the population, those who were already semicivilized being kept as labourers, those who were savages being left to themselves in their forests or half-desert prairies. No agricultural European population grew up in the settled districts. As there were aborigines on the spot to cultivate the land already improved, comparatively few negroes were transported from Africa, and these chiefly to the shores of the Caribbean and to Peru. It was only in the tropical regions of the Antilles and (somewhat later) of Brazil that negro slavery grew up on a large scale; and even there mining, rather than agriculture, was the first cause of their being brought from Africa. The need for negroes was not great in Mexico or Peru, because the native Indians were of a hardier stock than the feeble Arawaks of the Antilles, and lived on under their European masters, though ground down and reduced in numbers by ill treatment. Thus when at last the Spanish colonies asserted their independence, they started without that incubus of a mass of negro slaves which brought so much trouble upon the southern states of the North American Union.

Between the numerous aboriginal tribes there were the greatest differences not only in their degree of advancement toward civilization, but in intelligence, in virility, in fighting quality, and in that kind of resisting power which enables a people to survive under oppression. The best fighters seem to have been — I am not now including the tribes of eastern North America — the Aztecs of Mexico and the Mapoche or Araucanians of Chile. The Caribs in some of the Lesser Antilles and in Venezuela were fierce and tenacious, while their neighbours, the Arawaks of the other Antilles, seem to have become extinct under Spanish severities in half a century. We have no materials for even the vaguest guess at the numbers of these tribes, but it is evident that some disappeared altogether, and that others were greatly reduced. The Chibchas of Bogota, who were estimated at a million when first reached by the Conquerors, are said by a Spanish annalist to have been almost exterminated in twenty years. Of the Mochicas or Yuncas on the Peruvian coast, still numerous at the coming of Pizarro, though many had perished during their conquest by the Incas, few were left after half a century, and their cities have long been heaps of ruins, perhaps partly because the irrigation works which brought water to them were allowed to perish. A census taken in Peru by the Viceroy Toledo in A.D. 1575 is said to have shewed eight millions of Indians in what is now Peru and Bolivia. Two centuries later there were less than half that number. So it is stated that the Indians round Panama rapidly declined in number when the Spaniards established themselves there. The natives of northeastern Brazil were killed off in the end of the sixteenth century, though the tale that two millions were destroyed in about twenty years is scarcely credible; and the less numerous tribes of central Argentina and Uruguay have entirely vanished. The process still goes on, though to-day the means are usually less violent. It is intoxicating liquors and European diseases, not any ill treatment by the Chileans, that have been reducing the stalwart Araucanians to a fourth or fifth part of what they were eighty years ago, and the Tehuelches and other Patagonian tribes, including the wretched Fuegians, are dying out, largely from natural causes. But in the Amazonian forests along the Putumayo river — and that within the last few years — the cruelties and oppressions practised by the rubber gatherers upon the helpless Indians have destroyed many thousands of lives and apparently altogether blotted out some tribes.

How many aborigines now remain in Latin America, it is impossible to ascertain. Even in such advanced countries as Mexico and Peru, there are no trustworthy figures, not only because it is impossible to find means of counting the wild nomads of northwestern Mexico and the still wilder savages of eastern Peru, but also because, even in the civilized districts, it is hard to determine who is to be deemed an Indian and who a mestizo, or half-breed. However, any estimate, if clearly understood to be merely conjectural, is better than none at all, so I may say that in Mexico [1] there are probably, out of fifteen millions of people, about eight millions of Indians, with at least six millions of mixed blood, and the rest Spaniards; while in Peru and Bolivia, out of a total of about six millions, three and a half millions are Indians, one and a half millions mestizos,

[1] The more usual estimates (e.g. that in the Statesman's Year Book for 1912) give 19 per cent of pure Spaniards, 43 per cent mestizos, and 38 per cent Indians, but enquiries made from many well-informed people in Mexico led me to believe that the proportion of Indians is much larger, and probably about that stated in the text.

and the rest more or less pure Spaniards.[1] The one state which is almost wholly Indian, so that the Guarani language is the prevailing tongue, is the inland country of Paraguay, and the one which has no Indians at all is Uruguay, lying on the coast, not far from Paraguay. Of the total population of South America, estimated at forty-five millions, probably eight to nine millions may be pure Indians. Besides these there are, perhaps, thirteen millions of mestizos or half-breeds, and fifteen of persons who deem themselves white, even if a good many have some infusion of aboriginal blood.[2] But if we omit Argentina, almost entirely, and Uruguay entirely, white, as well as Brazil, and confine our view to the other eight republics in which the Indian element is larger, a probable estimate would put the number of pure Indians at more than double that of the whites, and a little less than that of the mestizos. Upon such a computation the total quantity of native blood would much exceed the European. Such an estimate, however, can make no claim to accuracy. I give it only because it seems, from all I could gather, to represent, in a rough sort of way, the

---

[1] Brazil is believed to have nearly two millions of aborigines, most of them savages, Argentina perhaps fifty thousand, Chile one hundred twenty thousand (including the Fuegians). For the four northern republics and for the five of Central America no figures exist, but the bulk of their population, which may be roughly taken at nine millions, is Indian, and pure whites constitute a small minority, which is probably largest in Costa Rica, Colombia, and Panama.

[2] There are also eight or nine millions of negroes and mulattoes (nearly all in Brazil).

proportions of the races.   Anyone who chooses to consider all the more educated mestizos as whites, and all Indians with any touch of white blood, as mestizos, would, of course, bring out different figures.   The tendency of official statistics is in that direction, for everybody wishes to be reckoned as a white man, but such a method does not truly represent the racial facts.

Of the total of about nine millions of Indians, two or three millions may be wild, *Indios bravos,* as the South Americans call them, and in little contact with civilized whites or mestizos.   To this class belong many of the aborigines in Brazil, Colombia, Ecuador, and Venezuela, as well as most of the far smaller number still left in Argentina.   Of the more or less civilized and settled Indians, more than one-half, about three and a half millions, are in Peru and Bolivia ; and it is of these that I shall now proceed to speak, as I had opportunities in these countries of ascertaining their position, and as they are themselves more interesting, because they are the descendants of what was, before the Spanish Conquest, a comparatively advanced people.   What is true of them is, moreover, true, in a general sense, as regards the settled aborigines of the northern republics.   In those states, however, there is no such solid mass of sedentary agricultural Indians as dwell on the plateaux and inter-Andean valleys of Peru and Bolivia.

Though at the time of the Conquest there were probably in the Inca empire many different tribes speaking different languages, all have now been fused into two, the Quichuas to the north of Lake Titicaca, and the

Aymarás, both around its shores and to the south of it in Bolivia. Having given some account of both races in earlier chapters,[1] I need only add that the two languages are generally spoken all over the central Andes from the frontiers of Ecuador on the north to those of Chile and Argentina on the south. Comparatively few of these Indians, probably less than a fifth, are able to talk Spanish. Some few live in the towns and practise handicrafts. Three-fourths of the population of La Paz is Aymará, while in Cuzco at least one-third is Quichua. The vast majority, however, are country folk cultivating the soil as tenants or labourers or tending sheep and cattle as herdsmen for the landowners, who are, of course, either of Spanish or of mixed blood. Comparatively few Indians own small plots of their own. The landlords, who in the colonial times oppressed the peasants so atrociously as from time to time to provoke even this naturally submissive people to rebellion, no longer venture to practise the exactions and cruelties of those days. Authority is not feared as it was then, and could not be used to support such flagrant injustice. Neither do the clergy wring money from their flocks, as in those old bad days, though even now the fees charged for marriages are so high that the rite is commonly neglected. The ancient tribal system has melted away and the *cacique*, as the Spaniards called him, who was the head of a local community down till the end of the eighteenth century, is now gone, but the old organization of the dwellers in a

[1] Chapters III–V.

village by brotherhoods, and resting, or supposed to rest, upon blood relationship, still exists, and local affairs are managed by the local officials mentioned in an earlier chapter.[1]   Thus, the Indian is left very much to himself, except that he pays rent to the landlord and is often bound to render him personal service at his residence during part of the year.   This is called the *Mita*.   His food is not very nutritious, consisting largely of *chuno, i.e.* frozen potatoes, usually ground into flour.   His clothing is scanty, his mode of life hard and wretched, especially on the bleak plateaux.   Yet he is not in that abject poverty which fears starvation; perhaps, indeed, not so near the minimum level of subsistence as are millions of the people in China and India.   He does not contrast his own evil case with the luxury of the rich, as do the slum dwellers of European cities, nor does he feel his case to be evil, for it is no worse than his forefathers have borne for ten generations, and he knows no other.

Not only the Quichuas and Aymarás, but the Indians of the northern republics and of southern Chile are quite illiterate, and, as respects education, just where they were under the Incas, perhaps rather farther back, because there was then a sort of national life which has been long since quenched.   There seems to be among them little or no desire for instruction.   Even should any seek to rise in life, he would find no means of doing so, unless perchance some kindly priest should give the rudiments of knowledge to a boy brighter

[1] See Chapter V, p. 180.

than the rest. Religion does nothing to stir their minds. They are nominally Christians, but of many of them that may be said to-day which was said in 1746, by the humane and orthodox Spaniard, Juan Ulloa, whose secret report upon the condition of the Indians in Peru and Ecuador, made to the king of Spain, was published in England a century later. This commissioner says : —

"Their religion does not resemble the Christian religion any more than it resembles that which they had while they were pagans, for if we examine the subject with care, it will be found that, notwithstanding the nominal conversion of these tribes, the progress they have made in knowledge is so inconsiderable that it will be difficult to discover any difference between the condition in which they now live and that in which they were found at the time of the Conquest." [1]

That the influence of the priesthood did not commend religion to the people nor relieve their misery may be gathered from this further extract from the same secret report.

"The wretched state of the Indian is to be attributed to the vices of the priests, the extortions of the corregidors, and the bad treatment which they generally receive from all Spaniards. Unable to endure the hardships, and longing to escape from bondage, many of them

[1] I quote this from the interesting book of Professor Bernard Moses, *South America on the Eve of Emancipation, The Southern Colonies*, p. 192. The extracts given there from the *Noticias Secretas* of Ulloa give a frightful description of the cruelties and oppressions then practised on the Indians. Professor Moses says there were two Ulloas : Juan and Antonio ; others hold there was but one.

have risen in rebellion and found their way to unconquered districts, there to continue in the barbarous
practices of their idolatrous neighbours, and in view of
the foregoing, what conclusions are they to form from
the scandalous lives of their parish priests, especially
when we reflect that the Indian is but partially civilized
and taught by example rather than by precept? . . .
In the town of Pimampiro the behaviour of the parish
priest drove the Indians to despair. Uniting in one
body, they rose in rebellion and proceeded by night to
the Cordilleras, where they merged themselves with the
Gentile Indians with whom they have continued until
the present time."[1]

It ought to be remembered that the avarice and moral
faults charged upon the clergy in these reports, as well
as in other accounts belonging to the eighteenth century are brought against the parish priests rather than
the religious orders, although Ulloa describes the level
of conduct as having sadly declined among these also.
To some of the orders, most of all to the Jesuits, and in a
less degree to the early Dominicans, great credit is due
for their efforts not only to spread the gospel, often at
the risk of their lives, but also to secure justice for the
unfortunate Indians. The great Las Casas was only
the most conspicuous among many admirable Spanish
churchmen who threw their hearts into this campaign
of humanity, though they seldom prevailed against the
hard-hearted rapacity of the land owners and mine
owners who wished to keep the Indians in serfdom and

[1] *Noticias Secretas*, at p. 192, of Bernard Moses, *ut supra*.

did not care how many perished under their hands. These worthy ecclesiastics sometimes secured good ordinances from the Council of the Indies in Spain, but the colonial governors found that the path of least resistance was to proclaim the ordinance and wink at its neglect. On many a law was the note made, "It is obeyed, but not executed" (*Se obedece pero no se ejecuta*). In Paraguay, where the population was almost wholly Indian, the reign of the Jesuits was generally beneficent. They could not do much for the education of the mass of their subjects, but while they trained some few of the promising youth, they impressed habits of industry and good conduct upon the rest. Perhaps it is to the excessive inculcation of obedience that the blind submissiveness of the later Paraguayans to such despots as Francia and Lopez may be partly attributed.[1]

The oppressions, both civil and ecclesiastical, referred to in the extracts given above, have long since ceased, but their consequences remain in the abject state of the aborigines and their ignorance of the truths and precepts of Christianity. As a learned student of Indian life observes, it is to them a kind of magic, more powerful for some purposes than their own ancient magic which was based on nature worship. "They believe in Dios (God)," says Mr. Bandelier,[2] "but believe more in Nuestra Señora de la Luz (Our Lady of the Light)

---

[1] Half the population of Paraguay perished in the war of the younger Lopez, the third of the dictators, who ruled the country from 1818 to 1870.

[2] *Islands of Titicaca and Koati*, quoted in Chapter IV.

2 H

at Copacavana." They worship evil spirits and make
offerings to the mountain *Achachilas* and to the Earth.
Even in Mexico, where the Indians are, as a rule, much
more subject to enlightening influences, I was told in
1901 that an archbishop, visiting the parishes of his dio-
cese not long before, had found the ancient idols hidden
away behind the altars and occasionally brought out at
night to receive marks of reverence. In Peru the people
had hardly advanced to the Mexican stage of a regular
mythology with images of their deities, so idols were
less common and prominent, while the worship of
the spirits immanent in natural objects held its
ground.

Where the church fails to stir the currents of intellectual life among the masses of such a people as this,
what other influence is there to make for progress?

These Peruvian races were specially unfortunate because their natural leaders, the *caciques* or local chieftains who had formed a sort of aristocracy before the
Conquest, were either slaughtered or, in some few cases,
incorporated into the colonial upper class, so that they
were lost, as protectors, to the subject class, who, having little force of character, sank unresistingly into serfdom. Once, in 1781-1783, under the leadership of Tupac Amaru, of whom I have spoken briefly in an earlier
chapter, they rose in a revolt which lasted for three
years. Being unwarlike and untrained, ill-armed and
ill-led, they were defeated with great slaughter, after
atrocious cruelties had been perpetrated on both sides.
But they accomplished one feat rare in the annals of

war in destroying, along with its Spanish garrison, the city of Sorata, which they had long besieged in vain, by damming up the course of a mountain torrent and turning its full stream on the place. Since those days, even the few chiefs that then remained have vanished, and the aboriginal race consists wholly of the poorest and most neglected part of the population. That which to them makes life tolerable is the incessant chewing of coca, a very old habit, but now less costly than in Inca days, because the leaf can be more easily imported from the hot country east of the Andes.

Their enjoyments are two. One is intoxication, mostly with chicha, the old native beverage, but now also with fiery alcohol, made from the sugar-cane. The other is dancing at their festivals. The priests, when they were converting the natives, thought it better not to disturb the ancient heathen dances, but to transfer them to the days which the church sets apart for its feasts, expunging, so far as they could, the more offensive features of the dance, though what remains is sufficiently repulsive. Such ceremonial performances are common among the Indians of North America, also, and used often to be kept up for days together before a declaration of war. The dances of the Hopi and other Indians which the visitor sees to-day in Arizona are dull and decorous affairs. A striking description of the dances which he saw at Tiahuanacu on Corpus Christi Day is given by Mr. Squier,[1] and the much more recent account given by Mr. Bandelier of those he witnessed on another

[1] *Travels in Peru*, p. 305 *sqq.*

festival at Copacavana shew that things are much the same to-day.[1] The music, of a drum-and-fife type, is loud, harsh, and discordant, but this does not imply that a taste for sweet sound is wanting, for the Indian often carries his simple flute or pipe with him on his journeys and enjoys the monotonous ditties which he makes it discourse.

Three other facts may be adduced to illustrate the condition of the aborigines. There is no recent literature in their languages, not even a newspaper or magazine. They seem to be very rarely ordained as priests, though I was told in Mexico that there are a good many Indian priests there ; and it scarcely ever happens that any one of them rises into the class of learned or cultivated. I heard of one such at Lima, who had a remarkable knowledge of natural history; there may have been others.

Whether owing to the character of the Indians, or to their fear of the white man, robberies and assaults are rare not only among the more gentle Quichuas, but also in Bolivia, where the Aymarás, a more dour and sullen race, frequently break the peace among themselves, village attacking village with sticks and slings, while the women carry bags of stones to supply ammunition for the men's slings. In fact, the safety of the solitary European traveller in most parts of South Amer-

---

[1] *Islands of Titicaca and Koati*, p. 40 *sqq.* This learned student of Indian customs thinks that the drinking may have originated in the ceremonial offerings of chicha to the spirits. Its continuance needs no explanation.

ica is almost as remarkable as the like circumstance in India.

In respect of civil rights, there is no legal distinction between the Indian and the white. Both enjoy the same citizenship for all private and public purposes, to both is granted the equal protection of the laws, equal suffrage, equal eligibility to office. This is to some extent a guarantee to the Indian against ill treatment, but it does not raise him in the social scale. He seldom casts a vote; not, indeed, that it makes much difference in these countries whether the citizen votes or not, for a paternal government takes charge of the elections. He is never — so far as I could learn — a candidate for any national office. The laws of the two republics interfere very little with his life, which is regulated by ancestral custom. Even in revolutions he does not seem to come to the front. He is, however, willing to fight, and a good fighter both in foreign and in civil wars, however little interest he may take in the cause. But for this fact there would have been fewer and shorter revolutions. Thus the Indian is a member of the nation for military, if not for political, purposes. The former are at least nearer to his comprehension than the latter, for he cares, and thinks of caring, about politics no more than did the needy knife-grinder in Canning's verses. No one has yet preached to him the gospel of democracy; no one has told him that he has anything to gain from action as a citizen. The whole thing is as completely out of his sphere as if he were still living under the Spanish viceroys, or, indeed, under the rule of the

Inca Huayna Capac. There is, therefore, not yet any "Indian question" in South America.[1] There ought to be an Indian question : that is to say, there ought to be an effort to raise the Indians economically and educationally. But they have not yet begun to ask to be raised.

So much for the Indian as he is in Peru and Bolivia; and, apparently, also in those settled parts of northwestern Argentina where Indians still remain. In Paraguay the position is so far different that the Indians form not the lowest class, but the bulk of the nation. In the forest-covered regions of the Amazon and its tributaries, the *Indios bravos* are outside civilization altogether.

To understand the social relations of the white and Indian races one must begin by remembering that there is in Spanish and Portuguese countries no such sharp colour line as exists where men of Teutonic stock are settled in countries outside Europe. As this is true of the negro, it is even more true of the Indian. He may be despised as a weakling, he may be ignored as a citizen, he may be, as he was at one time, abominably oppressed and ill treated, but he excites no personal repulsion. It is not his race that is against him, but his debased condition. Whatever he suffers, is suffered because he is ignorant or timid or helpless, not because he is of a different blood and colour. Accord-

[1] There has been formed in Lima a society for the protection of the Indians, but I could not learn that it has been able to do much in the parts of Peru that lie far from the capital.

ingly the Spanish Americans do not strive to keep off and keep down the Indian in such wise as the North Americans and the Dutch and the English — I do not mean the governments, but the individuals — treat their black subjects. There is not even such aversion to him as is shewn in California and Australia to the east Asiatic immigrants from Eastern Asia. The distinction between the races is in Spanish America a distinction of rank or class rather than of colour. Against intermarriage there is, therefore, no more feeling than that which exists against any union palpably below a man's or woman's own rank in life. If it is rare for a pure white to espouse a pure Indian, that is because they are of different ranks, just as it is rare for a well-born Englishman to marry a peasant girl. There is nothing in the law to oppose such a union, and though whites seldom marry pure Indians, because the classes come little into contact, the presence of an unmistakable Indian strain in a mestizo makes no difference to his acceptability to a white woman of the same class. Whether this contrast between the Spanish attitude towards the Indian and the Anglo-American attitude to the negro is due to differences between Roman Catholicism and Protestantism,[1] or to the fact that the

---

[1] The sense of membership in a concrete community (a Visible Church) consisting of persons of whatever race who participate in the same sacraments is stronger in the Roman than in the Protestant churches ; and as a member of a lower race who has been ordained a priest is thereby raised to a position which is in a sense above that of any layman, the race itself is raised in his person.

Indian was never legally a slave, or to the fact that the aboriginal American races shew a less marked divergence in colour and features from the white than does the negro, is a question which need not be here discussed. Possibly all three causes may contribute to the result; and probably the circumstance that most of the early Spaniards, having brought no wives with them, treated their numerous children by Indian women as being legitimate and belonging to their own race, was also a factor. Such a usage, established in the days of the Conquest, would naturally continue to affect men's attitude. The result is anyhow one of great significance, and makes the racial problem here quite different from what it is in the southern states of North America.

The most salient point of difference lies in the position of the half-breed or mestizo. In North America a mulatto, a quadroon, even an octoroon who is only one-eighth black, counts as a negro. Here, except perhaps in a few of the oldest cities, a mestizo counts as a white. His half-Indian blood is no disparagement to his social standing, no obstacle to his reaching any public position. One may remark of such and such a person that he has evidently a strong infusion of Indian blood, of such another that he looks a Spaniard through and through, and the latter doubtless cherishes a secret satisfaction in his pure Iberian stock. But for the practical purposes of business and politics, the two, supposing them to belong to the same educated class, stand upon the same level. The families which value their lineage so highly that they would deem the marriage of a child to a person of mixed blood, otherwise desirable, to be a *mésalliance*, must be now few, and hardly exist outside five or six cities — such as Bogotá, Lima, Arequipa, and Santiago.

Thus one may say that there is no "colour question" in South America. Its republics have political and economic problems enough, but they are spared a source of embarrassment and danger constantly present to the minds of thoughtful North Americans, and present also (though less painfully) to the minds of South Africans. Although, therefore, both in Spanish America and in the United States there are social distinctions which coincide with race distinctions, the character of those distinctions is different. In both countries there are two sections. But in the United States everyone who is not white is classed as coloured, however slight the trace. In Spanish America everyone who is not wholly Indian is classed as white, however marked the Indian tinge.[1] Thus the mixed population, which in the United States swells the negro element, is in Spanish America a part of the white nation, and helps to give that element its preponderance. And a further difference appears in the fact that whereas in the United States the man of colour is discriminated against for social purposes, irrespective of his wealth, educa-

---

[1] An infusion of negro blood, sometimes met with in the coast towns of Peru, is regarded with less favour than a like infusion of Indian blood, for while the first negro ancestor must have been a slave, the Indian ancestor may have been an Inca.

tion, or personal qualities, in Spanish countries race counts for so little that when he emerges out of the poverty and ignorance which mark the Indian, his equality with the white man is admitted. So rarely, however, does he emerge that one may broadly say that the Nation consists in these republics of white men and mestizos only, the Indian constituting, if not another nation, yet a separate nationality, marked off not merely by poverty, but by its language and the adherence of its members to ancient superstitions. They have nothing, except the worship of the saints and a fondness for liquor, in common with the class above them, for they speak a different language, think differently, feel differently, have their own amusements, and cherish, in a dim way, faint memories of a time when their forefathers were masters of the land. They are not actively hostile to the white people, and, indeed, get on better with their landlords than some European peasantries have done with theirs. But they live apart, inside the nation, but not of it. The Aymarás are silent, suspicious, sullen. The Quichuas are more kindly, but hardly less reserved. This reserve and suspicion characterize the Mexican Indian also, who is generally more intelligent than the Peruvian.[1] Both Aymarás and Quichuas are tenacious of their customs, and do not seek to assimi-

---

[1] A few years ago in northern Mexico a truck carrying a load of dynamite for use at a mine was suddenly discovered to be on fire at a village station. The risk was imminent, so the driver of a locomotive engine picked the truck up and ran it away into the country at all the speed he could put on. He bade the brakeman

late any of that modern life and lore which has found its slow way even into the recesses of the Andes. No one from without tries to give it to them, no one rises from among themselves stirred by a desire to acquire it and then impart it to his fellows.

This want of leading, and want not only of light but of a wish for light, is the feature of the Indian population which most surprises the traveller, because he knows of no parallel to it among the subject races of Europe in the past or those of western Asia to-day. The Greek and Armenian in Turkey have at times suffered as much from the Turk as the Quichua has suffered from his conquerors in Peru, but in intelligence and capacity for progress they have been the superiors of the Turk; and had there been more of them, they would before now have shaken off his control.

If it is asked how the presence of this solid Indian mass, unassimilated by the white nation, has affected that nation and the progress of the country as a whole, the answer is that in the first place it prevented all chance of the growth of a free European agricultural population, even in those high valleys where Europeans could work and thrive. Had the hardy and laborious peasantry of Galicia, Asturias, and Aragon settled in these regions, how much more robust, mentally and physically; might the nation have been! How much

---

jump off and save himself, adding, "I go to my death." When he had got a mile away, the dynamite exploded. Every window in the village was broken, and he was blown to atoms, but the inhabitants were saved. He was a pure-blooded Indian.

might agriculture have been improved had there been intelligent labour! But besides this want, and besides the weakening of the state by the lack of national spirit in half of its population, the presence of a large mass of ignorance and superstition has operated to reduce the general intellectual level. There have been countries where a small rich and ruling class, living on the toil of inferiors, has cultivated art and letters with brilliant success, but we find nothing of the sort here. The ignorant mass has depressed the whole, as a glacier chills the air of its valley.

Whether the Spanish stock has deteriorated through the mixture of Indian blood is a more difficult matter to determine. The Peruvians and Bolivians of to-day, both whites and mestizos — and the same thing is true of Venezuelans and Ecuadoreans — differ much from the Spaniards of the sixteenth century and from the European Spaniards of to-day. They are probably more excitable; they are naturally less industrious because they live in hot countries and have Indians to work for them. But in Spain itself there are great differences between the peoples of the north and the south and the east. The Catalans are more energetic than the Andalusians, the Gallegos more industrious than the Valencians. The conditions of colonial life in the presence of a large aboriginal population, coupled with long misgovernment and intellectual stagnation, account for a good deal of the variation from the Spanish type. It is a sound maxim never to lay weight upon uncertain causes when certain causes are available as explanations. Moreover our knowledge of heredity in its influence on race development is still imperfect. The Argentines, who are of an almost pure white stock, also differ much from the modern Spaniard.

It might seem natural to assume *a priori* that men of pure European race would continue to hold the foremost place in these countries, and would shew both greater talents and a more humane temper than those in whose veins Indian blood flows. But I doubt if the facts support such a view. Some of the most forceful leaders who have figured in the politics of these republics have been mestizos. I remember one, as capable and energetic and upright a man as I met anywhere in the continent, who looked at least half an Indian, and very little of a Spaniard. Nor have there been any more sinister figures in the history of South America since the days of Pedro de Arias the infamous governor of Darien who put to death Vasco Nuñez de Balboa, than some who were pure Spaniards. No half-breeds have shewn more ruthlessness than the Spanish Carbajal in the days of Pizarro, or than Rosas, the Argentine dictator of seventy years ago. And in this connection it deserves to be noticed that the ancient Peruvian Indians, though they thought nothing of indiscriminate slaughter and occasionally tortured captive enemies, did not generally shew the same taste for blood as the Aztecs shewed in their sacrifices nor the same propensity to methods of elaborate and long-drawn-out cruelty as did the Red men of North America.

As I have so far been speaking chiefly of Peru

and Bolivia, where the Indian population is larger and more civilized than elsewhere, a few observations ought to be added regarding the other republics in which a considerable aboriginal population remains. I omit Uruguay, because it has none at all. In Argentina there are some civilized Indians in the northwestern districts round the cities of Jujuy and Tucuman, and to these the remarks made regarding their neighbours, the Bolivian Indians, apply. There are also wild Indians, perhaps one hundred thousand, perhaps more, on the Gran Chaco of the far north,[1] and the scattered remnants of nomad Patagonians in the far south and in Tierra del Fuego. These seem to be disappearing. The Onas in that island have been freely killed off by the ranchmen on whose flocks they preyed, and tubercular disease is destroying the rest. In Chile, besides the Araucanians, described in Chapter VI, there are a few small tribes, in a low state of barbarism, left in the archipelago of wet and woody isles along the Pacific coast. The rural population of the republic — indeed, nearly all of the poorer and less educated part of it — is mestizo, a bold and vigorous race, good workers and fine fighters. Paraguay is an almost purely Indian country.

Of the four northern republics, Panama, Colombia, Venezuela, and Ecuador, I have seen only the first. In each of these the number of purely Spanish families is small. It is probably largest in Colombia. In Venezuela the Indians have been more largely absorbed into

---

[1] Some of these now come south to work on Argentine farms.

the general population than has happened in Colombia and Ecuador. In all four states such of the Indians as remain wild forest dwellers are passive, and practically outside the nation, which is, as a social and political entity, predominantly mestizo. What has been said of Peru and Bolivia is true of these states also: there is no colour line; the mestizos are treated as white and are not, as a class, intellectually inferior to the white. The Indian forms the lowest stratum, and seldom rises out of it.

There remains Brazil, distinguished from the other republics by the fact that in addition to her small mestizo population and her pure Indian population, most of it wild, she has a great mass of negroes and a still larger mass of mulattoes and quadroons. It is hardly too much to say that along the coast from Rio to Bahia and Pernambuco, as well as in parts of the interior behind these two cities, the black population predominates. In character and habits it somewhat resembles the negroes of the British West Indies and Santo Domingo, being superior to the Haytians, but inferior in education and enterprise to the coloured people of the southern states of North America. High as is its fecundity, its death-rate is also so high, owing to the general neglect of sanitary precautions, that it does not appear to be increasing relatively to the general population. It is well treated — slavery was seldom harsh among the kindly natured, easy-going Portuguese — and bears no ill-will to its former masters. Neither do they feel towards it that repulsion which marks the attitude of the whites to the negroes in North America and South Africa. The Brazilian lower class intermarries freely with the black people ; the Brazilian middle class intermarries with mulattoes and quadroons. Brazil is the one country in the world, besides the Portuguese colonies on the east and west coasts of Africa, in which a fusion of the European and African races is proceeding unchecked by law or custom. The doctrines of human equality and human solidarity have here their perfect work. The result is so far satisfactory that there is little or no class friction. The white man does not lynch or maltreat the negro : indeed, I have never heard of a lynching anywhere in South America except occasionally as part of a political convulsion. The negro is not accused of insolence and does not seem to develop any more criminality than naturally belongs to any ignorant population with loose notions of morality and property.

What ultimate effect the intermixture of blood will have on the European element in Brazil I will not venture to predict. If one may judge from a few remarkable cases, it will not necessarily reduce the intellectual standard. One of the ablest and most refined Brazilians I have known had some colour; and other such cases have been mentioned to me. Assumptions and preconceptions must be eschewed, however plausible they may seem.

The chief conclusions which the history of the relations of races in the South American continent suggests are the three following. The first may be thought doubtful. It is negative rather than positive, and though it seems worth stating, I state it with diffidence.

The fusion of two parent stocks, one more advanced, the other more backward, does not necessarily result in producing a race inferior to the stronger parent or superior to the weaker. The mestizo in Peru is not palpably inferior in intellect to the Spanish colonial of unmixed blood, but seems to be substantially his equal. The mestizo in Mexico is not palpably superior — some doubt if he is at all superior either physically, morally, or intellectually — to the pure Tarascan or Zapotec Indian, who is, no doubt, a stronger human being than the South American Quichua or Aymará.

The second conclusion is this: Conquest and control by a race of greater strength have upon some races a depressing and almost ruinous effect. The Peruvian subjects of the Incas had reached a state of advancement which, though much below that of the ancient Egyptians and Babylonians, was remarkable when one considers that their isolation deprived them of the enormous benefit of contact with other progressive peoples, and when one considers also the disadvantage of living at a great altitude, the absence of milk-yielding animals, and the paucity both of animals capable of domestication and of cereal plants. The impact of Spanish invasion not only shattered their own rudimentary civilization to pieces, but so took all the heart and spirit out of them that they have made practically no advances during four centuries, and have profited hardly at all

21

by the western civilization of their masters. The aborigines of Mexico, having more stamina of intellect and will, have suffered less by the shock, but have done almost as little to assimilate the arts and ideas of Europe.

Thirdly, the ease with which the Spaniards have intermingled by marriage with the Indian tribes—and the Portuguese have done the like, not only with the Indians, but with the more physically dissimilar negroes —shews that race repugnance is no such constant and permanent factor in human affairs as members of the Teutonic peoples are apt to assume. Instead of being, as we Teutons suppose, the rule in this matter, we are rather the exception, for in the ancient world there seems to have been little race repulsion; there is very little to-day among Mohammedans; there is none among Chinese. This seems to suggest that since the phenomenon is not of the essence of human nature, it may not be always as strong among the Teutonic peoples as it is to-day. Religion has been in the past almost as powerful a dissevering force as has racial antagonism. In the case of Spaniards and Portuguese, religion, so soon as the Indians had been baptized, made race differences seem insignificant. Islam has always done this in the East and in Africa.

As touching the future, it seems as certain as anything in human affairs can be that the races now inhabiting South America, aboriginal, European, and African, will be all ultimately fused. The Spanish republics (except the purely white Argentina and Uruguay) will be Ibero-American, Brazil will be Ibero-American-African. All present facts point that way, and that any hitherto unfelt repulsion will arise seems most improbable. When, however, will the process be complete? In the Spanish republics, hardly before two centuries, probably not even then. It seems not much nearer now than it was in 1810, when the revolutionary struggles began, though anything which stirred up the Andean population, such as the discovery of a large number of new and rich mines, bringing in foreign labour and increasing the demand for domestic labour, or anything that roused a spirit of economic and political change, might accelerate the consummation. .

Still less predictable is the quality of the mixed race that will emerge. One cannot but fear that the Portuguese of tropical Brazil may suffer from the further infusion of an element the moral fibre of which is conspicuously weak, though there are those who argue that the blood of the superior race must ultimately transmute the whole. It is not to be assumed that the peoples of the Spanish republics will necessarily decline, for the present degradation of the Indians may be due as much to their melancholy history as to inherent defects. It is still too soon to be despondent. There may be in the Indian stock a reserve of strength, dormant, but not extinct, ready to respond to a new stimulus and to shoot upwards under more inspiriting conditions.

PANAMA

By ALBERT EDWARDS

NEW AND CHEAPER EDITION OF THE BEST BOOK
ON PANAMA FOR THE GENERAL READER

*Profusely illustrated, decorated cloth, 12mo
$1.50 net; postpaid, $1.62*

"A thoroughly satisfactory book for one who is looking
for solid information." — *Boston Globe.*

"A most interesting picture of the country as it is
to-day." — *San Francisco Chronicle.*

"One of the very few books on any Latin-American
country that gives any idea of the whole land and people."
— *Los Angeles Times.*

"One of the very best of travel books."
— *Continent.*

"Lively and readable, containing the real atmosphere
of the tropics." — *Minneapolis Tribune.*

"A book which every American ought to read, both for
pleasure and profit." — *New York Herald.*

THE MACMILLAN COMPANY

Publishers   64–66 Fifth Avenue   New York

MACMILLAN'S NEW TRAVEL SERIES

With the re-issue of these popular volumes THE NEW TRAVEL SERIES is inaugurated, the purpose of which is to make available at the lowest price possible the best there is in the field of illustrated books of travel and description. They are welcome books, either for the traveller's use during his visit, or as a pleasant reminder of bygone days, or to bring the different districts vividly before the minds of intending travellers, or those who are unable to leave home.

EACH VOLUME PROFUSELY ILLUSTRATED

Decorated cloth, 12mo, boxed, $1.50 net; postpaid, $1.65

SPANISH HIGHWAYS AND BYWAYS. By Catharine Lee Bates.
" A classic in its domain." — *Chicago Record-Herald.*

MEXICO: THE WONDERLAND OF THE SOUTH. By W. E. Carson.
" The best popular book on Mexico that we have seen." — *America.*

STAGE-COACH AND TAVERN DAYS. By Alice Morse Earle.
" This book, with its profuse and interesting pictures, should prove a favorite."
— *Buffalo Express.*

LABRADOR: THE COUNTRY AND THE PEOPLE. By Wilfred T. Grenfell.
" Mr. Grenfell has put the very soul of picturesque Labrador into his pages."
— *Record-Herald.*

ALASKA: THE GREAT COUNTRY. By Ella Higginson.
" A great book on a great subject." — *Boston Transcript.*

BOSTON: THE PLACE AND THE PEOPLE. By M. A. DeWolfe Howe.
" One of the best all-round books about Boston yet published." — *Argonaut.*

ALONG FRENCH BYWAYS. By Clifton Johnson.
" Faithful, complete, and well-balanced idea of French rural life, manners, and customs."
— *Boston Herald.*

AMONG ENGLISH HEDGEROWS. By Clifton Johnson.
" The book deserves to succeed." — *The Spectator*, London.

THE ISLE OF THE SHAMROCK. By Clifton Johnson.
" A most interesting book, full of lively sketches and anecdotes."
— *London Daily News.*

THE LAND OF HEATHER. By Clifton Johnson.
" Every student of human nature will be pleased with this entertaining book."
— *Brooklyn Standard Union.*

NEW ENGLAND AND ITS NEIGHBORS. By Clifton Johnson.
" A book that ranks with the best in the author's long list of entertaining and picturesque works." — *Denver Republican.*

NEW ORLEANS: THE PLACE AND THE PEOPLE. By Grace King.
"A useful and attractive book." — *Daily Telegraph.*

CHARLESTON: THE PLACE AND THE PEOPLE. By Mrs. St. Julien Ravenel.
" Every page is pregnant with interesting fact and suggestion."
— *Philadelphia Public Ledger.*

PHILADELPHIA: THE PLACE AND THE PEOPLE. By Agnes Repplier.

CUBA. By Irene A. Wright.
" One of the most informing of all books on the subject." — *Pittsburg Gazette.*

THE MACMILLAN COMPANY

Publishers   **64–66 Fifth Avenue**   **New York**

Lightning Source UK Ltd.
Milton Keynes UK
UKOW06f0514291015

261584UK00009B/187/P